Sexing the World

Sexing the World

GRAMMATICAL GENDER AND BIOLOGICAL SEX IN ANCIENT ROME

Anthony Corbeill

PRINCETON UNIVERSITY PRESS

PRINCETON AND OXFORD

Copyright © 2015 by Princeton University Press
Published by Princeton University Press, 41 William Street, Princeton, New Jersey 08540
In the United Kingdom: Princeton University Press, 6 Oxford Street, Woodstock, Oxfordshire
OX20 1TW

press.princeton.edu

Jacket illustration: Copyright © Muamu/Shutterstock.

Library of Congress Cataloging-in-Publication Data

Corbeill, Anthony, 1960– author.
  Sexing the world : grammatical gender and biological sex in ancient Rome / Anthony Corbeill.
    pages cm
  Includes bibliographical references and index.
  ISBN 978-0-691-16322-2 (hardcover : alk. paper)   1. Latin literature—History and criticism.
2. Latin language—Gender.   3. Gender identity in literature.   I. Title.
  PA6029.E87C67 2015
  870.9′3538—dc23   2014019102

British Library Cataloging-in-Publication Data is available

This book has been composed in Minion Pro text with Myriad Pro display

Printed on acid-free paper. ∞

Printed in the United States of America

10 9 8 7 6 5 4 3 2 1

HDC
et
ESG
magistris optimis

Contents

Acknowledgments

Numerous institutions and individuals have allowed me to think and write about grammatical gender for the past decade. Initial research was conducted at the Institute for Research in the Humanities at the University of Wisconsin, Madison, during a time highlighted by frequent conversations with Michael Kulikowski and James McKeown. Additional research and writing were completed as a Visiting Fellow at All Souls College, Oxford, where the availability of James N. Adams could not help but stimulate serious thinking about the Latin language. A final draft was finished at my home institution, the University of Kansas, as a Fellow at the Hall Center for the Humanities; without the Hall Center, intellectual life in Lawrence would be much poorer and I am proud of my association with it over the past two decades. I also thank my hosts for invitations to speak at various colleges and universities. On these and other occasions the following people have considerably enriched my thinking by sharing thoughts and publications: David Blank, Amy Coker, Nancy de Grummond, Claudia Fernández, William Fitzgerald, Simon Goldhill, Philip Hardie, John Henderson, Lora Holland, Joshua Katz, Kezia Knauer, Jerzy Linderski, Marcos Martinho, Allen Miller, Robert Morstein-Marx, William Race, Robert Renehan, Emma Scioli, Alan Shapiro, Bert Smith, Joshua Smith, Emma Stafford, Jaana Vaahtera, and Brian Walters; special encouragement and advice always came from Nicholas Horsfall and Jocelyn Kitchen. I continue to remain thankful for my generous colleagues and patient students in the Classics Department at the University of Kansas; special gratitude goes to Lizzy Adams, whose care as a research assistant not only detected errors but also forced me to reevaluate several claims. Lastly, thanks to Rob Tempio of Princeton University Press for his interest, and for the detailed and challenging comments from one of the referees of the manuscript. An earlier version of chapter 1 has appeared in *Transactions of the American Philological Association* 138 (2008): 75–105.

This book could not have been written without the initial and continued inspiration of the two teachers in the dedication. Professor H. D. Cameron encouraged me as an undergraduate to follow my instincts; Professor Erich Gruen taught me as a graduate to rein in my excesses. Although neither has read a word of what follows, what I have taken from their example can be found on every page.

Sexing the World

Introduction

Latin Grammatical Gender Is Not Arbitrary

> In German, a young lady has no sex, while a turnip has. Think what
> overwrought reverence that shows for the turnip, and what callous
> disrespect for the girl. See how it looks in print—I translate this
> from a conversation in one of the best of the German Sunday-
> school books: "*Gretchen*. Wilhelm, where is the turnip? *Wilhelm*.
> She has gone to the kitchen. *Gretchen*. Where is the accomplished
> and beautiful English maiden? *Wilhelm*. It has gone to the opera."
> (Mark Twain, "The Awful German Language,"
> Appendix D of *A Tramp Abroad*)

To a speaker of Latin, the table at which I sit (*mensa*) is feminine, the cup from
which I drink (*poculum*) neuter, and the eyes with which I see (*oculi*) masculine. Every aspect of an ancient Roman's life was populated with nouns that
possessed at least one of these three genders. This linguistic phenomenon, of
course, hardly characterizes Latin alone. Grammatical gender is in fact so widespread that it takes the satire of a Mark Twain to remind us of the inherent
oddness of these categories. In explicitly drawing attention to a turnip's presumed sex, Twain questions the logic—and wonders about the origins—of one
of the basic categories that humans have used in the organization of language.[1]
Part of the humor of Twain's remarks lies in the fact that, presumably, the oddness to which he draws attention goes unnoticed in the daily usage of a German
speaker. The grammatical gender of inanimate objects, we are taught, is a convenient linguistic convention, having no correspondence with any sort of imagined sexual characteristics of those objects in the real world. I propose in this
book to offer some ancient evidence that runs contrary to this claim. In the
world of Latin grammatical gender, I will argue, the sex and sexuality behind a
given gender was always available for exploitation by the learned speaker.

According to the book of *Genesis*, the first act of Adam was to name the animals that God had assembled before him (2: 19–20). The author of this account

---

[1] Corbett 1991 has the best general discussion.

does not relate what principles the first man adopted in deciding upon the names that he chose, but apparently Adam's choices met with God's approval. For the Latin language, a story of the originary act of naming circulating in Rome of the late Republic offers a little more detail about what was thought to inform the decisions of these first speakers. From the extant books of the treatise *On the Latin Language* (*De lingua Latina*) by the scholar Marcus Terentius Varro, a coherent—albeit tantalizingly incomplete—narrative can be reconstructed concerning the origins of Latin vocabulary.[2] A group of "first-namers," guided by nature, generated a set of basic Latin nouns that were somehow expressive of the objects or ideas that they described in the real world. Verbal signifiers, in other words, had a perceptible relationship with their signifieds. Even at this elemental stage of the language, however, Varro suggests that mistakes may have been made. Among the types of mistakes committed is the occasional misapplication of grammatical gender—the apparently feminine noun for eagle (*aquila*), for example, confusedly designates both the male and the female bird (*ling.* 8.7). To Varro, then, not only the shape and sound of a word, but its grammatical gender as well, stem from some characteristic that inheres in the thing named, and it is this characteristic that these wise first-namers perceived by dint of their understanding of the natural world. So perhaps the feminine turnip deserves, if not overwrought reverence, at least serious scholarly consideration.

HUMAN LANGUAGE AND MORE-THAN-HUMAN REALITY

Much of my discussion in this book is predicated on a particular set of grammatical rules—those of grammatical gender—and attempts to demonstrate in detail how the Romans continually applied gender's apparent logic to an understanding of the world around them. A principle shared by many of the Roman scholars and grammarians who offer the bulk of my evidence is that the Latin language can both limit and determine the ways in which a person thinks about and perceives the external world, a notion now generally encompassed by the term "linguistic relativism." The most basic version of the modern manifestation of this view has become closely identified with the work of Edward Sapir and his student Benjamin Lee Whorf, and the areas of language to which this principle is applicable have been the subject of extensive speculation and controversy among scholars since the nineteenth century.[3] In recent years, linguists and cognitive scientists have become increasingly interested in demonstrating

[2] Varro presumably offered a fuller account in the lost portions of the treatise; for possible Stoic background see Allen 2005. Chapter 1 below goes into more detail concerning the reconstruction offered here, including evidence from the later grammatical tradition.

[3] For convenient overviews of the debate, see Gentner and Goldin-Meadow 2003; Deutscher 2010: 1–22.

those varied areas of human experience in which perception does indeed seem affected by the observer's native language, such as in the interpretation of the color spectrum or the ways in which spatial relationships are expressed.[4]

I intend to provide a historical perspective to this ongoing debate over the extent to which the structure of language affects perception of the world. Using as my laboratory the stable data of the Latin language and Latin literature, I will be focusing on understanding a single pervasive but often neglected aspect of the Latin learner's world: Roman attitudes toward grammatical gender. Grammatical gender forced speakers of Latin, beginning from when they first learned to talk, to classify all the objects and concepts encountered in, or invented for, the external world into one (and, occasionally, two) of three categories: the masculine, the feminine, or the neuter. This linguistic process of sexing the universe, of providing gendered categories for each of its elements, assisted the native speaker in turn by providing labels through which that named universe could be further interpreted and understood. To offer two clear and especially prominent examples: positing the earth (*terra*) as feminine, and reinforcing this conception through daily usage, contributes to the notion that the natural world reproduces itself in ways analogous to the human; positing the powers of fertility as having both male and female grammatical gender, as with the native Roman deities Liber and Libera, extends that same analogy to the workings of the gods. In these two instances, grammatical gender works to organize the realms of both the human and the more-than-human.

The system of grammatical gender in a given language often strikes even native speakers of that language as serving no obvious purpose. Indeed, a language such as English seems to function perfectly well as a means of sharing information even though its gender system has largely disappeared, and on the daily occasions when non-native speakers communicate in a gendered language, errors of gender rarely cause their basic points to be misunderstood.[5] Such uncertainty over the function of genders among contemporary language users renders attempts to reconstruct their origins all the more difficult.[6] But if gender possesses no obvious pragmatic function in rendering communication more efficient, why do gender systems survive in so many of the world's languages? A possible answer explored in this book is that grammatical gender, whatever its origin, persists for underlying cognitive reasons, ones that have little to do with making speakers mutually intelligible. Numerous studies in linguistics have shown that, even though native speakers are no closer than scholars to being able to account for the purpose of grammatical gender, this

---

[4] Deutscher 2010: 25–98, 217–232 (color); Gentner and Goldin-Meadow 2003: 7–8 (space).

[5] Examples in Yaguello 1978: 92–93.

[6] The two basic approaches to origins are associated with Grimm 1890: 307–555 (gender arises from personification) and Brugmann 1889 (gender arises from morphology and analogy, with biological sex playing only a minor role). For later refinements to each side of this dichotomy see Yaguello 1978, citing in particular the work of Sapir, Meillet, and Jakobson.

ignorance does not prevent them from seeing gender, either consciously or not, as a "reflection of a vision of the universe."[7] I will be citing numerous examples from both ancient and modern languages of this fundamental desire of human beings to "make sense" of everyday speech by relating it to the external reality that that speech attempts to describe. In particular, I will be exploring rationalizations of grammatical gender by speakers and writers of Latin, rationalizations that I do not necessarily claim have any correspondence with the actual historical origins of the gender system, but that can tell us much about Roman attitudes toward not only grammatical gender but also biological sex.

I have no doubt that, by the classical period, Latin scholars and speakers both sensed and exploited a relationship between linguistic gender and physical sex. Perhaps seduced by the need to see a more-than-human logic at work in the creation of their language, they used grammatical gender to create a world that is divided, like language, into opposing categories of male (masculine) and female (feminine).[8] This drive toward rationalization exposes a problem inherent in the antiquarian reconstructions that have pervaded Roman scholarship since the late Republic. In their desire to attribute meaning to grammatical gender, scholars of ancient Rome reconstruct an ideal prehistory, one in which Latin's original speakers sex the world by assigning specific genders to nouns, both inanimate and animate. In creating such an early etiology of grammatical gender, the Latin grammarians established assumptions that necessarily restricted contemporary and future perceptions about what grammatical gender can mean.[9] I intend to make this potential for confusion into a virtue. The tendency to seek an originary function in gender creates a self-reinforcing circuit, as a natural world filled with the dichotomy of masculine and feminine is constructed to correspond with the grammatical world of masculine and feminine.[10] The workings of genesis amnesia can also contribute to this circuit: if a given noun, though not "born a woman," assumes a grammatically feminine gender, over time this gender can facilitate the process by which the thing named accrues sexed qualities that speakers ultimately choose to identify as socially "feminine." A recent survey of laboratory research on grammatical gender shows that the mere creation of categories causes human subjects to create meaningful similarities among the members of each category. For example, when learning that an unfamiliar word for "violin" was feminine, English speakers chose as descriptors of the word adjectives such as "beautiful," "curvy," and "elegant"; when told that the unfamiliar word was masculine, sub-

[7] Yaguello 1978: 93 ("Le genre est-il le reflet d'une vision de l'univers?").
[8] Yaguello 1978: 91–113 offers a fascinating account of how this dichotomy in modern French plays itself out in French society.
[9] Cf. Butler 1990: 46–47.
[10] For efforts in antiquity and beyond to construct "nature" in ways that match the perceived realities of the social world, see Flemming 2000: 1–28.

jects described the object as "difficult," "impressive," and "noisy."[11] Experiments such as this show how the grammatical categories of "masculine" and "feminine" can help reinforce a normative dichotomy of "masculine" and "feminine" in society at large. One particularly visible consequence of these associations is that a number of inanimate nouns come to acquire anthropomorphic features associated with animal, and particularly human, sexuality. To cite one familiar example, the American Statue of Liberty ultimately owes its female manifestation to the grammatical gender of the virtue that it personifies, the Latin feminine noun *libertas*. In this context, I will explore how Latin grammatical gender, regardless of origins, allows the Romans to create order by sexing their world.

SEX (*SEXUS*) AND GENDER (*GENUS*)

The consistent overlap, and even occasional identification, of grammatical gender with biological sex by speakers in ancient Rome finds an analogue in the Latin nouns commonly used to denote "gender" and "sex." In a distinction that prevails throughout Latinity, *genus* is the normal Latin noun for the grammatical category, while *sexus* indicates the biological division of male and female humans and animals. Variations within this basic distinction, however, do occur. Unsurprisingly, from the beginnings of their literature Latin speakers have no qualms about applying the more general noun, *genus*, meaning "type" or "category," to the particular categories of "male" and "female" human beings and animals—to "sex," in other words—and this practice continues across a broad range of texts and genres throughout Latinity.[12] The word *sexus*, by contrast, has a history that is both more circumscribed and more revealing. In Varro's *On the Latin Language*, the earliest formal discussion of Latin grammar, the noun *sexus* denotes grammatical gender. In introducing those properties that characterize the various parts of speech, Varro writes that three features mark each noun and pronoun: gender (*sexus*), number, and case (*ling.* 8.46). As Roman grammar develops a more specialized vocabulary after Varro, *genus* entirely replaces *sexus* as the default term for referring to grammatical gender, but *sexus* does makes its appearance in these philological texts when the writers choose to echo a preexistent tradition—one that seemingly dates back to Varro—in affirming that grammatical gender and biological sex are to be closely identified.[13] Hence, even as *genus* develops a specialized meaning for the

---

[11] Boroditsky et al. 2003; this example, one of several offered, is from 71–72.

[12] ThLL vol. VI, 2 1895.32–72 (O. Hey).

[13] Serv. *gramm.* IV 408.1, Serg. *gramm.* IV 493.8, Cledon. *gramm.* V 10.19, Frg. Bob. *gramm.* V 652.9. For details, see the discussion in chapter 1 of Consent. *gramm.* V 343.7–344.37.

grammarians, the notion of biological sex as an explanatory principle is never too distant to access.

This tendency for the scholarly tradition to identify grammatical gender with biological sex explains in part the grammarians' neglect of the neuter gender as an active participant in their worldview. It is here that another etymology comes into play. In deriving the word for grammatical gender (*genus*) from the verb that denotes human procreation (*genero*), Varro leads later grammarians to assume that there must be only two "proper" genders, the masculine and the feminine. The neuter, as inherently non-procreative, becomes viewed as a non-integral part of the gender system.[14] This neglect of the neuter receives further impetus from the restricted semantic range of those Latin words categorized as neuter. The types of words that tend to be marked with this gender include those describing classes or collections of objects and ideas (such as the neuter noun *genus* itself), those with functions perceived as passive (the internal organs), or those that are the product of becoming (e.g., neuter fruits are normally conceived of as the product of feminine trees).[15] Such classes would account for a relatively small percentage of those Latin nouns in active daily use. More importantly, however, none of these classes of the neuter is understood to bifurcate or to be actively involved in production in the same ways as those Latin nouns that fluctuate between masculine and feminine (see further chapter 2). An ancillary indication that the neuter may have had less powerful semantic connotations than the other two genders resides in its gradual disappearance during the final centuries of Latin's existence as a living language, a development for which traces survive from as early as the beginning of the second century AD.[16] The consequences of this development are most readily visible in the fact that none of the modern Romance languages has a morphologically distinct neuter gender.[17] This neglect by the grammarians—and by native speakers of the language—carries over into the other major areas upon which I focus in my final three chapters: the manipulation of grammatical gender by poets, its role in naming deities, and the treatment of hermaphrodites. As a result, I will follow my sources in treating the neuter only occasionally throughout the following pages, with emphasis placed instead on the role of the grammatical genders of masculine and feminine in creating and reaffirming the role of the male and female in the Roman world.

---

[14] Varro frg. 245 in Funaioli (1907), who provides testimony from the later tradition; cf. too Don. *gramm. mai.* IV 375.20 (Keil): *vel principalia vel sola genera duo sunt, masculinum et femininum*. For more details, see chapter 1.

[15] LHS 8–10.

[16] Adams 2013: 428–431.

[17] Adams 2013: 383–384; for Romance languages, see Maiden 2013: 167–174.

THE LATIN LANGUAGE AND THE ROMAN SOCIAL WORLD

Monique Wittig, in her 1985 article "The Mark of Gender," discusses the role of grammatical gender in contemporary French and English as "a sociological category that does not speak its name."[18] Her discussion concentrates principally upon the absence of a commonly agreed upon epicene third-person singular pronoun in English—that is, the failed attempts to replace the common-gendered "he" or the cumbersome "he or she" with something equivalent to the French "on," such as that pariah of English grammar teachers, the pronoun "one." Her argument will be familiar because of its subsequent influence. By using simply "he" to refer to an indefinite grammatical subject, regardless of that subject's biological sex, language becomes constructed daily as a site for reinforcing sexual hierarchies in the real world, even in a relatively genderless language such as English.[19] This phenomenon, by which the masculine represents the default gender for groups of mixed sex, also receives attention in Roman antiquity, as do the consequences of the practice. In his commentary on Vergil's *Aeneid*, Servius promotes the use of the masculine default on the grounds that the masculine constitutes the "better sex," a formulation that reaffirms the ease with which the artificial rules of grammar can be applied to real-world relationships between the sexes.[20]

I would like to suggest that Wittig's approach can be applied to grammatical gender in Latin, but not in order to claim that the inherent structures of Latin allow it to serve as a tool for sexism. Rather, I would like to suggest that the tendency of orthodox Latin grammar to explain a noun's gender by reference to the corresponding biological sex combines with the daily usage of writers and speakers to succeed in heterosexualizing Roman culture's worldview.[21] As I discuss fully in chapter 1, the division of the world into male and female begins with how Roman scholars etymologize the very Latin word that means "gender." *Genus*, Roman students were told repeatedly and at an early stage in their education, derives from the verb *genero*, the verb describing the act of sexual reproduction. Furthermore, the invariable listing of the genders in antiquity—with masculine first, followed by feminine and neuter, an order so familiar to modern language learners—was constructed by the ancient grammatical tradition as "not merely a traditional order in which to treat the genders, but a natural linguistic order."[22] The stability of this grammatical organization through

---

[18] Wittig 1985: 4.

[19] Corbett 1991: 219–221 provides, with bibliography, an interesting analysis of the issue from a historical and linguistic point of view.

[20] Serv. *Aen.* 2.457: *meliori sexui . . . , id est masculino*; other examples in Vaahtera 2008: 257–259.

[21] Butler 1990: esp. 11, 45–48.

[22] Vaahtera 2008: 248; her entire discussion is relevant to this point.

the millennia informs other types of orderliness that arise from the creation of categories along the lines of sex/gender.

And yet, as Bourdieu says, "to bring order is to bring division, to divide the universe into opposing entities"; but any process of division simplifies, inevitably promoting misrecognition of the original reasons for creating that order.[23] A second etymology further contributes to naturalizing this process of division. The word dividing the physical sexes—*sexus*—likely originates from the verb meaning "to cut" (*seco*). Although there is no evidence that the Romans were aware of this particular etymology, they nevertheless recognize at work behind the noun the principle of mutually exclusive division: an earlier neuter form (*secus*) appears in its extant occurrences exclusively with adjectives meaning "manly" (*virile*) or "womanly" (*muliebre, femineum*). "Sex," then, describes a "cutting" in two, a splitting of the human world into mutually opposing camps.[24] And yet, as has been aptly observed, these sorts of mutually opposing divisions in fact exaggerate the difference between a man and woman: "men and women are closer to each other than either is to anything else—for instance, mountains, kangaroos, or coconut palms."[25] The division by sex, then, would seem to serve as means to another set of ends. Beginning with the overtly innocent instances of etymologizing the nouns *genus* and *sexus*, one sees not only Latin vocabulary, but the dominant means by which Romans make sense of their world, divided into the categories male/female, masculine/feminine, active/passive, dry/wet, and so on. In this process of identifying grammatical rules with social categories, cultural divisions become naturalized, and there is created a normative view of the separation of the sexes, another step in the invention, so to speak, of heterosexuality.[26] These mythically stable oppositions constructed along the lines of sex contribute to the separation of male and female into exclusive areas, and the history of injustices arising from this separation need not be rehearsed here. But some of the implications of the situations in which these categories are played out, in the creation and reinforcement of what has been called the "heterosexual matrix," will be examined in the following chapters.[27]

OUTLINE OF BOOK

Saint Gregory the Great concludes the introductory epistle to his *Magna Moralia* with a famous assessment of the relationship between the rules of grammar

[23] Bourdieu 1990: 210.

[24] Szemerényi 1969: 977–978; Vaan 2008: 560–561.

[25] Rubin 1975: 179.

[26] I derive the phrase "invention of heterosexuality" from Katz 2007. For the invention of heterosexuality in the Augustan Age (and the concurrent abasement of homosexuality), see Habinek 1997.

[27] Butler 1990: 9.

and an understanding of the divine: "I consider it most unworthy to confine the language of the heavenly oracle within the rules of Donatus."[28] At the time Gregory was writing in the late sixth century AD, the evolution of Latin into the various dialects that were to become the Romance languages had reached an advanced stage, and in opposition to this perceived decline there had been developing a full corpus of grammatical writings that strove to preserve and enforce the rules of classical Latin usage. In rejecting a strict adherence to this corpus, which he identifies here with one of its great exponents, the fourth-century grammarian Donatus, Gregory eschews rule-bound strictures and superfluous rhetoric in favor of a writing style that will accord with the needs of his subject matter in the *Magna Moralia*, an exposition of Christian morality through a thorough exegesis of the Book of Job. Judging in accordance with these standards, Gregory would deem the following pages, which depend heavily upon these "rules of Donatus," eminently unworthy.

Chapter 1 begins by reconstructing how the Romans imagined that the earliest Latin speakers employed grammatical gender. From as early as Varro, scholars and grammarians occupied themselves with cataloguing the peculiarities of grammatical gender—instances, for example, when gender assignment seems counterintuitive, or where one noun can vary between masculine, feminine, and neuter. This scholarly activity, with little extant precedent in Greek tradition, finds grammarians consistently placing great importance upon the identification of grammatical gender with biological sex. I attempt to explain this fascination with "sex and gender" by examining the reasons posited for the fluid gender of nouns, and by considering the commonest practitioners of grammatical gender bending (in particular Vergil). By dividing the world into discrete sexual categories, Latin vocabulary works to encourage the pervasive heterosexualization of Roman culture.

Extant texts from the late Republic and early Empire attribute to poets writing in Latin a power that the Roman grammarians do not recognize either for writers of prose or for speakers of Latin in general: the ability to manipulate, apparently at whim, the standard gender of a noun. Vergil, for instance, uses the word for "tree bark" (*cortex*) in both the masculine and the feminine for no clear semantic reason; rather he does it, we are told by later commentators, because that is what Vergil does. In chapter 2, I survey eight different explanations—ranging from metrical considerations to the desire to allude to a Greek intertext—that scholars have suggested since antiquity for the literary phenomenon of the non-standard gender. In my conclusion I follow an assumption that lies unexplored in several of these explanations. Roman scholars attributed to poets the privileged knowledge of an early poetic language, one that had access to mythic and folkloric associations dating back to the period when the Latin

---

[28] Greg. M. *moral. epist.* 5: *indignum vehementer existimo, ut verba caelestis oraculi restringam sub regulis Donati.*

language was first coming into existence. During this period, grammatical genders were fluid, and could be applied to various items in the world in accordance with the privileged knowledge of these ur-speakers.

Chapter 3 provides an opportunity for speculation about places in the poets where fluid grammatical gender has not received much attention. I begin with a survey of visual evidence from antiquity to demonstrate that, with only apparent exceptions, personifications in ancient Rome are depicted with the sex that corresponds to the grammatical gender of the noun that describes them (the masculine noun *honos*, for example, appears in representations only as a man, the feminine *virtus* only as a woman). After establishing this point, I examine poetic texts that offer an array of examples in which a poet plays with the notion of personification through the exploitation of a noun's gender. My approach builds on the conclusions of the previous chapter, as I show poets using grammatical gender as a shorthand to recall situations or episodes from the mythic past. I conclude with an analysis of Catullus 6, where sensitivity to grammatical gender contributes to the riddling nature of this short poem.

In chapter 4 I move from literature to a broader consideration of the role of grammatical gender in daily religious experience. Not surprisingly in light of the preceding chapter's discussion of personifications, the grammatical gender of a god's name matches the perceived sex of its imagined incarnation. I extend this observation to an analysis of the *indigetes*, a set of minor deities—nearly 150 are attested in our sources—who seem to have ruled every aspect of daily life, and to whom the Romans appealed, in particular at significant transitional stages such as birth, marriage, and death. There is detectible in the numerous extant allusions to these deities, as well as to other divine powers, a tendency to group gods in sexed pairs, such as that of the feminine goddess of purification, Februa, and her masculine consort, Februus. Further support for these pairings is found in ancient philosophical speculation that deities must encompass within themselves the characteristics of both sexes in order to best represent the nature of the physical world. I close by showing how this originary state of divine androgyny—whether historical or the product of intellectual speculation—collapses over time in ways analogous to the loss of fluid gender for nouns, as the relentless dichotomy of masculine and feminine drives different aspects of reality to become associated with one particular sex. Passivity and nurture become characteristic features of female deities, activity and culture of male.

My fifth chapter closes the book by looking once again at mixed sex, but this time as manifest in the human body. I begin by surveying the different attitudes toward human intersexuality in the Greek world in order to highlight the difference from Roman conceptions. During the Roman Republic the human hermaphrodite enjoyed a dual existence in more ways than the obvious. The slippery nature of its sexuality placed the hermaphrodite in the category of the religious sacred, capable of having unimaginable effects on the real world; at the same time its status as a prodigy of nature made it a concern of the political elite. This divided existence was regularly resolved by a complex religious and political process employed to ensure the prodigy's banishment to outside the boundaries of the Roman state. Here again the combination of the sacred and the mysterious finds analogues with the fluid-gendered nouns and the androgynous divinities of the Roman past. And, just as those once fluid gods and nouns come to occupy over time the rigid categories of masculine and feminine, so too with the dawn of the Empire the treatment of the hermaphrodite as a prodigy ceases. Concurrent with the ending of the prodigy process, our sources also locate the end of the awe once felt for the hermaphrodite, as it devolves into a mere curiosity, a plaything for the privileged.

While each of these chapters can be read as an independent case study, I intend them together to present a diachronic narrative of the imagined development of sex and gender in ancient Rome. Latin's earliest stages are perceived as extraordinarily fluid regarding both grammatical gender and physical sex, and this fluidity is expressed in the practice of the vatic poets who have alleged access to this early stage of the language, and by the sex of the numerous minor deities who were created in order to watch over the daily life of the Romans. As time went on, however, grammatical gender and—by a necessary corollary—the roles associated with biological sex came to be reified into rigid categories, the violation of which was thus deemed an action contrary to nature. Nouns adopt fixed genders; the sex of gods correlate to fixed roles; the mysterious hermaphrodite no longer reflects a lost, sacred age of flux and fluidity. Unlike Saint Gregory, I believe that it is an eminently worthy enterprise, and one of continued relevance, to disentangle the ways in which speakers of Latin constructed their society in accordance with the "rules of Donatus." Grammatical gender may have originated as an innocent accident of morphology. In practice, however, its system provided Latin speakers a means of organizing, categorizing, delineating—and in many cases marginalizing—features of the world around them.

Chapter 1

Roman Scholars on Grammatical Gender and Biological Sex

[Francis I, on improving diplomatic relations between France and Switzerland]

—I'll pay *Switzerland* the honour of standing godfather for my next child.

—Your majesty, said the minister, in so doing, would have all the grammarians in *Europe* upon your back; *Switzerland*, as a republick, being a female, can in no construction be godfather.

—She may be godmother, replied *Francis*, hastily—so announce my intentions by a courier to-morrow morning.
(Lawrence Sterne, *The Life and Opinions of Tristram Shandy, Gentleman*, vol. 4, ch. 21)[1]

Sterne offers here a transparent play on the relationship between grammatical gender and biological sex. Names of countries, regularly gendered feminine in the Romance languages, accordingly take on the features of females in both visual representations and the imaginings of native speakers. Just as it would have been unthinkable for a Roman artist to portray the personified city *Roma* as a man, so too does Francis's minister identify the king's proposal to make Switzerland a godfather as grammatically impossible. Two assumptions underlying this exchange will inform the following chapter: first, that to equate biological sex with grammatical gender marks a natural and self-evident move; second, that those who busy themselves with the study of grammar have strong opinions regarding the historical validity of this first assumption.

---

[1] The French "source" (Ménage 1715: 2.214) that Sterne cites for his anecdote does not mention this confusion over Switzerland's sex.

INTRODUCTION

I shall echo the practice of the ancient grammarians by beginning with one of their preferred research methods: etymology. The earliest extant attempt to locate the origins of the Latin word for grammatical gender, *genus*, dates to the late Republic. Varro derives the noun from the verb *generare* "to beget," since genders "are only those things that give birth" (Varro frg. 245 Funaioli: *Varro ait genera tantum illa esse quae generant*). As is the case with most of his etymologies, Varro does not simply appeal to metaphor here, but he envisions words as organic bodies with a life of their own.[2] Concordant with that life is the ability to age, die, and give birth to related word forms. Unlike many other aspects of Varronian grammatical theory, this etymology comes to wield significant influence as it reverberates throughout the lexicographical and grammatical traditions. The *Thesaurus Linguae Latinae* lists nine direct citations, and a number of additional allusions can be found in ancient commentaries and scholia.[3] This scholarly tradition will continue to offer more explicit examples of the ways in which grammatical gender allows words themselves to participate in a biology of sexual reproduction. And yet, while modern scholars confirm Varro's conclusion that the word *genus* is related to the notion of creation and procreation, they do not consider why this finding holds sway over the subsequent grammatical tradition. I intend in this book to identify some of the sources for this fascination with reproducing genders.

Exploring what grammatical gender meant in ancient Rome requires both patient philology and an openness to the theoretical possibilities of the ways in which sex and gender are able to coexist. The philological aspect derives from the fact that, in the absence of any full discussion of fluid gender in Latin,[4] my research has entailed poring through the corpus of the Roman grammarians and cataloguing the several hundred instances of nouns with variable gender and the opinions expressed about them by both ancient and modern commen-

---

[2] Ahl 1985: 22–28.

[3] ThLL vol. VI, 2 1885.28–35, with related etymologies from γῆ and *gens* at 35–43 (O. Hey, with fuller testimonia than Funaioli). The earliest such reference that I have found in the Greek grammatical tradition is among the Byzantine commentaries on Dionysius Thrax (*Sch. in D.T.*, GG 1.3: 361.29): πόθεν γένος; ἀπὸ τοῦ γείνω, ὅ δηλοῖ τὸ γεννῶ.

[4] The most helpful general surveys are Wackernagel 1926–1928: 2.1–51, Garcia de Diego López 1945–1946, LHS 5–12, and Renehan 1998. Lunelli 1969: 100–102 n. 17 has bibliography on select issues, and NW 889–1019 contains nearly all relevant data. For individual texts and authors, see Catone 1964: 57–60 (Ennius), Koterba 1905: 136 (Pacuvius and Accius), Cartault 1898: 49–51, 53–55 (Lucretius), Woytek 1970: 30–35 (Varro *Men.*), *ILS* 5: 857–858 (inscriptions), Tolkiehn 1901: 181–182 (epigraphic poetry), Jeanneret 1917: 54–57 (curse tablets), Väänänen 1982: 182–188 (vulgar Latin). It is worth noting that the recent development of the online ThLL, which allows a search under the lexicon's category *de genere*, would make a comprehensive survey of fluid gender considerably more feasible (at least for those letters already covered by the lexicon).

tators. At the same time, this apparently unprocessed material provides much room for theoretical extrapolation: I hope to demonstrate how the ancient conceptualizing of grammatical gender offers an attractive model through which to understand aspects of human sexuality and constructed social gender. This chapter concludes with the suggestion that the choices that the Romans made in essentializing the concept of grammatical gender—that is, positing origins from nature that correspond with the workings of biological sex—form part of a heterosexualization of the world. This creation of a grammatical world of "compulsory heterosexuality," as recent critics have put it, shapes in turn the treatment of human sex and gender throughout Roman antiquity. In subsequent chapters, I intend to outline how this kind of essentializing of gender takes place in other areas of Roman culture as well, from poetry to religion to political attitudes toward the human hermaphrodite.

If one were to ask of a modern linguist the formulaic question of the Latin grammarians, "*Genus quid est?*" ("What is gender?"), the response would be something like the following:

Genders are classes of nouns reflected in the behavior of associated words.[5]

This standard linguistic definition of gender is strictly formalist, in much the way that we might classify in English those nouns that form their plurals by adding the letter "s" (one cat / two cats) separately from those that do so through the change of an internal vowel sound (one mouse / two mice). The Latin grammarians demonstrate an awareness of this type of formalism, often presenting nouns in conjunction with a pronoun (e.g., *hic vir, huius viri,* etc.); in this practice the "associated word" (in this case a form of the pronoun *hic*), demonstrates gender independently from the morphology of the noun itself (e.g., Varro *ling.* 9.41). As should even now be clear, however, I am interested less in the morphology of nouns than in the semantic connotations of their grammatical gender: how native speakers of Latin conceived of the categories of "masculine" or "feminine" or, in many cases, the category "neither of these" (that is, *neuter*).

The modern scholarly definition of gender given above, if strictly applied, implies that a word unaccompanied by an associated adjective or pronoun has no gender in that particular context. The elasticity of this definition proves especially useful for hybrid nouns such as the German *Mädchen* ("girl"). Although formally neuter, semantic grounds frequently prompt native speakers, in informal contexts, to use the feminine pronoun *sie* ("she") when referring back to the neuter noun.[6] An analogous hybrid common in English is the word "baby." In most cases, of course, the pronouns "she" or "he" are applied accord-

---

[5] Hockett 1958: 231.
[6] Corbett 1991: 183–184, 225–260.

ing to the child's sex, but the alternative neuter pronoun "it" is often used by those for whom the semantic fact of the baby's sex is not essential (e.g., those who are not the baby's parents). This contest between semantics and lexical choice is also a feature of Latin. The phenomenon appears particularly often in Roman comedy, in apparent imitation of Greek models. The comic playwright Terence, for example, describes a young lover, Pamphilus, addressing his girl-friend as *mea Glycerium* ("my Glycerium"). Since Glycerium's biological sex is undoubtedly important to him, Pamphilus uses the feminine adjective *mea* to describe her despite the fact that it formally disagrees with the neuter gender of her proper name.[7] As the fourth-century commentator Donatus remarks on another passage of Terence, Pamphilus has here "rendered the form that cor-responds with [the noun's] meaning" rather than adhered to strict grammatical categories (Don. Ter. *Eun.* 302.2: *declinationem ad intellectum rettulit*). The oc-currence of analogous gender changes in inscriptions shows that the desire to match grammar and biology extended beyond the comic stage. The nouns *delicium* and *deliciae* ("sweetie") function in Latin as terms of endearment for a single male or female beloved, normally young, despite the fact that the nouns are respectively neuter singular and feminine plural. As happens in Terence, however, meaning can take precedence over grammar: the masculine and femi-nine singular forms *delicius* and *delicia* occasionally surface in order to corre-spond more closely with the physical reality of the boy or girl so designated (e.g., *ILS* 7668, 9346).[8] None of these examples of hybrid nouns, from modern Germany to ancient Rome, will occasion much surprise. Each refers to an ani-mate being whose biological sex prompts the violation of strict rules of agree-ment. As we shall see, however, speakers and writers in Rome could extend this practice to so-called inanimate words as well, words that would seem to have no sexual characteristics. It was simply necessary that these variations in gen-der had sufficient authority (*auctoritas*) to back up the change. I will touch upon the nature of this peculiar authority in the final section of this chapter, and treat it more fully in the following chapter on the use of grammatical gen-der among Roman poets.

Grammatical gender can be found in many disparate language groups—not just in Indo-European, but in two-thirds of surviving African languages, as well as in several hundred of the native families spoken in Australia and New Guin-ea.[9] The major Asiatic families and most indigenous North American languages provide the principal exceptions to the prevalence of gender categories. Among several Indo-European languages with gender, including Latin, there are three active genders—masculine, feminine, and neuter—while in others various ad-ditions to and modifications of these categories exist. Most Romance languages,

---

[7] Ter. *Andr.* 134; cf. NW 889–890; Wackernagel 1926–1928: 2.18–19.
[8] For details from *CIL* 6, see Harrod 1909: 74 n. 78, 77.
[9] Corbett 1991: 1–2; for PIE, Matasović 2004.

such as French and Italian, have lost neuter forms, while in English the only significant expression of gender that survives is in the third-person personal pronouns, where the singular forms "he," "she," and "it" normally denote biological sex or, in the case of "it," the lack thereof. This chapter concentrates on nouns in Latin, and in order to maintain focus on the sex and gender equation, I will follow the Varronian tradition in restricting my examples principally to nouns with the ability to procreate: that is, those identified in the extant Latin material as normally masculine and feminine.[10]

Some nouns belong to intuitive gender categories. For example, the commonest Latin word for "man"—*vir*—is masculine and those for "woman"—*femina* and *mulier*—are feminine. But beyond such clear cases, matters frequently become less intuitive and even utterly baffling. The male eagle, *aquila*, is designated only by the first-declension female form, and the commonest vulgar term for the female genitalia, *cunnus*, is masculine, while that for the penis, *mentula*, is feminine. When presented with cases such as these, the temptation to reconstruct situations in which gender assignment makes a particular point about sexualities is nearly irresistible. And indeed on a broader level, scholars have made various attempts to explain the assignment of words to specific gender categories as indicative of some sort of systematic view of how each element of the external world possesses or reflects discernible sexual characteristics. Perhaps the most ambitious example of this quest for systematization is that of Jacob Grimm (1785–1863, best known today as one of the Brothers Grimm). Grimm famously attempted to explain the assignment of gender to non-animate nouns in Proto-Indo-European (PIE) through, among other things, a comparison of the various daughter languages.[11] Grimm posited that grammatical gender originated in the practice of the earliest speakers of PIE, who personified all the inanimate objects of the world, deeming "masculine" those with harsh and active qualities, while the things denoted by "feminine" nouns were characterized by passive traits such as gentleness and softness. As time progressed, Grimm argued, these

[10] See, for example, Pomp. *gramm.* V 159.24–26: "If we follow [Varro's] authority, there will be only two genders, masculine and feminine. Only these two genders can procreate" (*quodsi sequemur auctoritatem ipsius [sc. Varronis], non erunt genera nisi duo, masculinum et femininum. nulla enim genera creare possunt nisi haec duo*). Most post-Varronian grammarians in fact divide Latin nouns into not two or even three but five *genera*: masculine, feminine, neuter, common, and epicene, a division already found in the *Techne* of Dionysius Thrax (*GG* 1.1: 24.8–25.2; on this treatise, see Dickey 2007: 77–80). The categories of both common nouns (where gender depends on accompanying words, not morphology of the noun; e.g., *hic equus* for a stallion, *haec equus* for a mare) and epicene nouns (see the example of *columba* in the text below) clearly assume the identification of sex with gender. Ahlquist 1996 offers a history of these categories.

[11] Grimm 1890: 307–551, in particular 345–357 ("Personification"; originally published 1831). Brugmann (1889 and, in English summary, 1897) counters that non-animate nouns obtain gender purely by analogy with the morphology of animate categories; among later discussions see in particular Fodor 1959. For ancient debates, see Blank 1998: 176–185, Baynes 2002.

associations were largely forgotten, but traces remained in the survival of gender categories.

Although Grimm's conclusions remained popular for several decades, constructing such a worldview for societies deep in prehistory must inevitably lead to special pleading, and the categories constructed likely reveal as much about the way the researcher organizes his or her own world as about the belief-system of early speakers of a given language. One can imagine the heady atmosphere that must have prevailed in Grimm's day, when the notion of a Proto-Indo-European language was first raised; the headiness, indeed, spawned much wild speculation. Rampant enthusiasm over reconstructing the earliest stages of language development presumably explains why, when the Linguistic Society of Paris drafted its bylaws in 1865, article eleven included the following provision: "The Society will accept no communication dealing with . . . the origin of language."[12] Examples in the next chapter will document clearly that the scholarly backlash against romanticizing the origins of grammatical gender still holds sway in the traditions of classical scholarship, where standard commentaries on the Roman poets faithfully cite parallels when an unusual gender is encountered, and then pass on without further comment. Oddly assigned genders are worth noting, but apparently the uncertainties attendant in attempting to evaluate their meaning is too great.[13] Nobody wishes to be labeled the new Grimm. Fortunately, however, the speculations of Roman scholars and grammarians remain free of this type of self-conscious caution, and it is with these speculations, rather than with linguistic "truth," that this chapter will primarily engage.

The first European who is recorded to have divided his language up into the categories of "males" (ἄρρενα), "females" (θήλεα), and "things" (σκεύη) is the fifth-century BC Greek philosopher Protagoras.[14] The principal extant reference to his activity in this area finds Protagoras criticizing the logic employed in assigning gender to inanimate objects. Aristotle reports that the philosopher accused Homer of a "grammatical solecism" for putting the introductory word of the *Iliad*, μῆνις ("wrath"), into the feminine gender, and he raised a similar objection to the feminine noun πήληξ ("helmet"). Protagoras "corrects" Homer by maintaining that the two words must in fact be masculine (Arist. *SE* 14.173b = DK A28). Although Aristotle is tantalizingly concise in preserving this information, it seems clear that Protagoras argues here for more than a regularization of morphology. One may grant the possibility that purely morphological considerations account for Protagoras's mention of the word πήληξ; although exclusively feminine in its extant occurrences, the termination of the nomina-

---

[12] Kendon 1991: 199.

[13] LHS 1: 404: "die Stufen sind nicht mehr zu rekonstruieren"; Sihler 1995: 245 ("most ideas on the question are necessarily very speculative").

[14] Arist. *Rh.* 3.5.5 (DK A27). Aristotle uses μεταξύ to signify neuter; the term οὐδέτερον (Latin *neutrum*) first appears in the later grammarians.

tive in -ξ in fact fits more closely a masculine paradigm. The same principle, however, does not apply to μῆνις, for which both morphology and status as an abstract concept anticipate the feminine gender.[15] Instead, Protagoras wishes for language consistently to identify biological sex with grammatical gender and, by extension, to equate stereotypically male contexts—such as those involving Achilles's vengeful wrath, or a warrior's helmet—with a corresponding masculine gender. An ancient commentator on Vergil may be making an analogous association when he remarks confidently that the poet uses *clipeus* ("shield") in the masculine, even though no accompanying adjective makes clear the noun's gender in this particular context (Serv. Auct. *Aen.* 3.286).

Intriguing parallels for Protagoras's dictum may be found in modern languages as well. In French, for instance, the word for "lightning" (*foudre*) normally possesses the feminine gender in both its literal and figurative senses. That gender can, however, shift to the masculine when the word occurs in contexts identifiable with traditional male activity, such as when denoting Jupiter's thunderbolt, or in metaphorically describing a warrior as "battle lightning" (*foudre de guerre*).[16]

Corresponding debates about the equivalence of gender and semantics underlie a parody by the playwright Aristophanes that is contemporary with Protagoras. In the *Clouds* (658–693), the character Socrates unwittingly convinces Strepsiades that the gender and the sex of nouns must coincide. A man whose name becomes feminine (Amynia) when you address him, for example, must necessarily have feminine characteristics (686–692).[17] Strepsiades's existence in the world of the concrete and sensual makes it intuitive for him to expect such correspondences between word and thing. He concludes his lesson by objecting that Socrates's teaching is useless: "why should I learn things that everybody knows?"[18]

Roman writers resumed with gusto this controversial dispute about the relationship between real-world sex and linguistic gender, as can be seen from silent poetic practice and abundant scholarly discussion. Before turning to some of these texts, it will be helpful to devote a few words to chronology in order to remind us of the great timespan that separates the grammarians and scholars

[15] I follow here Wackernagel 1926–1928: 2.4–5 against those who argue that Protagoras's objections are either purely morphological (e.g., Gomperz 1901–1912: 1.441–445, for whom μῆνις requires special pleading) or do not reflect a fully thought-out system (e.g., Fehling 1965: 214–215). Compare the discussion of Hom. *Il.* 15.626 below.

[16] Grevisse 1969: 199, who offers historical explanations for the variation.

[17] For a play on this idea in Rome, see Cic. *De orat.* 2.277 (Egilia); Porph. Hor. *sat.* 1.8.39 (Pediatia); Corbeill 1996: 97 with n. 115.

[18] Aristoph. *Nu.* 693 (ἀτὰρ τί ταῦθ᾽ ἃ πάντες ἴσμεν μανθάνω;); for the intellectual context, see Green 1979, esp. 20. That even "Socrates" suspects that biological sex determines grammatical gender is shown by the ease with which he segues from male and female animals to "male" and "female" objects to names of men and women.

that I will be mentioning from the poetic sources that they cite. The earliest extant texts written in an identifiable form of Latin date to the fifth century BC, while the Romans themselves traditionally dated the origins of Latin literature to the mid-third century. This puts the beginnings of Latin literature about 500 years after Homer, who normally marks the beginning of Greek literature. In contrast, the extant Latin grammatical tradition upon which I shall be concentrating begins for our purposes with Varro in the late first century BC, and then skips forward four centuries to a series of texts conveniently referred to collectively as the "Latin grammarians" (*Grammatici Latini*). These teachers and scholars, who now survive for the most part as little more than names, compiled their texts in the fourth, fifth, and later centuries AD, but based their work in large part on that of predecessors from the first centuries BC and AD whose works are now mostly lost, in particular the grammatical writings of Remmius Palaemon and Pliny the Elder.[19] When the *Grammatici Latini* discuss the use of grammatical gender in Latin, therefore, they refer to authors writing as much as five to seven hundred years earlier (the majority of whose texts they possess only in excerpts and who have been recognized as canonical since the first century BC) and about a language whose origins can be dated an approximate two hundred years before that. It should therefore be clear that, in attempting to reconstruct what these grammarians thought about grammatical gender, I am not attempting to recover the true "origins" of this phenomenon. These scholars clearly had no better access to such information than we do today. Rather my discussion, both in this chapter and later, aims to offer reasons why they posit the origins that they do.

GETTING UPTIGHT ABOUT GRAMMATICAL GENDER

As the epigraph from *Tristram Shandy* shows, grammatical gender comes up in unexpected situations, as the association of grammatical gender with biological sex offers ways for people to make sense of the world around them. Another modern example more closely reflects the concerns of the Roman grammarians. In adapting to film Henri-Pierre Roché's novel *Jules et Jim*, François Truffaut chose to emphasize those features of the relationship among the three main characters that best dramatize the precarious uncertainties of sex, love, and gender. The following exchange, new to the film, occurs between the two male protagonists, the German-speaking Jules and the Frenchman Jim, who alternate, confusedly, often painfully, and ultimately tragically, as the lovers of Catherine:

[19] Nettleship 1886. The attempt of Barwick 1922 to identify the *Ars grammatica* of Remmius Palaemon as a particularly prominent source has recently come under scrutiny; cf. Schenkeveld 2004: 17–27, with bibliography. North 2007 argues cautiously that quotations (as opposed to simple citations) in Festus derive from collections made in the early first century BC.

JULES: You will note that words cannot have the same significance in two different
   languages as they don't have the same gender. In German, war, death, the moon,
   are all masculine, while the sun and love are feminine. Life is neuter.
JIM: Life? Neuter? That's a nice concept, and very logical too.[20]

Here the inexorable logic of grammar offers bemused solace that, despite appearances to the contrary, there does indeed exist order in the world of sex and
gender (or at least German gender). This type of play can also sting—as the
remark that "life is neuter" seems to imply. A sensitivity similar to that attested
by this example surrounded the implications of grammatical gender in Roman
antiquity.

Two ancient anecdotes will convey the extent to which thinking about grammatical gender could get a Roman all excited. The dramatic date of the first
example is the early to mid-second century AD. In his *Attic Nights* (4.1), Aulus
Gellius describes a group of Romans who have assembled in the vestibule of the
imperial palace on the Palatine hill to pay their daily early-morning respects to
the emperor. As the crowd is waiting for the emperor to get out of bed, an excit-
able scholar is described. He has raised eyebrows and a serious voice, with a
look reminiscent of the official interpreter of the divinely inspired Sibylline
oracles (*interpres et arbiter Sibyllae oraculorum*). The subject of his discourse?
Latin grammar.[21] In particular, he expounds on the proper use of case endings
and gender for irregular Latin nouns, and his exhibition evokes in turn an excited response and lengthy debate from a prominent philosopher of the time,
Favorinus. Favorinus, whose notorious reputation as a hermaphrodite may
have made him particularly sensitive to a discussion about uncertain genders,
immediately shifts the argument from the subject at hand.[22] What is really important, he stresses, is not the command of grammatical niceties but the ability
to form a correct definition. In the debate that follows, Favorinus proceeds to
define the Latin word *penus*, a technical term designating personal property, by
quoting from a series of classical Latin texts.

The second example comes from a treatise written in the fifth or sixth century by an otherwise unknown schoolteacher from North Africa named Pompeius. As part of his commentary on Donatus's authoritative grammar of Latin,
Pompeius has just been discussing how Varro's derivation of *genus* from *genero*
dictates that there are only two proper genders, the masculine and the feminine. The exposition rapidly becomes less calm and conventional, until Pom-

---

[20] Truffaut 1968: 56.

[21] Vardi 2001 discusses the motif of the ridiculed scholar (usually a grammarian) in Gellius. For
a chronological consideration of the social position of the grammarian, in particular his ambiguous
status as both authority and object of ridicule, see Kaster 1988: 32–95, esp. 50–70.

[22] Keulen 2009: 126–134 offers a full discussion of Favorinus's alleged hermaphroditism. The
disputed historicity of the views that Gellius attributes to Favorinus does not affect my point here;
see Holford-Strevens 2003: 98–130, esp. 99–100 (Favorinus's physique) and 123–124 (on Gell. 4.1);
Beall 2001: 88–89 (Gellius's Favorinus on grammar).

peius exclaims to his pupils as follows (my translation attempts to reflect Pompeius's repetitive and awkward Latin):

> *hinc nascitur, id est hinc inventum est, ut possimus nos excusare, ut, quotienscumque circa genera peccaverimus, excusatio sit, non inperitia. puta si dicam "haec" paries, possum me excusare et dicere quod licet mihi hoc dicere. si . . . paries . . . non generat nec generatur, licet mihi pro voluntate mea quem ad modum voluero dicere.* (Pomp. gramm. V 159.27–33)

> As a result—that is, we've discovered from this that we can excuse ourselves of ignorance whenever we have made errors regarding the genders [of inanimate objects]. For example, if I should refer to a wall (*paries*) as feminine [*which is incorrect*], I can excuse myself and say that it's permissible for me to say this. [Since] . . . a wall can neither beget nor be begotten (*non generat nec generatur*), it's fine to say whatever I want to say in accordance with my own wishes.

There can be no doubt that Pompeius knows that the gender of *paries* is masculine and not feminine. Latin grammarians commonly use the word, at least since Varro (*ling.* 9.41), as an example of an inanimate noun whose morphology prevents its masculine gender from being intuitively obvious.[23] Rather, in feigning ignorance Pompeius seems here to be using a standard example to make a striking pedagogical point—a point that is, so far as I know, unique among the grammarians—that any given speaker of Latin, even a student, may chose a noun's gender in accordance with his own will (*pro voluntate*).

Pompeius continues, again using traditional material to make a nontraditional argument. Like Quintilian centuries earlier (*inst.* 1.5.35, discussed in chapter 2), the grammarian cites Vergil as an authority who can, apparently at will, assign non-standard genders to inanimate objects. Yet while Quintilian emphatically teaches his pupils not to follow poetic practice in this case, Pompeius seemingly recommends the Vergilian example to his own classroom and reiterates that "we can defend ourselves" when mistaking the gender of an inanimate object, since these sorts of gender do not arise from nature (V 160.7–9). His closing recommendation, however, retreats from this confident position, meekly asserting: "So if anybody asks us [about those genders] that do not arise from nature, we shouldn't say anything until we have an authoritative parallel to back up our choice" (*si haec omnia . . . interrogati fuerimus, quae non a naturali ratione veniunt, non ante debemus respondere nisi etiam exempla nobis occurrerint; V 160.16–19*).

It is difficult to evaluate what Pompeius seems to be advising with this final assertion—are we to imagine that a student really cannot mention the wall (*paries*) of the classroom unless a ready quotation from an authoritative poet is at hand to support whatever gender is chosen? Such harsh prescriptions on

---

[23] The word *paries* was occasionally construed as feminine in Pompeius's time, which may have led him to choose this particular example (ThLL vol. X, 1 387.36–38 [P. Gatti]; Stotz 1998: 4.141).

language use surely would strike even the strictest grammarian as impractica-
ble. Rather, the most probable interpretation is that, like the grammatical debate in the halls of the emperor recorded by Gellius, the frustration of Pompeius in his classroom ultimately serves to reaffirm what it would seem to deny.
In the first anecdote, Favorinus is surely being disingenuous when he claims
that a true philosopher need not be concerned about grammatical gender. Favorinus was well known for arguing in the Socratic manner and, within the
debate itself, his quotation of Vergil (*Aen.* 1.703–704) betrays an acquaintance
with the controversy regarding the gender of *penus*.[24] Elsewhere, as well, Gellius
depicts Favorinus's familiarity with the technicalities of Latin diction (Gell. 8.2,
13.25, 18.7), and throughout the *Attic Nights* the philosopher demonstrates that
"detailed linguistic knowledge was the indispensable basis of culture."[25] Indeed,
the very fact that the Sibylline grammarian attracted a crowd of learned men, as
Gellius says, shows that the issue of grammatical gender could arouse interest
among the educated elite and become part of a verbal skirmish about intellectual (and social) propriety. As for our schoolteacher Pompeius, his diatribe
against gender occurred in a context that had occupied grammarians at least
since the time of Varro five hundred years earlier: the *de rigueur* topos of "uncertain genders" (*indiscreta genera*).[26]

Discussions of words of uncertain gender were a favorite occupation of both
the teacher's classroom and the scholar's study, and their efforts supply a significant percentage of the fragments that we possess of the third- and second-
century BC Latin poets. Nonius Marcellus devotes seventy pages (in modern
editions) of his treatise on Latin grammar and vocabulary to the subject, with
terse entries such as the following: "GREGES is often masculine; Lucretius uses
it in the feminine in book 2" (Non. p. 208.22–25: *GREGES, ut saepe, generis
masculini sunt. Feminini. Lucretius lib. II: "lanigerae pecudes et equorum duellica
proles / buceriaeque greges"*). In the sixth century, Priscian's highly influential
Institutiones spends thirty pages on the topic (Keil's edition), and this scholarly
activity culminates in Neue-Wagener's 1902 *Formenlehre*, which offers a compendium of the rules and exceptions for Latin gender, published in 130 tightly
packed pages. The brief empowerment that Pompeius offers his suffering pupils, therefore, is likely a clever pedagogical move that consciously winks at
tradition to catch their attention and to drive home that learning correct genders is in fact essential.[27] Indeed, the absurdly exasperated conclusion of his

---

[24] Gell. 4.1.15; for Vergil's use of *penus* see Char. *gramm.* 94.24–25 B, Prisc. *gramm.* II 163.12–13,
Serv. *Aen.* 1.703. These sophistic tendencies apply also to the historical Favorinus (Beall 2001:
88–92).

[25] Swain 2004: 33.

[26] Barwick 1922: 268 n. 3 asserts that discussions of gender were part of the grammatical tradition by the first century BC.

[27] I suspect that a similar pedagogical technique underlies Pompeius's momentarily "forgetting"
the gender of *periodos* (*gramm.* V 281.22–24; *pace* Kaster 1988: 157).

account affirms the importance of the topic: if you cannot support a gender by citing an authority, avoid using the word![28]

In contrast with so many other features of the Roman grammatical tradition, no such preoccupation with the fluidity of grammatical gender seems to be anticipated by Greek precedents. This relative silence is attributable in large part to the fact that very few instances of ambiguous gender survive in extant archaic and classical Greek texts. The greater stability of gender in ancient Greek is no doubt partly a function of that language's early development of the definite article, a part of speech that provides an unambiguous indication of a noun's gender in those cases when its morphology may raise doubts.[29] Nevertheless, despite the stabilizing influence of the article, a few instances of variable gender do occur in Greek texts. Two unrelated factors account for these extant examples. First, as in many other languages, gender can be used to create semantic distinctions. For example, beginning with the Homeric epics the masculine form ὁ ἅλς, "salt," contrasts with the feminine ἡ ἅλς "sea" (one can compare the well-known example in Republican Latin of feminine *dies*, "day as prearranged deadline or goal," vs. the masculine "day as particular period of time").[30] Second, the gender assigned to a noun could vary depending on the particular dialect. The word λιμός ("hunger"), for example, seems to be uniformly masculine in Attic, but appears in the feminine in non-Attic dialects.[31]

Dialectal explanations for gender flux receive scant attention from the Roman grammarians, who consistently view Latin as a monolithic creation, variations from which offer evidence only for barbarism. The sole reference to dialectal differences in gender known to me occurs not in the grammarians, but in the rhetor Fortunatianus (whose work is tentatively dated to the fourth century): "native Romans use several formerly neuter words in the masculine gender instead, such as *hunc theatrum* and *hunc prodigium*" (Fortun. *rhet.* 3.4: *Romani vernaculi plurima ex neutris masculino genere potius enuntiant, ut "hunc theatrum" et "hunc prodigium"*).[32] The scholarly bias against linguistic variation in Latin derives, not surprisingly, from the worldview of the privileged: in the early centuries AD the members of the Roman intellectual elite imagined themselves to be speaking a form of Latin that was standard across the entire expanse of their vast empire.[33]

[28] Compare Pompeius's similarly exasperated appeal to *auctoritas* when discussing the quantity of the first syllable of a given Latin word (*gramm.* V 106.30–107.3).

[29] Schwyzer 1966: 2.28–29.

[30] Wackernagel 1926–1928: 2.14–15; Schwyzer 1966, 2: 37; Coker 2010 argues that literary genre plays a key role in Greek gender fluctuation; Fraenkel 1917 (*dies*). For examples in other languages, see Albrecht 1895–1896 (Hebrew); Garcia de Diego López 1946a: 143–150 (Spanish); Grevisse 1969: 196–206 (French).

[31] See Schwyzer 1966, 2: 37, with additional examples.

[32] For the abundant evidence for regional variations in Latin outside the educated elite, see Adams 2007 (220–222 on Fortun. *rhet.* 3.4).

[33] Clackson and Horrocks 2007: 229–231.

The comparative rarity—and observable regularity—of gender flux in Greek corresponds with the relative lack of interest that ancient scholars of that language display toward the phenomenon. The only discussions of variable gender known to me in the Greek grammatical tradition in fact date to the Roman period.[34] The grammarian Herodian (mid-second century AD) remarks that poets have the authority (ἐξουσία) to change a noun's gender and cites Homer as an example. Interestingly, and particularly in light of an analogous tendency among the Romans, Herodian records only changes from masculine to feminine.[35] The literary essays of Dionysius of Halicarnassus, written during the Augustan era and probably in Rome, contain two peculiar references to gender fluctuation in classical Greek that make clear how much the practice differed between the two languages. In the *Second Letter to Ammaeus* Dionysius cites five examples of gender "changes" (ἀντιμετατάξεις) in Thucydides, four of which in fact find Thucydides varying gender by changing the part of speech rather than the gender of a single noun (e.g., the neuter participial form τὸ βουλόμενον in place of the feminine noun ἡ βούλησις), whereas the fifth instance does not occur in extant texts of Thucydides (D. H. *Amm.* 2.10).[36] In any case, the practice as described by Dionysius seems aimed more at preserving euphony—in particular by avoiding homoioteleuton—than at achieving the kinds of deep semantic significance that influences Latin usage.

Despite these suggestive examples, the fact remains that the extant texts of the Greek grammarians are few and late, and so caution is advised in deriving firm conclusions from their silences.[37] Nevertheless, yet another piece of silent evidence provides strong indications that varying grammatical gender received little attention in the Greek tradition. In the numerous discussions of fluid gender that occur among Roman scholars, at no point does a grammarian offer Greek evidence for comparanda. Priscian, for example, freely acknowledges throughout the *Institutiones Grammaticae* his indebtedness to the second-century Greek grammarian Apollonius Dyscolus. Yet in his full discussion *De generibus* ("On Genders") the Latin author does not cite a single Greek parallel for gender fluidity, although he continues to cite Greek texts throughout this section for other reasons.[38] The other Roman grammarians are also silent, making it all but certain that they found little or no treatment of the topic in their Greek predecessors.

In the ancient exegesis of Greek texts as well, the few instances of fluid gender that do occur rarely receive extensive commentary; the remarks are largely

---

[34] For a full discussion, see Coker 2010.

[35] Hdn. Gr. *GG* 3.2: 747.19–26; I discuss in chapter 3 how Roman neoteric poets seem to have made gender changes in the same direction.

[36] Roberts 1901: 180; cf. Roberts 1910: 107–108 (on D. H. *Comp.* 6).

[37] For a succinct survey of the extant Greek grammarians see Dickey 2007: 72–87.

[38] Prisc. *gramm.* II 141–171. For the closeness of Priscian's treatment of gender to Apollonius in other respects, see *GG* II iii, 58–60.

neutral, with no perceived need for explanation. The scholiast's remark preserved for a passage in Homer's *Iliad* is typical. The full comment reads simply: "it should be noted that [Homer] refers to stones (τοὺς λίθους) in the feminine."[39] When the scholar does venture to offer an explanation, as in the *scholia vetera* to Pindar, odd genders are given only a vague literary significance, being attributed to the poet's "own practice."[40] The Alexandrian scholar Aristarchus provides a notable exception. He considered it a regular feature of Homeric style to accompany a feminine noun with a masculine adjective, and used this claim to defend readings in the transmitted text. His example is the phrase δεινὸς ἀήτη ("harsh gust") instead of the expected and better attested δεινὸς ἀήτης, where the noun ἀήτης is masculine (Hom. *Il.* 15.626).[41] It is regarding this same line that I have discovered the only exegetical comment in the Greek tradition that resembles the Roman tendency to equate the characteristics of biological sex and grammatical gender. One anonymous scholiast remarks on the line that the unusual juxtaposition of masculine adjective and feminine substantive "makes the expression more forceful and reveals the wind to be more violent."[42] Even in this example, however, the noun is not perceived as being of variable gender, but as receiving a different semantic nuance by the addition of the incongruous adjective.

By contrast, the Roman tradition placed great importance upon a noun's variable gender and how it manifested itself in the literary sphere, attributing to poets an authority (*auctoritas*) that connected the practice with specific poetic techniques and intentions. As a result, analyzing the tradition's grammatical remarks on gender can offer rare insight into how Roman critics operated when working outside the tradition inherited from their Greek predecessors.[43]

These remarks on the contrasting ways in which the earliest Greek and Roman scholars viewed grammatical gender in their respective languages may

[39] Scholia A to Hom. *Il.* 12.287b (Erbse 1969–1988); cf. Scholia Theoc. 7.26. My claim here is based on checking the scholia, in particular for Homer, where a comment on gender change would be likely to occur, and by checking word indices. Compare the twelfth-century commentator Eustathius on Hom. *Od.* 1.53, who attributes the Homeric practice to dialectal variation and adds that "countless (μυρία) such examples survive among the poets." He cites as his authority the second-century AD lexicographer Aelius Dionysius, whose involvement in the Asianist/Atticist controversy further indicates that concerns about gender entered only late into the Greek tradition.

[40] Schol. ad *Pyth.* 1.29a, 4.331 (τὸ ἴδιον ἔθος).

[41] Jonge 2008: 234, citing Aristarchus fr. 33 Matthaios. For the construction see West 1978: 324, Janko 1992: 297.

[42] Schol. Hom. *Il.* 15.626c, cited in Sluiter 1990: 8 n. 22.

[43] Contrast Mühmelt's 1965 contention that extant commentaries on Vergil owe everything "clever and useful" to the Greek exegetical tradition (136: "So ergibt sich das Paradoxon, daß, was zur Erklärung Vergils an Klugem und Brauchbarem, in der Substanz wie in der Wahl der Ansatzpunkte und Beobachtungsformen, gesagt worden ist, letztlich von Griechen gesagt wurde"). His monograph contains no evidence that the Vergilian commentators borrowed their many remarks on gender from Greek predecessors, nor have I found traces of Greek influence in those Latin discussions not involving Vergilian exegesis.

cast some light on a noteworthy difference between some basic elements of Greek and Latin vocabulary. Comparative linguists have demonstrated that PIE had two separate words to describe fire, depending upon which property of fire the speaker chose to emphasize.[44] Its conception as a strictly physical, non-animate entity was ascribed the neuter gender, whereas the masculine gender was used when fire was viewed as a living and animate force of nature. What is of interest in the present context is that the Greeks adopted as the normal word for fire the form in the neuter gender (Gr. πῦρ; cf. Germ. *Feuer*, Eng. "fire"), whereas the Romans came to use the animate, masculine form (Lat. *ignis*; cf. *Agni*, the male Vedic fire-god). An analogous tendency can be observed in the two PIE words for water, which again have both inanimate (neuter) and animate manifestations (in this case, feminine): Greek adopted the neuter form as the dominant word (Gr. ὕδωρ; cf. Germ. *Wasser*), whereas the Latin word is feminine and originally animate (Lat. *aqua*; cf. Goth. *ahva*, denoting flowing water). In Latin, the PIE neuter form of "water" acquired a specialized meaning (*unda*, "wave") and, perhaps unsurprisingly, it had passed into the feminine gender by the historical period. This tendency to ascribe sexual characteristics to primal elements of nature continues into the late Republic. Varro attributes the presence of fire and water (*ignis et aqua*) in Roman marriage ritual to their symbolic significance: fire promotes the union of the male seed (*semen*) with the watery moisture of the female, a union that is necessary for proper development of the human fetus (*ling*. 5.61). Indeed, it is worth noting further that, despite its ambiguous morphology, the noun *ignis* is never attested throughout classical Latinity as anything other than masculine. The temptation to attribute to our earliest Latin speakers a desire to sexualize the natural world—and to see that desire perpetuated in Latin's poetical and scholarly traditions—proves almost irresistible.

Dissenting voices do speak out however. In a note on Catullus that displays characteristically deep learning, George Goold exclaims "But enough of fantasy! The fact is that ambiguous genders in Latin have no literary significance but constitute a morphological problem."[45] Such an unambiguous assertion of "fact" by a renowned scholar of the Latin textual tradition presents a serious challenge to the above remarks, even after Renehan's careful defense of the poetic potential of fluid gender, on which we will elaborate in more detail in chapters 2 and 3.[46] I would like now, however, to redirect attention away from practice and toward ancient interpretations of that practice. It is possible to outline the statements, speculations, and explanations offered by the ancient scholarly tradition as a means of reconstructing what the grammarians thought to be the

---

[44] Wackernagel 1926–1928: 2.15–16, following Meillet 1920, and Schulze 1934, esp. 194–196. For a modern linguistic account of this dual vocabulary in PIE, see Lehmann 1989, esp. 232–233 (he does not speculate on *why* daughter languages adopt different forms for "fire" and "water").

[45] Goold 1981: 234.

[46] Renehan 1998.

historical significance of grammatical gender. This evidence shows that, when confronted with the appearance of an unusual gender, Roman scholars typically approach the issue as a problem less of grammatical morphology than of human biology.

THE NATURE OF THE EVIDENCE

The literary practice of playing on Latin genders is likely even more ubiquitous than the hundreds of examples offered by our extant evidence would already indicate. A number of surviving instances suggest that the manuscript traditions of our extant poets, as well as of some prose writers, originally contained peculiarities of gender that centuries of copying have regularized.[47] A particularly notorious example is Catullus's alleged use of *pumex* ("pumice") in the feminine in the second line of his dedicatory poem to Cornelius Nepos (1.2: *arido* vel *arida . . . pumice*). The regular, masculine form of the noun enjoys support not only from the extant manuscripts of the poet and of the six grammarians who quote the lines, but also from a clear imitation of the verse in Martial (8.72.2).[48] An indirect reference provided by the fifth-century commentator Servius, however, has prompted several modern editors of Catullus to import the feminine form into his text. Despite the fact that every other occurrence of *pumex* in both prose and poetry throughout Latinity is masculine, some scholars justify the gender change on the basis of Servius's single testimony. If this claim is true, one line of argument proposes that Catullus intends here to allude to the feminine gender of the Greek word for pumice (κίσηρις). In this case, remarks one esteemed authority, the simple change of gender represents "an unobtrusive announcement of Catullus' mastery of Greek, with the implication that his work is written for readers literate in both languages."[49] The ground rules that underlie this lively debate over Catullus depend upon a number of far-from-certain factors. The trustworthiness of the grammatical tradition must be weighed not only against the tendency for manuscripts to simplify texts over the course of transmission, but in particular against our own perception of the limits that can and cannot be placed on the resourcefulness of

---

[47] In addition to Catull. 1.2, see the *apparatus criticus* of Winterbottom 1994 for Cic. *off.* 3.112 (*primo luci*), where the editor accepts, against MS authority, Nonius's unique evidence for the unusual gender (Non. p. 210.17); Gell. 6.20.6 also argues (apparently) for a non-standard gender at Catull. 27.4 that is not in the MS tradition. See Thomson 1998: 273–275; Bardon 1973 follows Gellius.

[48] For the possibility that the Veronese MS (V) contained the feminine reading, see Thomson 1998: 197; contra Kiss (forthcoming). Goold 1981: 233–235 (with Kaster 1978: 199 n. 48) defends the reading *arido* by offering a reconstruction for Servius's recommendation *arida*; contra Renehan 1998, esp. 224–227.

[49] Wiseman 1979: 169.

Roman poets. Modern commentators sometimes choose to assume that unique attestations of gender fluctuation, such as Servius's lone comment on feminine *pumex*, reflect one of the occasional instances where ancient scholars either misrepresent or misunderstand their source. And yet the sheer number of examples of fluid gender discussed in this and the following chapter, and those present elsewhere in the tradition, should cause us to begin with the assumption that these authorities preserve accurate information unless there arises a clear reason to doubt them.

Nevertheless, the simple fact remains that, despite all the feverish activity devoted to cataloguing odd genders, no ancient scholar directly explains why the issue appeals to him. While there surely exists the compulsion to standardize the Latin language, to establish and reaffirm rules of proper usage, this compulsion exists in continual tension with a recognition of the beauty and respect owed to Latin's innate irregularities, and a drive toward exposing what one text cryptically refers to as "the rules behind the irregularities" (*defectionis regula*).[50] If one examines this desire for a uniformity that must simultaneously accept anomaly, it is possible to detect in these texts a deeper motivation than the wish simply to teach proper modes of speaking.[51] One possible explanation of their efforts can apparently be ruled out: perhaps counterintuitively, these remarks on gender are unlikely to be meant to aid students in the reading of the particular texts cited. Ennius, the third most frequently quoted early Latin poet in the grammarians (after Plautus and Terence), had become increasingly neglected after the death of Vergil and by the fifth century, when many of the grammarians were writing, his works were either difficult to obtain or perhaps no longer even extant.[52] Even as early as the second century, a discussion of Ennius preserved by Gellius implies that the poet's texts were neither easily accessible nor widely read.[53] Writing a century or two after Gellius, Nonius clearly did not directly consult a text of Ennius's *Annales* while he was compiling his work.[54] Indeed, as with Servius's testimony over Catullus's use of *pumex*, the uncertainty over the accuracy of the information that these ancient scholars provide is such that many modern critics might echo Skutsch's assertion (speaking of Nonius) that their words can only be securely trusted when independent testimony provides corroboration.[55] Secure ancient precedent supports Skutsch's

---

[50] Char. *gramm.* 62.13–14 B (for which see most recently Schenkeveld 1998). On the regard for irregular forms among the ancient grammarians, see Fehling 1956, esp. 254–258.

[51] On the grammarians as "guardians of language," see Kaster 1988, esp. the summary remarks at 196–197.

[52] Decline in popularity of Ennius after Vergil: Kaster 1995: 257–258; status in subsequent centuries: Skutsch 1985: 10. Jocelyn 1964: 282–286 finds no positive evidence that Ennius or other early Republican authors were commonly read as of the fourth century.

[53] Gell. 6.2; more generally Skutsch 1985: 30–31, 448, 676.

[54] Skutsch 1985: 38–40.

[55] Skutsch 1985: 525, on Nonius recording Ennius's use of *crux* in the masculine (Non. p.

caution: Gellius records how a grammarian under Hadrian, Caesellius Vindex, mistakenly claimed that Ennius used in the masculine the neuter noun meaning "heart" (*cor*), and this misreading crept into the text of Nonius as an unqualified assertion (Gell. 6.2.3 on Enn. *ann.* 371–373; Non. p. 195.17–20). In an analogous fashion, an anonymous grammarian writing a few centuries after Caesellius lists as feminine the otherwise exclusively masculine noun *penis* ("penis"); in this case it is clear that his assertion rests upon an elementary misconstrual of Sallust's collocation *pene bona* at *Bellum Catilinae* 14.2.[56] Yet such anecdotes also allow us to glimpse the attractions offered to ancient scholars by aberrations of gender. Given both the general neglect of the early Latin poets in the Latin canon and the known potential for errors of transmission, the repeated notes we find on their fluid use of gender—Ennius is cited for providing an uncustomary gender for approximately twenty-five words, Pacuvius and Accius for ten[57]—call out for an explanation. This interest clearly must respond to something other than a need to guide students to an explication of these individual lines of text. Fluid grammatical gender must have a significance that reaches outside its occurrence in any given author.

The popularity of the unread Ennius among these scholars raises an issue concerning the grammatical tradition whose very familiarity may forestall its direct confrontation. It is well known that ancient Greek and Roman prose treatises on oratory and style often, with apparent inconsistency, take their illustrations of correct speech and effective rhetoric from poetic texts. The grammatical tradition concerning gender does not provide an exception: the overwhelming majority of odd genders handed down to us by antiquarians and grammarians occur in poetry. One of the reasons for this preference is highly practical. While Roman prose authors may offer a technical writer clear examples of varying levels of style, there are a very limited number of cases in which they seem to be changing gender consciously. The more conceptual reason for citing poetry involves the common perception that it predates prose in the development of the language (Varro frg. 319 Funaioli). As a result, the deviations from normal Latin vocabulary and syntax found in poetic texts should be regarded with greater tolerance and even, for certain poets, with reverence. It is clear that the grammarians—and, we may presume, the poets—placed a great deal of significance in the malleability of grammatical gender. The next section of this chapter attempts to reconstruct the scholarly notion prevailing in Rome about the possible origins of grammatical gender and to assess what bearing those origins have on correct expression.

195.12–13: *malo crucei, fatur, uti des / Iuppiter!*), a gender also used by Gaius Gracchus (Fest. p. 136): "If it were not for Gracchus we should probably defy Nonius and declare *malo* to be the verb."

[56] Exc. Bob. *gramm.* I 553.29–30; cf. ThLL vol. X, 1 1074.40–42 (N. Bruun).

[57] Catone 1964: 57–60 (Ennius) and Koterba 1905: 136 (Pacuvius and Accius) give full lists (without analysis).

THE GRAMMARIANS ON ORIGINS

Four hundred years after Protagoras critiqued Homeric practice in order to make his radical claim for the internal logic of grammatical gender, another fragment of a great thinker presents an analogous assertion. The Roman polymath Marcus Terentius Varro writes the following in a lost portion of his treatise *On the Latin Language*:

> *potestatis nostrae est illis rebus dare genera, quae ex natura genus non habent.* (Varro frg. 24 Funaioli)

> It is in our power to give gender to those things that do not have it by nature.

Varro envisions here a narrative of language development whose outline is preserved most clearly in the *Ars grammatica* of Charisius, according to which the Latin language, "born together with human beings," contains minor inconsistencies that, over time, specialists in the language are able to resolve.[58] In the particular case of grammatical gender, one commentator on Donatus's grammar explains observable inconsistencies as places where these ancestors "nodded" (Explan. *gramm.* IV 493.6: *in his plerumque auctoritas nutat*). Varro explicitly includes a lapse in assigning proper gender among his examples of the negligence of these "first namers" (*illi qui primi nomina imposuerunt rebus*), citing in particular the absence of a recognizably masculine form to describe the male eagle (*aquila*; *ling.* 8.7). Although for us Varro's pronouncement of the learned speaker's power to change gender survives only as an isolated fragment, he and the many grammarians who refer to his assertion make clear how the Latin grammarian imagined his role in the archaeology of grammatical gender.[59]

The category of gender that Varro mentions as given to nouns "by nature" (*ex natura*) corresponds to the modern conception of biological sex—the word for man is masculine, for mother feminine, and so on. In fact, in an apparent calque of the designations employed by Protagoras, Varro labels the categories of gender not with the denotations *masculinum* ("masculine") and *femininum* ("feminine") that will become standard in the later grammatical tradition, but with the specifically sexual designations *virile* and *muliebre* ("manly" and "womanly"; *ling.* 8.46). Over five hundred years after Varro, it is clear that the grammarian Consentius still considers gender as a grammatical category with ramifications in the real world. In discussing the application of grammatical

---

[58] Char. *gramm.* 62.2–14 B (cf. Isid. *orig.* 1.7.28: *cetera [sc.* other than masculine and feminine*] nomina non sunt genera, sed hoc <u>nominum ratio et auctoritas</u> voluit*). Schenkeveld 1996 and 1998 offer a new text, translation, and discussion of this complex passage.

[59] Nine later treatises contain variations of Varro's statement (Funaioli 1907: 196); for analogous assertions in the extant treatise see, e.g., *ling.* 6.3, 8.10, 10.53. Lomanto 1998, esp. 94–96, 101–102, analyzes the ways in which Stoic theories of natural language—in particular the natural link between signifier and signified and the existence of "first namers"—influenced Varro's conception of gender. For Philo's analogous application of Stoic theory to scriptural exegesis, see Baynes 2002: 39–47.

gender to language, he begins in the typical way outlined above. After review-ing the Varronian etymology that derived "gender" from the verb "to generate," Consentius then describes the "natural" application of gender, which encom-passes words describing males and females of any species. He designates this class of words as possessing the "original genders" (*genera principalia*):

> *quoniam ita <sc. genera principalia> appellari coepta sunt in nominibus animantium,*
> *extenta res est consuetudine, ut etiam haec quae essent sexuum expertia masculino*
> *genere aut feminino genere censerentur ut aer portus terra domus.* (Consent. *gramm.*
> V 343.21–24; cf. Serv. *gramm.* IV 408.1–3)

> Since [these original genders] were applied first to those nouns that describe animate beings, the practice was extended by custom (*consuetudo*), so that also the nouns that lack sex would be classed in the masculine or feminine gender—for example, "air," "port," "earth," or "house."

Typically, Consentius does not proceed to conjecture what precise principles compelled the posited first-namers to assign for these four examples the gen-ders that they did. His list of nouns hardly clarifies the issue, since they follow no predictable pattern either semantically or morphologically. The normally masculine *aer* occurs in the feminine in Ennius; *portus* and *domus* are mascu-line and feminine respectively, despite sharing many features of inflection. The word for earth, *terra*, is the only one listed that has a long tradition of being feminine on account of its universal personification in the Roman world as fe-male.[60] The best that Consentius can conjecture in explaining the assignment of gender is that grammatical *ars* followed some sort of *ratio*, some logic of what is fitting in each instance, although he is unwilling to commit to whether *ars* followed this logic "willfully or fittingly" (*seu licenter seu decenter*; V 343.30–344.3). Consentius, in fact, seems to approach the modern linguistic under-standing of the origins of PIE gender: in applying gender, the earliest speakers classified the non-animate beings of the world around them into categories by analogy with beings that have true biological sex.[61]

A passage from Priscian demonstrates clearly this process of analogy at work. In Priscian's discussion, notions of procreation prevail over grammatical morphology in the assignment of gender (Prisc. *gramm.* II 154.7–14). In his discussion of third-declension nouns whose nominative ends in *-or*, Priscian observes that this class normally possesses masculine gender, with the excep-tion of three nouns. Two of these exceptions have ready explanations: *soror*

---

[60] See, e.g., Varro's explicit account as preserved in Aug. *civ.* 7.28 (Cardauns fg. 263): *caelum esse quod faciat, terram quae patiatur, et ideo illi masculinam vim tribuit, huic femininam* ("[Varro] at-tributes masculine power to the sky because it acts, feminine to *terra* because it is acted upon"; see further Wissowa 1916–1924d, esp. 331–332).

[61] I owe thanks to Vaahtera 2008: 254–257 and *per litteras* for helping me refine my earlier ex-planation of Consentius's account (Corbeill 2008: 92–93).

("sister") and *uxor* ("wife") denote human beings of female sex and therefore, Priscian concludes, "their very nature prevents these two from possessing the opposing gender" (*quorum duo ipsa natura alterius esse generis prohibet*). For the remaining noun, *arbor* ("tree"), Priscian appeals to the principle of analogy: *arbor* "is justly enumerated as feminine because each individual tree is said to be the 'mother' of its own offspring" (*iure inter feminina connumeratur, quod "mater" quoque dicitur proprii fetus unaquaeque arbor*). A passage from Vergil is then enlisted to confirm the point (*georg.* 2.19). Employing a familiar technique, Priscian uses *natura*, buttressed by Vergil's poetic *auctoritas*, to attribute sex and gender to an inanimate noun. This example further underscores the principle that sensitivity to the ties between sex and gender constitutes a method of gender assignment that characterizes classical Latinity in particular (for in the majority of its Romance reflexes, the Latin noun *arbor* yields to morphology and transforms into a predictable, masculine form).[62] This passage from Priscian provides valuable insight into the processes that were imagined to have taken place in the assignment of gender by the earliest speakers in Latin.[63]

In accordance with this impulse by grammarians to equate sex and gender, the exegetical tradition on several occasions attempts to explain how such a sexed gender applies to elements in the world that we would consider nonanimate. A striking example of the belief that nouns can "have sex" (in both senses of the term) is offered by an ancient scholarly note on Vergil's *Aeneid*. In the epic, Dido is underscoring the insensitivity of her lover Aeneas by saying that the Caucasus mountain—a masculine noun—gave birth to him. Her invective provokes a learned comment in the Servius Auctus tradition. The commentator notes that Vergil has here altered his Homeric inspiration, in which Patroclus accuses Achilles of having a mother who was not human. Homer, he notes, has avoided inconcinnity by having Patroclus imagine Achilles's mother as a noun of feminine gender, the sea (θάλασσα). Feminine, in other words, matches female. And yet the commentator further remarks that Vergil's adaptation does not stem from some oversight on the poet's part but in fact has particular point. Dido makes Aeneas's origins more incredible and unnatural even than those of Achilles when she posits his birth as arising from a singular—and masculine—parent: "Dido took care to make more incredible 'giving birth' from a mountain of masculine gender" (Serv. Auct. *Aen.* 4.367: *elaboravit dicendo "genuit" incredibilius facere de monte masculini generis*). The verb used by Vergil to which the commentator's quotation draws attention, *genuit* (*gigno*), commonly refers to both the male and female roles in procreation, and almost certainly alludes to the Varronian etymology of *genus* from *generare* that Servius shows awareness of elsewhere (*gramm.* IV 407.39).

---

[62] The only exceptions are Portuguese and Logudorese (Löfstedt 1961: 243).

[63] For the (different) understanding of "masculine" and "feminine" trees among the Greeks, see Foxhall 1998.

A note by Servius on another passage of the *Aeneid* finds the commentator again self-consciously conflating grammatical gender and biological sex. In describing the murderous rage of his enemy Mezentius, the Etruscan king Evander remarks on how this warrior "had widowed the city of so many citizens" (Verg. *Aen.* 8.571: *tam multis viduasset civibus urbem*). Servius points out that the verb "to widow" (*viduo*) is particularly apt in this context since the Latin word for city, *urbs*, is feminine and it is therefore fitting for the noun to take on the role of a widow (Serv. *Aen.* 8.571: *proprie "viduasset" dixit, quia urbs generis est feminini*). Examples such as these confirm that the attempt to relate a noun's *genus* to sexual reproduction insinuated itself into the grammatical and literary tradition subsequent to Varro as an explanatory model for clarifying the relationship between word and thing. As a result, it becomes legitimate to ascribe a sexual connotation to the grammatical gender of any random Latin signified. As Consentius makes explicit in his own discussion, "nouns don't 'generate,' but the bodies that are named [by the nouns] do."[64] Put in more modern terms, the signified enacts the sexual implications of the signifier.

These ancient scholarly reflections on Vergil should not be dismissed as the product of an outlandish antiquarianism, for such a sexual division of language is restricted neither to poetic expression nor to ancient exegesis. On the contrary, a recent lengthy compendium of modern linguistic research into gender in over two hundred extant languages reaches the following conclusion: "gender always has a semantic core: there are no gender systems in which the genders are purely formal categories."[65] Similarly, even when grammarians confess openly to seeing no correlation between grammatical gender and physical sex, they often equivocate in ways reminiscent of the advice Pompeius renders in his classroom. Servius, for instance, affirms in his commentary on Donatus that for words like "wall" (*paries*) and "window" (*fenestra*) "we recognize no natural sex." Unable to proceed further by reason—there would seem, after all, to be no intuitively female characteristics shared by a wall and a window—he takes refuge in *auctoritas* in order to determine the genders of these nouns (*gramm.* IV 408.2–5; cf. Explan. in Don. *gramm.* IV 493.4–10). When *ratio* fails, the authority of the ancients provides an explanatory principle with which the scholar must remain content. What seems implicit yet again is an understood narrative that Roman scholars have adopted concerning Latin's origins. Someone, somewhere, at some time, decided to designate a noun with a specific gender. Indeed, the outline presented by Consentius, and implied by others, of how this assignment may have occurred aligns well with what modern studies of gendered languages have shown, namely, that a given gender

---

[64] Consent. *gramm.* V 343.16: *non enim nomina generant, sed corpora, quorum illa sunt nomina.* Vaahtera 2008: 255–257 interprets this passage differently.

[65] Corbett 1991: 307.

would have arisen from a semantic notion of what the word *meant* in some sexual sense.[66]

This insistence on correlating meaning with gender and sex also explains an oddity found in extant discussions. As I have mentioned above, variation in gender seems to have been an infrequent phenomenon among writers of Latin prose. Nevertheless, the treatises composed "On Uncertain Genders" (*De indiscretis generibus*) do often cite examples from prose authors, but in a manner distinct from the poetic citations. One instance cited at random will clarify the difference: "**CERTAMEN** is in the neuter gender. It is feminine in the fourth book of Sisenna's *Histories*: "having swiftly used up their spears, they brought the contest (*certationem*) back to swords" (Nonius pp. 195.29–196.1: *CERTAMEN generis est neutri. Feminini. Sisenna Historiarum lib. IV: "iaculis celeriter consumptis ad gladios certationem revocaverunt"*). In this example the compiler Nonius does not cite a feminine use to correspond with the neuter noun *certamen*, as would be the case were he citing a gender variation from a poetic text, such as when he records the variable gender of *greges* (quoted above under "Getting Uptight"). Rather, Nonius gives a noun form that is built on the same stem *certa-*, but one whose suffix makes the word unquestionably feminine: *certatio*. Nonius alone contains over fifty examples of this kind of listing, although such nouns of allegedly different genders would be considered, in modern terms, two separate words. In this particular instance, Nonius certainly recognized that the *-io* suffix would make *certatio* a feminine noun. In fact, the absence in the Sisenna passage of an accusative adjective or pronoun referring to *certationem* makes clear that he must be deriving the gender in his example from the suffix alone. Why then does he offer examples such as this one, which on the surface seems to claim speciously that a neuter form (*certamen*) has become feminine (*certatio*)? Our account of the relationship between meaning and gender provides an explanation. In the case of the neuter noun *certamen* and the feminine *certatio*, I would suggest that the semantic notion of "struggle," regardless of the morphological shape it adopts, has associated with it an inherent gender, in this instance the neuter. Although no extant text expresses this notion explicitly in regard to gender, the hypothesis accords with ancient treatments of the origins of Latin vocabulary more generally. Varro writes that an originally small set of words—approximately one thousand—constituted the elemental building blocks of the lexicon (*ling.* 6.36: *verborum . . . primigenia*). From this source, all other words, constituting as many as five hundred

---

[66] The discovery that Anatolian has only two genders—common and neuter—has sparked debate over whether this reflects early PIE or an anomaly in the internal development of Anatolian. See Matasović 2004: 33–41, esp. 33: "Late (perhaps post-Anatolian) PIE had three genders . . . although there is now a majority opinion, approaching consensus, to the effect that this system developed from an earlier one with only two genders." This historical issue does not have direct bearing on my discussion here since the grammarians always identify the feminine and masculine in Latin as discrete entities.

times the original number, were created by adding various suffixes and prefix-es.[67] Just as this theory of an elemental vocabulary could legitimize etymology as a tool for reconstituting language origins, so too would it have allowed theoretical access to a noun's original gender.

Further support for a model positing that the original semantic association of a lexeme can determine a noun's true gender is offered by Nonius's perplexing lemma for the word *reditus* ("return"; pp. 222.11–17). After citing Vergil for this noun's occurrence in the masculine—a gender that it retains exclusively throughout Latinity—Nonius proceeds to list examples from prose authors. Alongside the feminine *reditio* from Varro, he adds two synonyms for "return" that are formed from completely unrelated stems, *regressio* (Cicero) and *reversio* (Varro). Even a scholar from ancient Rome would acknowledge that these nouns are formed on three distinct stems. The only characteristic that these words share, aside from the prefix *re-*, is meaning; Nonius, using Vergil as his authority, seems to be claiming that something about "returns" is masculine.[68] Once again, a poet provides evidence for a semantic notion being traditionally associated with a specific, "correct" grammatical gender.

Examination of gender use in modern languages provides a parallel for this phenomenon of speakers perceiving that non-animate nouns are able to exhibit a demonstrable "masculinity" or "femininity." In modern German, for example, the suffix *-mut* is no longer productive in the creation of masculine abstract nouns. Without familiar morphology as a guide, one study has shown, contemporary German speakers opt to assign gender to a given compound in *-mut* according to whether it expresses "introversion" or "extroversion." "Introverted" nouns, such as *Anmut* ("gracefulness") and *Wehmut* ("sadness"), are regularly gendered by native speakers as feminine, whereas "extroverted" nouns—*Hochmut* ("arrogance"), *Übermut* ("bravado")—are understood to be masculine.[69] In other words, grammatical gender for these German speakers, as for scholars such as Nonius, seem to arise from meaning and not morphology.[70]

If we accept the hypothesis that Latin nouns had inherent sexual connotations that it is the job of the ancient scholar to excavate, then let us make our-

---

[67] O'Hara 1996: 48–50.

[68] This explanation of Nonius's lemma for *reditus*, as odd as it may appear, seems preferable to others (see the *apparatus criticus* in Lindsay 1903: 328–329; White 1980: 148–149; Rosén 1999: 70–74), since it also accounts for the related lemmata such as that of *certamen* discussed in the text above.

[69] Corbett 1991: 94, citing Zubin and Köpcke 1984, who are careful not to assert that their findings prove conclusively a correlation between gender and sex: "there could be a deep-rooted polarity in our understanding of personality and affect which influences the assignment of a gender on the one hand, and influences our stereotypic attitudes about maleness and femaleness on the other" (94).

[70] Boroditsky et al. 2003 concisely survey recent scientific attempts to prove the validity of this claim for speakers of other gendered languages.

selves Latin schoolteachers like Pompeius, faced with an uncertain gender, but lacking confidence in our intuitive capacity to assign one. What do we do? In such cases, later grammarians had recourse to four criteria developed by Varro.[71] In descending order of importance these are: first, *natura*, or the perception of the natural sex of a given noun, as understood by native speakers; then *ratio*, the application of the "logic" of morphology or etymology, which can be considered in tandem with the third criterion, *consuetudo* or "usage"; finally, when all else fails, recourse is had to the often elusive *auctoritas*. The first category, that of *natura*, is most straightforward.[72] As remarked above, animate beings with sex are "naturally" categorized as masculine or feminine. Servius notes explicitly that "nowhere in Latinity does the word for an animal have a neuter gender"; as his mention of "Latinity" indicates, Servius here explicitly stresses that this generic phenomenon distinguishes Roman from Greek practice and thus was to become a central tenet of the Roman grammarians' understanding of gender.[73] Parts of the seemingly inanimate natural world also have consistent sexual associations for Romans: as noted above, mountains like the Caucasus are normally masculine whereas the earth (*terra*) and trees are regularly sexed as feminine.

The second criterion, *ratio*, includes the rules and analogies offered by the structure of Latin.[74] One indication of gender passed on by the *ratio* of the earliest speakers of the language—an inconsistent one, as numerous grammatical works make clear, but one that modern speakers of gendered languages still tend to rely on—is morphology. As one late treatise puts it with cautious optimism (but demonstrable inaccuracy): "our ancestors decided that nouns which end in 'us' or 'r' usually (*magis*) belong to the masculine gender" (*decreverunt auctores, ut ea nomina, quae in us vel in r exeunt, magis masculino genere pronuntientur*; Commentum Einsidlense VIII 235.36–37 [saec. IX–X]). Servius, furthermore, praises the "ancestors" for using gender to create semantic distinctions. For example, he notes that the *maiores* used gender to distinguish the feminine singular form of the noun *insomnia* ("insomnia") from its neuter plural homonym *insomnia* ("dreams"; Serv. *Aen.* 4.9). Comparative philology and

---

[71] The application of these criteria differs throughout the grammatical tradition; I discuss here solely how they apply in assessment of grammatical gender. For more general discussions see: Varro and Quintilian (Cavazza 1981: 143–152, Vainio 1999: 47–61); Charisius (Schenkenveld 1996: 27–29); Servius (Kaster 1988: 177–178). For their broader application, and adaptation from Greek precedent, see Siebenborn 1976 *passim*.

[72] On the far more ambiguous meaning of *natura* in other branches of Latin grammar, see Siebenborn 1976: 151–154. I follow here Julianus Toletanus's seventh-century commentary on Donatus (V 318.26–33, likely derivative of Varro's discussion) in outlining how to determine the gender of nouns that do not have sex by nature (*ex arte descendentia*).

[73] Serv. *georg.* 1.207 (the neuter plural *ostrea* as Grecism); cf. Serv. *Aen.* 5.822 (*cete*), Serg. *gramm.* IV 493.14–28, Isid. *orig.* 12.6.52; Wackernagel 1926–1928: 2.17, with Adams 2013: 408 n. 2.

[74] Diom. *gramm.* I 439.16–17, who lists Varro's criteria as *natura, analogia, consuetudo,* and *auctoritas. Analogia* is equivalent to *ratio* (Cavazza 1981: 140–153).

the systematic collection of exceptions allow modern scholars to create categories that may describe the language more precisely, but the basic morphological tendencies noted by ancient scholars such as these remain the best guide for the student.[75]

Consuetudo, or the usage of the educated speaker, possesses in Varro's scheme an importance equivalent to *ratio*, although, in contrast with the fixed rules of *ratio*, he is aware that even learned usage is continually subject to change.[76] In the treatise *On the Latin Language*, Varro demonstrates his awareness of how an understanding of grammatical gender can adapt in accordance with the changing experience of human speakers. Originally, he writes, doves of both sexes were designated by the formally feminine word *columba*; within his own recent memory, however, the domestication of doves has caused human beings to care about the bird's sex and so the masculine form *columbus* has begun to be used for males (*ling.* 9.56).[77]

Fourth and finally, there remain those instances in which no clear guide is offered by biology, morphology, or usage, those places where ambiguity rules and where sometimes, as noted above, "those who first gave names to things made mistakes" (Varro *ling.* 8.7). Here, Charisius tells us, the speaker runs to the "sacred altar" of *auctoritas*, that is, usage again, but usage by those who matter.[78] The Latin speaker, like the Roman politician, agrees in designating as the ultimate authority a quality at once perceptible and ineffable.[79] To determine which practitioners of the Latin language wielded this authority, our sole recourse is to turn to the contexts in which extant grammarians use the term. To begin with, and perhaps counterintuitively, for the grammarians it is the *poets* who provide the overwhelming majority of examples of controversial gender. The usage of canonical poets such as Terence, Lucretius, and Horace is often cited with approval, but Vergil, who became a standard school text almost immediately upon his death, represents an ideal that is only rarely contested.[80] In

---

[75] NW 965 begin their discussion of Latin declensions with the statement that "The gender of most nouns can be determined through their endings" ("Das grammatische Genus der Nomina wird grossenteils durch die Endungen bestimmt") and then spend fifty-four pages qualifying "most" (cf. *magis* of the *Commentum Einsidlense*, quoted above in the text).

[76] *Consuetudo* as practice of the *eruditi*: Quint. *inst.* 1.6.43–45; Char. *gramm.* 63.9–11 B. Varro frg. 43 (Funaioli) provides as an example of *consuetudo* conflicting with *ratio/analogia* the adverbs *mutuo* and *mutue*; usage favors *mutuo*, but *mutue* is more rational (*ut docte*).

[77] Discussion in Wackernagel 1926–1928: 2.26–27; similarly, Paul. Fest. p. 6 (*agnus ... apud maiores communis erat generis, sicut et lupus*). Garcia de Diego López 1945: 136–137.

[78] Char. *gramm.* 63.3–5 B: *ubi omnia defecerint, sic ad illam [sc. auctoritatem] quem ad modum ad aram sacram decurritur*; cf. Prisc. *gramm.* II 169.6–8 on *vetustissimi* changing genders "by auctoritas alone."

[79] Barwick 1922: 184: "*auctoritas* ...; d.i. der Sprachgebrauch eines Schriftstellers, der sich weder auf *natura* noch auf die *ratio* oder *consuetudo* stützt. Er bleibt als letzte Zuflucht übrig, wenn die drei ersten Instanzen versagen."

[80] Jocelyn 1985: 159 n. 140 notes that "the first clear sign" of Vergil being considered a classic occurs in Suetonius (*Cal.* 34.2, *gramm.* 23.4); Horsfall 1981: 48–51 critically surveys early diffusion

fact, Vergilian usage can wield sufficient authority to cast doubt consistently on the gender that one would expect from the application of established grammatical criteria (*ratio*).[81] Well-known poets of the classical age, such as Ovid, seem to run at best a distant second to Vergil, whereas the authority of others— including a group that one grammarian refers to obliquely as "the highest writers"—are ascribed authority that is "dubious" and "lesser" and "obscure."[82] Another ancient source pits those "of received authority" against the "learned" (*doctos*; Non. p. 215.9–10). Lastly, and perhaps surprisingly, the antiquity of a poet does not necessarily contribute to authoritative status—the testimony of the nameless *vetustissimi* ("the oldest ones") can be rejected, and that of the *antiqui* ("the ancients") can be driven out by everyday usage, while the poet Ennius, Vergil's precursor in Latin epic, is normally treated as a respectable anomaly.[83] In chapter 2 I will analyze in detail what features seem to characterize this poetic authority, and why that authority allows some poets to transgress seemingly immutable grammatical categories.

CONCLUSION

The views that can be reconstructed from these grammatical and exegetical texts, while spanning several centuries, nevertheless possess certain commonalities. First, the assignment of grammatical gender rests on an understanding that some type of sexual essence inheres in certain objects, regardless of whether that object is animate or inanimate. Second, several authors allude to an early time when genders were fluid, and assume that their eventual fixedness arose from the authority of anonymous *maiores* or other "first-namers." Third, this same authority is possessed by certain poets, in particular Vergil, who can use an uncommon gender of a noun without being accused of either ignorance or error. With this summary in mind, I would like to close with two final speculations. I would like first to offer, briefly, a possible historical parallel to this con-

---

of Vergil, including epigraphic evidence. For Vergil as grammatical authority, see Vainio 1999: 140–142, and for resistance see, e.g., Serv. *Aen.* 6.104 with Kaster 1978: 199–200. For Quintilian's understandable privileging of prose authors, in particular his distinction between *auctoritas* and *vetustas*, see Vainio 1999: 47–82.

[81] Prisc. *gramm.* II 141.16–19; Gell. 13.21 discusses how euphony allows Vergil to ignore *ratio* and *consuetudo*.

[82] Ovid's authority for gender: Char. *gramm.* 102.9–11 B; *summi scriptores*: Non. p. 229.11; *dubia*: Memmius at Non. p. 194.30; *minus*: Celsus at Non. p. 195.5–6; *obscurae auctoritatis*: Non. p. 229.11; see further White 1980: 182–183. For ancient scholars, in particular Gellius and Servius, using such terms indiscriminately to prove a point, see Kaster 1978.

[83] *Vetustissimi*: Prisc. *gramm.* II 160.17; everyday usage: Serv. *Aen.* 10.377; a sample of the many non-judgmental references to Ennius's idiosyncrasies: Gell. 13.21.14, Macr. *Sat.* 6.4.17–18, Prisc. *gramm.* II 30.4–6. Dionisotti 1984: 207 and Chin 2008: 20–25 discuss the grammarians' varying use of labels such as *veteres* and *antiquissimi*.

cern with gender from outside the Roman grammatical tradition that has been my focus. I will then consider the broader ramifications that this fixation on gender may have for Roman society.

The lexicographer Pompeius Festus provides several examples from both poetry and prose of the existence of uncertain gender in archaic Rome. He stresses, however, that the phenomenon should be regarded not as an error (*vitium*) but as an example of "ancient practice" (*antiqua consuetudo*; Fest. p. 286). Once again we have, as with Vergil, the notion of an archaic manipulation of gender to which the informed have access. One may compare here Quintilian's discussion of the four elements upon which rest the rules for both spoken and written language (*sermo*): reason (*ratio*), antiquity (*vetustas*), authority (*auctoritas*), and usage (*consuetudo*). He encapsulates the role of "antiquity" in the briefest terms and hence in those that are least helpful for trying to understand the rules underlying its use: "A certain majesty and, if I may say so, religious awe commends [the mention of] ancient things" (*vetera maiestas quaedam et, ut sic dixerim, religio commendat*; *inst.* 1.6.1; cf. 1.6.39–41). If an observable practice cannot be understood, it presumably operates under a different, inscrutable, set of criteria.

While Quintilian's appeal to intangible principles to describe the authority of the ancestors anticipates my discussion of androgynous gods and hermaphrodites in chapters 4 and 5, it also has relevance to variable grammatical gender. The authority attached to language in translating sacred texts provides a comparandum from another area of antiquity for this compulsion to recall earlier, hallowed, practice. Here the style of translating word for word (*verbum e verbo*) tends to take precedence over endeavors to translate according to sense (*sensus de sensu*). As is famously expressed in Jerome's fifty-seventh letter, the word-for-word translation of sacred texts serves to protect the translator not only from misrepresentation but also from accusations of spreading heretical views when the original text contains potentially controversial doctrine.[84] A wide range of practices among early Christian writers characterizes these obsessively literal translations, practices that frequently result in lack of clarity in the resulting text: individual lexemes from the parent text can be rendered etymologically to create a neologism, or its syntax and word-order may be retained in the often unrelated new language of the translation. "The logical consequences for the translation of a text regarded as verbally inspired" can result in illogicality of grammar and inscrutability of expression.[85] Such practices can include changing a noun's normal gender in the target language to correspond with that in the original text. As Adams has noted regarding the transformation of gram-

---

[84] Hier. *epist.* 57.1: *[inperita lingua] obicit mihi vel ignorantiam vel mendacium, si aut nescivi alienas litteras vere interpretari aut nolui: quorum alterum error, alterum crimen est.* On translation *verbum e verbo* (and its variants), see further Brock 1979, esp. 78, Bartelink 1980: 36, 46–47, 52.

[85] Brock 1979: 87. For examples of the *Vetus latina* imitating the syntax of the Septuagint, see Mohrmann 1965: 93–94.

matical gender in the Latin Psalter to match the Hebrew original, "the imitation of Hebrew should not be put down to [the translator's] incompetence in Latin, but reflects a deliberate policy of translation: the form of the Latin is meant to suggest that of the Hebrew original, which had of course the status of a sacred text."[86] In an analogous fashion, I suggest, Vergil and a select few other poets are deemed to have access to an ur-gender, to a notion of the original sexual connotations of any given signifier. As we shall see in the next chapter, this ability to discern and therefore assign genders that may seem unusual to contemporaries both peaks and dies with Vergil's poetry. For those students of Latin who study the chronologically younger arts of prose and oratory, or for those poets lamentably post-Vergilian—just as for those early Christians who are not working to preserve the original nature of a sacred text—assigning an uncommon gender is a fault that must be avoided.

Vergil, then, marks the zenith of the play of Latin gender. Some time before him, the Roman grammarians envision a period of uncertain fluidity in grammatical gender, while afterward begins the establishment of rigid categories of the masculine and feminine and, inevitably, of what is male and female—of sex. Can the implications of this imagined development be extended beyond the boundaries of ancient scholarship and reach out, like the inherent sex of gender itself, into broader areas of Roman society?

In the remaining chapters, I will attempt to illustrate the workings of just such a type of linguistic determinism. An understanding of grammatical gender as possessing archaic fluidity, a fluidity subsequently lost, has effects that are felt throughout a wide array of cultural activities during Rome's classical period. This construction of grammatical gender offers Latin poets a means of establishing a poetic authority that puts them on a par with their Greek predecessors (chapter 2); it organizes a world of otherwise mysterious Roman deities whose connection with the external world becomes blurred by the adoption of Greek notions of a divine pantheon (chapter 4); and, finally, in the realm of human sexuality we may witness a development that parallels the understood narrative of grammatical gender, as the hermaphrodite transforms from a figure whose fluid sex demands reverence to one that presents an improper model for a world of clear-cut sexualities (chapter 5). In other words I hope to demonstrate, in the seemingly innocent arena of grammatical gender, that there is at least some validity to the claim that "as the language is, so also is the nation."[87]

---

[86] Adams 2003: 273; see Ammassari 1987: 25–32, esp. 29. Meershoek 1966: 62–63 has an example of Jerome changing gender in the Vulgate as a concession to popular speech.

[87] Jespersen 1967: 16.

Roman Poets on Grammatical Gender

INTRODUCTION

The previous chapter illustrated how inherent aspects of the Latin language during the classical period, particularly the absence of a definite article to accompany nouns, contributed to the perception that grammatical gender in the earliest stages of the language must have been fluid, a perception that did not exist in the Greek tradition. In turn, the Roman grammarians busied themselves with cataloging each attested variation in gender, and developed a set of criteria to determine whether in any particular instance the literary source for the variation simply offered a dubious deviation from the normal gender—and could thereby be ignored—or whether the source wielded sufficient authority (*auctoritas*) to make the exception acceptable. These grammarians and other ancient scholars gave special credence to those nouns whose characteristics were supported by the educated usage of the elite or by the single authority of a respected Roman author. In the vast majority of cases, it was a poet of the Republic or early Empire who was perceived as having the ability to violate otherwise inviolable laws of grammar. In this chapter I would like to survey in what areas our ancient sources located this poetic authority, and to inquire why some poets were thought to have greater access to it than others. Informing these various ancient explanations is an assumption that the desire and ability of the most highly respected poets to transform grammatical gender provides tangible evidence of the superior knowledge that these poets possess of the relationship between language and the natural world.

EXPLAINING GENDER IN THE POETS

In assessing what considerations might drive a Latin poet to alter an established grammatical gender it would seem most convenient to begin with what the poets themselves report. Unfortunately, there survives no statement—or even allusion—in an ancient Roman poet concerning the practice. There do, however, exist certain observable facts from which inferences about intention can be made. First, writers of poetry will not infrequently use the same word, but in different genders, at various points in their corpus. I discuss below Quintilian's perplexed deference to Vergil's use of two conflicting genders for the noun *cortex* ("tree bark"). Second, although instances of variation of gender in poetry are numerous, only a minute proportion of these nouns would have been used in other than the standard gender by the educated Latin speaker, or even by the most stylized of prose writers. One prominent example of such a noun of unfixed gender is *finis* ("end"). The grammatical gender of *finis* fluctuates unpredictably between masculine and feminine in prose and poetic texts throughout Latinity. While it is possible in this and other cases to reconstruct plausible historical reasons for such variation, these explanations fail to account for why Roman poets manipulate the phenomenon as an acceptable poetic device.[1] In most cases, moreover, the change effected by the poet is a rarity (and not infrequently constitutes a unique example) that challenges ancient and modern scholars alike to ascribe a satisfactory reason for its existence.

An example mentioned in chapter 1 is the alleged use of the word "pumice" (*pumex*) in the feminine in the second line of Catullus's first poem. The noun is universally masculine elsewhere throughout Latinity, including in the manuscript tradition of Catullus itself, with the attestation of a feminine form deriving solely from an imprecise aside in Servius's commentary on the *Aeneid*. This apparent exception has exercised the ingenuity of numerous scholars, who have offered solutions that range from accusing Servius of scholarly incompetence to attributing the existence of the variation to the Catullan echo of a (lost) Greek intertext. The existence of feminine pumice awaits, and will likely never enjoy, a universally approved explanation. Yet regardless of how this case may be resolved—or explained away—the mere fact that a commentator of such wide reading as Servius could allow for the possibility of such gender manipulation provides us with the courage to assume that varying grammatical gender had literary significance.[2] Indeed, the shift in the gender of a word within the extant corpus of a single poet, such as the example of Vergil's manipulation of tree bark, all but guarantees that the practice constitutes a self-conscious literary device.

And yet as sound as this assumption may appear, not all modern scholars would agree. Such resistance to attributing poetic significance is hardly new; it would seem to be shared by the many catalogues of uncertain gender made in antiquity. As in the vast majority of modern commentaries on Latin poetic texts, ancient scholars duly note gender variation and then pass over that observation without further comment. Therefore, in response to this established stance of cautious agnosticism, or reasoned skepticism, it is necessary to preface my own discussion with two assertions about assigning meaning to the

---

[1] For *finis*, see ThLL vol. VI, 1 787.33–82 (H. Bauer). Adams 2013: 383–452 traces various historical explanations for fluctuating gender for several Latin nouns.

[2] Sharrock 2008 reevaluates Servius's much maligned status as a literary critic.

practice of fluctuating genders. First, I assume that the poets knew well the standard genders of the nouns that they used, with only a few limited exceptions.[3] These exceptions include uncommon loan words and toponyms, where morphological analogy or semantic differences from the parent language may cause the Latin author to derive an incorrect gender.[4] Second, in the absence of evidence to the contrary, I assume that poetic intent underlies the variations on offer. What follows, then, is a short survey of the commonest explanations for fluid gender that have found advocates from antiquity to the present.[5] I conclude this survey by showing how each explanation contains an element of a larger truth, and by suggesting that this practice derives its significance from the same kinds of attitudes reconstructed in chapter 1 regarding the relationship between language and the external world.

EXPLANATION 1: SEMANTIC DISTINCTIONS

As mentioned in the previous chapter, speakers of both ancient and modern languages manipulate noun gender to create semantic distinctions (e.g., ancient Greek ἅλς, meaning "salt" in the masculine but "sea" in the feminine).[6] Ancient writers also recognized this phenomenon, and they could be impressively specific in locating the source of such variations. In Servius's commentary on book 4 of the *Aeneid*, the commentator wishes to argue that Dido, newly enamored of Aeneas, is plagued by dreams rather than troubling wakefulness after hearing the hero recount his adventures since Troy. Servius delineates a clear and traditional grammatical distinction to prove his case:

> hoc . . . maiores inter vigilias et ea quae videmus in somnis interesse voluerunt, ut "insomnia" generis feminini numeri singularis vigiliam significaret, "insomnia" vero generis neutri numeri pluralis ea quae per somnium videmus. (Serv. Aen. 4.9)

> Our ancestors wished to observe the following difference between wakefulness and what we see in our dreams:[7] *insomnia* (feminine singular) means wakefulness, but *insomnia* (neuter plural) refers to what we see while dreaming.

Notice how Servius stresses a point that has been a recurring theme in ancient Roman reconstructions of the origins of gender: the practice of altering gender

---

[3] Contrast, for example, Jocelyn 1967: 314 on *salum* masculine at Enn. *scaen.* 162 rather than the expected neuter: "Ennius may have been unsure of the gender."

[4] Morphological analogy: see, for several examples, the discussion of toponyms such as *Argos* in NW 940–959; for semantic differences see, e.g., Nisbet and Hubbard 1978: 175 on Hor. *carm.* 2.11.16–17 (*nardo*).

[5] Adams 2013: 384–392 offers an analogous survey from the perspective of historical linguistics.

[6] For Latin examples see Adams 2013: 386.

[7] For *in somnis* as "in dreams," see Brown 1987: 236.

to accord with meaning stems from a conscious decision of the earliest speakers of Latin (*maiores*), and this decision has hardened into a principle that contemporary speakers are expected to follow. What makes this example particularly salient is that Servius's claims here, which are echoed elsewhere in the exegetical tradition, are demonstrably incorrect, since a one-to-one correspondence between gender and meaning proves untenable in the case of *insomnia*.[8] Servius surely was himself aware that the distinction he draws represents more a theoretical ideal than observable linguistic fact. For the grammarians, the ideology of the sage ancestors overshadows daily usage as *auctoritas* once again trumps customary practice.

EXPLANATION 2: MORPHOLOGY AND ANALOGY

The previous example offers an instance of both gender and number affecting a noun's meaning. The majority of cases upon which I shall focus in this chapter, by contrast, treat variation in gender alone and, more significantly, they involve instances where a new and unexpected gender does not alter a noun's basic meaning. Occasionally when an ancient Latin author defies commonly attested gender, Roman grammarians do not ascribe literary motives, noting instead that these writers are simply adapting the word in question to match the gender that would be expected from the noun's morphology. This type of change receives abundant illustration from the alterations that gender undergoes in the transition from Latin to the descendant Romance languages. The vast majority of tree names, for example, have feminine gender in Latin despite having an inflection identical with a masculine second-declension noun. For instance, the word for the pine tree (*pinus, -i*) has masculine terminations but in fact attracts feminine modifiers. We have already seen this historical tendency toward accommodating gender to morphology in modern explanations for why Protagoras accused Homer of a solecism in construing the noun πήληξ as feminine. Protagoras, according to some modern scholars, simply wished to regularize Greek usage by having all inanimate nouns with a nominative ending in -ξ be masculine.

A clear example from Roman antiquity illustrating this type of analogical change involves the word denoting "forehead" or "countenance" (*frons*). Aulus Gellius provides a particularly detailed account of the issues and scholarly concerns that must have lain behind distinctions such as Servius's succinct semantic discussion of the two different forms of *insomnia*. Gellius records an occasion when, in the company of a group of well-educated young men, he quoted some verses of the comic poet Caecilius that included the characterization that "the worst enemies are those with a happy expression (*fronte hilaro*) but a bitter heart" (Gell. 15.9.1: *hi sunt inimici pessumi, fronte hilaro, corde tristi*). In response to this tag, a member of Gellius's audience—"one from the crowd of

---

[8] Details in Getty 1933.

grammarians, a man not undistinguished"—takes Caecilius to task not for the inaptness of his epigram but for a grammatical idiosyncrasy. The anonymous scholar rebukes the playwright for his "bold license" in committing an outrageous grammatical solecism by construing the noun *frons* in the masculine rather than the feminine. A debate ensues, in which Gellius defends Caecilius's grammar, asserting that in fact it is Gellius's own contemporary Romans, not a playwright active over three hundred years earlier, who are "bold and licentious" for not recognizing that *frons* should in fact be construed in the masculine. Gellius offers two arguments in support of the masculine gender: analogy and the authority of the ancients.[9] For use of the masculine form he cites Cato the Elder and then, incensed at his interlocutor's lack of respect for arguments from ancient authority, he turns to the argument from analogy: all other third-declension nouns having nominative and genitive singular in *-ons/-ontis*, he claims, are masculine, and regularity demands that *frons* be so too. Although the argument from analogy successfully silences all objections, it is intriguing to note that Gellius willingly admits to his readers that it is based on false pretences (15.9.7: *audi . . . rationem falsam*).[10] The moral stands clear: when an argument from analogy cannot offer a decisive proof, respect for the authority of the ancestors will be the determining criterion.

In the vast majority of cases of fluctuating gender, in fact, the Roman author gives relatively little weight to arguments from analogy. Another example of how the violation of morphological expectations confounds the ancient scholar—this time from outside Gellius's insular world—involves the neuter noun *vulgus* ("crowd"). This noun's nominative singular ending in *-us* and genitive in *-i* anticipate a masculine gender, and such an incongruous morphology for the neuter perplexes grammarians. The word appears frequently among lists of exceptions, occasionally eliciting clearly prescriptive remarks such as Charisius's "*vulgus* should be construed in the masculine rather than the neuter" (*gramm.* 55.22–23 B: "*vulgus*" *masculini generis potius quam neutralis dicendum est*; cf. Prob. *nom. gramm.* IV 208.7–15). As will by now be expected, Vergil, who employs the noun in both genders in the *Aeneid* (1.149, 2.98), compels Charisius to deem the exceptional palatable (*gramm.* 94.10–12 B).[11]

EXPLANATION 3: THEY JUST DO IT

And yet to recognize the practice as palatable does not necessarily make it comprehensible. The remaining explanations found in ancient grammar and exege-

---

[9]ThLL vol. VI, 1 1352.80–1353.17 (L. Robbert) surveys attested usage; although almost universally feminine, masculine forms occur throughout Latinity without a clear difference in meaning.

[10]Gellius likely has two mutually consistent reasons for this admission: first, he has in mind the exception **spons, spontis* (Holford-Strevens 2003: 174 n. 12), and, second, he is elsewhere suspicious of arguments from analogy (cf. 5.21; Marache 1952: 208–213; cf. Vardi 2001).

[11]NW 972–973 catalogues uses of *vulgus* as masculine.

sis that I will consider locate the reason for gender change in a conscious, but frequently enigmatic, manipulation on the part of the author. A striking example of the mysterious power that a poet wields over grammar comes from Quintilian's treatise on the training of the orator. Quintilian, who normally warns his fledgling speakers not to attempt to imitate poetic diction and figures, nevertheless refrains from criticizing Vergil when he seems to lapse from rhetorical norms. In discussing how the orator should avoid solecisms in public speaking, Quintilian presents Vergil as a counterexample. He points out that the poet commits what he calls a "solecism in gender" (*per genus facit soloecismum*) when he uses the noun *cortex* ("tree bark") in the feminine in his *Eclogues*, while using the more commonly attested masculine form in his later poem, the *Georgics*. Seeming to realize that his students might misconstrue the implications of this statement as a critique of Vergil, Quintilian immediately adds: "I don't in fact reprehend either of these uses, since Vergil is the authority for both; but let's pretend that one of them is incorrect" (*inst.* 1.5.35: *quorum neutrum quidem reprehendo, cum sit utriusque Vergilius auctor; sed fingamus utrumlibet non recte dictum*; cf. Serv. *ecl.* 6.63). In this instance, authority does not help determine what preferred usage should be for the budding orator, but it does allow the authority figure, Vergil, apparently at will, to use whatever gender he deems suitable for his poetic context.[12] The elder Pliny states in one of his lost grammatical works that only intellectual discernment on the part of a speaker (*intellegentia*) separates a solecism from a trope.[13] It is Vergil's wisdom that allows him to transform what should be an embarrassing error of public speech into a poetic figure.

Pompeius, the source that preserves Pliny's statement, follows Quintilian in citing Vergil's authority in order to forgive another solecism, this time the use of a singular subject with a plural verb (*pars . . . secant*; *Aen.* 1.212). The literary effect achieved, he notes, is "novelty." As with Quintilian, however, the intellectual curiosity that might ask why Vergil would seek such an effect in this context shrinks in the face of Vergil's authority: "it is unscrupulous (*nefas*) to believe that so great a man did this out of ignorance, rather than that he used his knowledge (*sapientia*) to aspire to novelty."[14] In neither of these cases does the ancient scholar attempt to isolate the reasons for Vergil's choices, to attempt to reconstruct more precisely the scope and source of the *sapientia* that informs the poet's preference in each instance. This critical neutrality resembles the definition for poetic figure that recurs throughout the tradition: "what is called a solecism in prose is a trope in poetry."[15]

[12] Vainio 1999: 123–148.

[13] Plin. *dub. serm.* frg. 124 Mazzarino, as quoted in Pomp. *gramm.* V 292.13–14: "*quando sit soloecismus, quando sit schema, sola intellegentia discernit.*" Pomp. *gramm.* V 289.20–22 includes mistaken gender (in this case, *hanc* for a man) as a solecism.

[14] Pomp. *gramm.* V 292.22–23: *nefas est autem de isto tanto viro credere per inperitiam hoc fecisse, non per scientiam adfectasse novitatem.*

[15] E.g., Don. *gramm.* IV 394.23–24: *soloecismus in prosa oratione, in poemate schema nominatur.*

The respectful ambivalence that Quintilian expresses about Vergil's inappro-priately correct diction reemerges later in the treatise when he comes to discuss more explicitly the role of authority (*auctoritas*) in determining proper speech. Again, Vergil's ostensible violation of gender intrudes on the exposition awk-wardly, and for no apparent reason.

> *auctoritas ab oratoribus vel historicis peti solet. (nam poetas metri necessitas excusat,*
> *nisi si quando nihil impediente in utroque modulatione pedum alterum malunt. qualia*
> *sunt "imo de stirpe recisum" et "aeriae quo congessere palumbes" et "silice in nuda" et*
> *similia.)* (Quint. *inst.* 1.6.2)

> Authority is normally obtained from orators and historians. (Metrical necessity ex-empts poets, except sometimes they choose one construction over another despite there being no compulsion from the meter. Examples include "*imo de stirpe recisum*" and "*aeriae quo congessere palumbes*" and "*silice in nuda*" and similar instances.)

After establishing, with seeming good sense, that orators should consider prose writers their ultimate authority for usage, Quintilian explains that poets do not automatically have such authority since their practice must occasionally yield to metrical necessity. There follows, however, an unnecessary addendum: poets will alter grammatical gender even when meter does not require it. In the po-etic passages quoted, the unnamed Vergil has used the non-standard gender for the nouns *stirps* (*Aen.* 12.208), *palumbes* (*ecl.* 3.69), and *silex* (*ecl.* 1.15). Vergil-ian practice regarding gender stands outside commonly accepted usage, but once again Quintilian cannot begin to form a basis for criticizing it, let alone for understanding the poet's intention. The practice remains ineffable.

Servius offers an even greater assertion of Vergilian authority in his discus-sion of one of the words that Quintilian includes in his list. *Silex*—a noun de-scribing a hard stone such as flint, or an outcropping of the same—occurs seven times in the Vergilian corpus, always in the feminine when the gender can be determined from context.[16] Servius's note on this usage is worth quoting in full:

> *paene omnes hunc silicem dixerunt: nam et Varro et Lucretius ita dicunt. tanta tamen*
> *est Vergilii auctoritas, ut persuadeat nobis etiam hanc silicem dici.* (Serv. *Aen.* 8.233)

> Almost everyone used to speak of *silex* in the masculine; that's the form that both Varro and Lucretius use. Yet Vergil's authority is so great that we've become con-vinced that we should also speak of *silex* in the feminine.

The substance of Servius's remark is demonstrably true. The earliest extant use of *silex* in the feminine occurs in Vergil, and this form then quickly becomes well attested, in conjunction with the masculine, among writers of both prose and poetry.[17] What occasions surprise is Servius's inference from this piece of

---

[16] Feminine: *ecl.* 1.15; *Aen.* 6.471, 6.602, 8.233. Gender not marked: *georg.* 1.135; *Aen.* 1.174, 6.7.
[17] Serv. *Aen.* 10.377 records the gender of *obex* changing in the opposite direction.

data. In the same way that Varro attests to the power that "good poets" (*boni poetae*) possess in correcting the grammatical irregularities perpetuated in the daily speech of the forum (*ling.* 9.17), so too does Servius see Vergil as wielding influence in the more restricted sphere of grammatical gender. Simply by means of his authority as a poet, Vergil becomes credited with single-handedly creating a new linguistic habit. Nor is this a case of the Vergilian commentators overemphasizing the importance of their subject. Nonius also cites Vergil's usage to show that, by the fourth century, the word *silex* has become feminine "by the agreement of everyone" (*omnium consensu*; Non. p. 225.19–24).[18]

And yet as unusual as it may seem to ascribe such power to a single writer, the claim does find tangible support in the practice of post-Augustan poets. An analysis of their use of grammatical gender in general finds them considerably less imaginative than many of their poetic predecessors. The instances of uncommon gender found in the post-Vergilian hexameter poets are not only rare, but they normally have a precedent in Vergil or another respected precursor.[19] In contrast with the unstable genders found in early writers such as Plautus and the extant fragments of Ennius (approximately eighty-one and twenty-four instances, respectively), genuine gender fluidity among these imperial writers is limited.[20] Instances that do occur are restricted to cases in which the gender of a noun seems to have been legitimately flexible, such as that of *finis* mentioned above. Another particularly significant group where gender varies includes terms that are often of non-Latin origin such as proper names, or words for exotic plants and minerals.[21] Other instances involve cases where a parallel tendency in prose texts suggests that the gender change reflects historical developments taking place within the language rather than artistic intent on the individual poet's part.[22] Of special interest are those cases that seem to be iconoclastic but in fact reflect a usage already established as poetic or for which there is an

---

[18] For details on *silex*, see NW 985–986, who include a discussion of *cortex,* another *bête noire* of the grammarians (for which see further ThLL vol. IV 1069.15–33 [O. Probst]). Both words appear interchangeably as masculine and feminine for no apparent semantic reason in both prose and poetry, and not infrequently in the same author. Several grammarians treat *silex* as possessing common gender (NW 985); only Diom. *gramm.* I 453.35 considers the feminine a solecism.

[19] This conclusion rests on examination of the comprehensive lists at NW 889–1019, a reading of all relevant sections of the *Grammatici Latini*, and a consultation of modern scholarly commentaries on post-Vergilian epic.

[20] Plautus: Hodgman 1902: 302, who notes that all but six of these eighty-one examples have parallels elsewhere; see now Adams 2013: 392–419. The count from Ennius is my own. Terence provides a conspicuous exception to this tendency; apparent examples are easily accounted for (of the type *mea Glycerium* or *cum primo luci*; see Allardice 1929: 4–5, and Don. Ter. *Eun.* 400). Other apparent exceptions at *Eun.* 310 (*penus*) and *Eun.* 970 (*ordo*) are normally emended.

[21] Numerous examples at NW 931–960 (e.g., *Abydus/-um* neuter at Verg. *georg.* 1.207 but feminine at Val. Fl. 1.285).

[22] E.g., *clipeus/clipeum* (ThLL vol. III 1351.35–45 [H. Hoppe]); *margo* (NW 975); *phaselus* (NW 972); *torquis* (NW 1005–1006). On this general topic, see Adams 2013: 383–452.

attested use by an earlier poet.[23] I know of no instance, however, where a post-Vergilian poet innovates by varying grammatical gender to create a literary effect independent of his predecessors.[24] In other words, Servius's claim in his remark on *silex* about the power of Vergilian *auctoritas* seems to be applicable not just to himself and his fellow grammarians, but also to poets writing in the century or two following Vergil's death.

Statistical evidence further supports this seemingly counterintuitive claim. Consider the much-discussed case of the gender of the noun *dies* ("day"). The feminine form of this word originally designated in the late Republic a particular or prearranged date. This circumscribed semantic meaning restricted the appearance of the feminine—Cicero, for example, uses the masculine 663 times, the feminine only 75; the similar ratio in Caesar is 133 to 17. The situation begins to change with Lucretius, who, regardless of meaning, uses only the feminine; Vergil, also in contrast with the overwhelming tendencies of earlier prose writers, prefers the feminine by a proportion of 17 to 20. The trend continues with the post-Vergilian epicists.[25] The conservatism of these later poets concerning grammatical gender matches other observable phenomena, such as the avoidance of metrical peculiarities that have no precedent in an earlier, canonical poet.[26] Indeed, even when they try to innovate, it seems that these later writers just can't win. The grammarian Consentius cites an unnamed Lucan for employing an unusual diaeresis for the sake of the meter, and criticizes him for doing so since he lacks sufficient *auctoritas*.[27] The same poet receives criticism from Servius for employing the noun *scrobis* ("ditch") in the feminine; the usage is "contrary to art" and "of lesser authority."[28] It should by now be unnecessary to add that Vergilian usage does not support the feminine gender for this noun.[29]

EXPLANATION 4: METRICAL CONVENIENCE

A fourth explanation addresses the alteration of certain word forms to accommodate a poem's prosody. We have just seen Quintilian warning his students of

[23] E.g., *callis*, masculine in prose only at Varro *rust.* 2.2.9; later occurrences, all in post-Vergilian epic, would seem to follow Vergil (*Aen.* 4.405, 6.443, 9.383; cf. Ov. *met.* 7.626, Val. Fl. 3.568, 5.394); *calx* (NW 991).

[24] The Augustan epic poet Cornelius Severus is cited five times for genders that do not have Vergilian precedent (fgs. 1, 3, 6, 8, 14 Courtney). Each example does, however, occur in other previous authors; cf. Courtney 1993: 321–328, Hollis 2007: 340–367.

[25] For statistics see table at ThLL vol. IV 1024 (K. Pflugbeil) and for discussion Fraenkel 1917.

[26] E.g., Müller 1894: 78, 144–145, 252, 254 (on Stat. *Theb.* 5.140).

[27] Consent. *gramm.* p. 6.17–19 Niedermann (V 389.16–17 Keil): *dixisse Phoëbum*, with p. 26.19 Niedermann (V 400.23–24 Keil): *dixisse Phoëbos*. The citation is from a lost work (frg. 12 Blänsdorf).

[28] Serv. *georg.* 2.50 (*contra artem*); 2.288 (*minor . . . est Lucani . . . auctoritas*); Kaster 1978: 197–199. Full collection on *scrobis* at NW 1004–1005.

[29] The gender is unmarked at every occurrence (*georg.* 2.50, 235, 260, 288).

rhetoric to be aware that metrical necessity often prevents poets from acting as authoritative models (*inst.* 1.6.2). Servius seems to provide an example in which metrical considerations offer a plausible explanation for an instance of unusual gender. He explains that Horace uses the masculine form of the noun *cupido* to describe "greed" instead of the more normal (and feminine) form because the adjective accompanying the feminine would not have fit into the Sapphic meter of the ode. Aside from being incorrect in this particular instance—there is no evidence that gender affects the semantic range of *cupido*—this type of testimony is also uncommon.[30] In fact, it is rare in the extant material for an uncommon gender to change a line's scansion—an unarguable exception is offered by the poetic word for "bird" (*ales*), where masculine and feminine alternate, apparently only for the sake of metrical convenience.[31] Metrical necessity is, therefore, not a major, and certainly not the principal, factor driving poets to manipulate grammatical gender.

EXPLANATION 5: SOUND

Valerius Probus, an influential grammarian of the first century AD and author of a work—regrettably lost—*On Uncertain Genders* (Prisc. *gramm.* II 171.14–15), was once asked how a speaker should choose between alternative spellings of a word in Vergil when both seem technically correct.[32] In reply, Probus advises avoiding the "overly rotten and smelly distinctions of the grammarians"; instead, he says, whether writing prose or poetry, you should "ask your ear" (*aurem tuam interroga*; Gell. 13.21.1). In garnering evidence to support Probus's contention that euphony is an important tool in textual criticism, Gellius, our source for this anecdote, quotes the beginning of Vergil's famous epitaph of Priam at *Aeneid* 2.554: *haec finis Priami fatorum* ("This is the end of Priam's destiny"). In noting that Vergil employs the feminine form *haec finis* over the standard masculine *hic finis*, Gellius contends that if we correct Vergil's line to read the expected gender, our ears will "spit it out" because of the harshly dissonant sound that will result (*durum atque absonum erit respuentque aures quod mutaveris*: Gell. 13.21.12).[33] Furthermore, in a move that would surprise

---

[30]Serv. *Aen.* 5.122: *metri ratione.* See too Porph. Hor. *carm.* 2.16.15 (who wonders about the gender change but offers no explanation). For the inaccuracy of Servius's claim, see Nisbet and Hubbard 1978: 261–262, with ThLL vol. IV 1423.45–49 (H. Hoppe).

[31]ThLL I 1524.83–1525.7 (W. Bannier); contrast the inaccurate statement at Schol. Hor. *epod.* 10.1.

[32]Jocelyn 1984 and 1985 provides evidence for this episode being "entirely fictional" (1984: 465), while Holford-Strevens 2003: 34 is more optimistic. In any case, authenticity is not essential to my point here.

[33]Bauer 1920 convincingly explains the origins of feminine *finis.* Less persuasively, Klotz 1931: 343 suggests that Vergil echoes Homer's βιότοιο τελευτή (*Il.* 7.104, 15.787); see too Hanssen 1942: 98–100.

later grammarians, Gellius adds that this concern for euphony can trump both grammatical rules (*ratio*) and customary usage (*consuetudo*).[34] It is not surprising, then, to find later grammarians providing different explanations for this Vergilian collocution. The Servian tradition ascribes the gender to semantic factors, falsely asserting that *finis* in the feminine refers to a long period of time (Serv. Auct. *Aen.* 2.554), whereas Pseudo-Probus claims that Vergil's choice was dictated by metrical considerations, a judgment that is difficult to interpret since the scansions of *hic finis* and *haec finis* are identical.[35]

Ancient scholars preserve other alleged examples of poets changing gender for the sake of sound and again, as one might expect, basic aesthetic principles stand in conflict.[36] Servius maintains that Vergil referred to timid deer as *timidi dammae* rather than with the more standard *timidae dammae* to avoid homoioteleuton, the sing-songy effect of ending consecutive words with the same syllable, here the final *-ae*.[37] Quintilian's discussion of this phrase, by contrast, is silent about euphony. Rather, he lists *timidi dammae* as a figure of speech that allows the poet to refer to both the male and female deer simultaneously since *damma* is a common noun that admits both sexes under the single feminine morphological form (*inst.* 9.3.6).

Another note in the Servian tradition reveals more explicitly an ancient controversy about a claim for euphony. Servius discusses the possible reasons why Vergil used the phrase *foederă porcā* even though the combination *foederă porcō*, involving the sacrifice of a male rather than a female pig, accords better with Roman ritual.[38] After reviewing several possibilities for the substitution, a final consideration from the Servius Auctus tradition opines that the combination *foederă porcā* simply sounds better. Porphyrio, a commentator on Horace, offers an assertion about the same juxtaposition that is at once more specific and more vague: "certain expressions using the feminine gender are somehow more pleasing."[39] Even if we ignore that these explanations potentially contradict that given above for the phrase *timidi dammae*, where consecutive vowel sounds are said to displease the ear, the very mention of euphony as an alternative explanation makes a clear point. As might be expected, euphony, then as now, is dictated largely by personal taste. In fact, this moral can be drawn from the conclusion of Gellius's story about Probus's sensitive ear with which I began

---

[34] Gell. 13.21.23: *usque adeo in quibusdam neque rationem verbi neque consuetudinem, sed solam aurem secuti sunt suis verba modulis pensitantem.*

[35] Prob. *inst. gramm.* IV 124.21: *propter metrum hoc fecisse Vergilium declarabimus* (this treatise is traditionally, but falsely, attributed to Valerius Probus; I assume that a note about euphony has here been misunderstood or incorrectly transmitted).

[36] For the general statement, see Serv. *Aen.* 1.480 (*licet alia euphoniae causa varientur . . . in generibus*).

[37] Serv. *georg.* 3.539: *mutavit genus, ut vitaret homoeoteleuton* (cf. Serv. Auct. *ecl.* 8.28).

[38] Serv. Auct. *Aen.* 8.641; on the ritual, Fordyce 1977: 272.

[39] Porph. Hor. *carm.* 1.4.12: *nescio quid . . . quaedam eloquutiones per femininum genus gratiores fiunt*; cf. Porph. Hor. *epod.* 9.22.

this section, a conclusion that provides wonderful proof—if such were needed—that not all would-be critics could agree on what "sounds right." A brave soul listening to Probus's remarks on the euphonious qualities of Vergil's *haec finis* objected that he could not in fact detect any difference between this combination and that of the allegedly less pleasing *hic finis*. To this Probus reacted with a common pedagogical move: he dismissed the listener as ignorant and unteachable (13.21.7–9).[40]

EXPLANATION 6: GRANDEUR

In discussing the limitations imposed on contemporary practice by the borrowing of oratorical precedents, Quintilian cites a series of examples in which great speakers of the past employed words or grammatical forms that have become obsolete by his own day. Included in this list are Pollio's unique use of *lodix* ("blanket") in the masculine, and Calvus's employment of the masculine plural of *collus* ("neck").[41] Quintilian does not suggest reasons for these apparent archaisms, simply noting them as instances that the original speakers would avoid if they were his contemporaries in the first century AD (*inst.* 1.6.42: *quae nec ipsi iam dicerent*). Lack of any historical and literary context—Quintilian quotes only the individual words—prevents us from offering any further judgment on whether Pollio and Calvus were attempting to make a special point through the unusual genders. Their general attitude, however, can perhaps be reconstructed from the comments that Festus makes about an orator from an even earlier period, the tribune Gaius Gracchus.

Festus records that Gracchus, in a public oration of the late second century BC, deemed someone as "worthy of dying on an evil cross" (Fest. p. 150: *dignus fuit, qui malo cruce periret*). A separate fragment of the same orator consists only of the phrase *malo cruce*.[42] These two citations constitute the only surviving instances of *crux* ("cross") being used in the masculine in all of extant Latin prose literature. The immediate contexts for these fragments are unknown, but one indication that Gaius was being deliberately provocative in changing genders is his use in each instance of the accompanying adjective *malus* ("evil"). This combination would have been jarring to his original audience, which would have doubtless been familiar with the frequent use in curses of the feminine form of the adjective *mala* with *crux* (especially in the phrase *in malam*

---

[40]See too the (confusing) discussion at Gell. 6.20.6 with Thomson 1998: 273–274. For informative, if inconclusive, surveys on euphony in Latin and other poetry, see, e.g., Hanssen 1942, Herescu 1960: 32–81, Wilkinson 1963: esp. 9–34.

[41]ThLL vol. VII, 2 1609.69–71 (H. Beikircher) lists masculine *lodix* only here, and ThLL vol. III 1658.74–80 (O. Probst) attributes the masculine *collus* exclusively to *vetustiores*.

[42]Malcovati 1953: 185 argues that both fragments derive from a speech delivered against Publius Popillius (ORF 6.36 and 38).

crucem—"Get painfully crucified," an approximate Latin equivalent of "Damn you").[43] Festus contends that Gracchus's use of the non-standard gender evoked here archaic usage, thereby allowing the orator, one presumes, to achieve a "higher stylistic level."[44] Perhaps, as we shall discuss more fully in the next section, the fact that the Greek equivalent of *crux*, σταυρός, is masculine also contributes to this heightened style, although the Greek word seems never to have been used in a curse.[45] While it does seem reasonable to conclude that a grammatical aberration such as this could be interpreted as archaic and therefore elegant, such claims remain impossible to evaluate fully in the absence of concrete evidence. Festus's allusion to archaic usage does, however, introduce a new and fascinating notion: the possibility that noun genders could change through time. This possibility is related to the final point I shall raise from scholars of antiquity: that poets change genders in conscious imitation of Greek models.

EXPLANATION 7: GREEK INTERTEXTUALITY

A more sophisticated claim that ancient scholars have made, and one that resonates well with recent scholarly approaches to the study of Roman poetry, is that a poet will alter the gender of a Latin word in order to imitate or recall a literary forebear writing in Greek. In his study of etymological wordplay in Vergil, O'Hara has well established Vergil's exploitation of an analogous practice, by which a poet writing in Latin "plays upon or reproduces the sound of words in a Greek model." In the *Georgics* (1.277), for example, Vergil employs the proper name of the god *Orcus* as a way of echoing the unrelated word Ὅρκος (the personified "Oath") from Hesiod's *Works and Days* (804).[46]

One way in which a Roman poet could use gender to allude to a Greek context involved changing the normal morphology of a Latin word. The Greek noun ὁ χάρτας, describing the leaf of the papyrus plant as prepared for writing, is universally masculine. As is the case with most Greek to Latin calques of this type, however, the noun's Latin equivalent, *c(h)arta*, becomes construed as a feminine noun of the first declension because of its nominative termination in *-a*.[47] The sole extant exception to this gender transformation occurs in a frag-

---

[43] ThLL vol. IV 1258.84–1259.12 (O. Hey).

[44] Skutsch 1985: 525, following Fest. p. 150. Despite the explicit testimony of Festus and Nonius, Bergk 1870: 150 derives, ingeniously but unconvincingly, the combination *malo cruce* from a presumed archaic formula *malo cruci(s)* ("to the evil of the cross"). For a fluid gender that does seem falsely attributed to Gracchus (Serv. *Georg.* 2.288) see Kaster 1978: 199 n. 48.

[45] Cf. Exc. Bob. *gramm.* I 552.35, 37–38: *apud Romanos femina, apud Graecos masculina . . . crux*, σταυρός.

[46] O'Hara 1996: 63 ("translation with paronomasia").

[47] NW 965–966.

ment of the second-century BC writer Lucilius: *Graeci ubi nunc Socratici carti?* ("Where now are the Greek Socratic writings?" Lucil. 709). Lucilius's fragments display much concern with linguistic and grammatical niceties, particularly in matters of orthography (e.g., Lucil. 349–381). The recourse taken in fragment 709—to alter the Latin morphology of the expected *carta* to the unparalleled *cartus* as a way of recalling the masculine gender of a linguistic ancestor—was unusual.[48] More often, as we have seen, poets referred to an original Greek gender through the less drastic measure of altering grammatical gender only, without a corresponding change of lexical form. The content of the quoted passage—the writings of the Greek philosopher Socrates—seems to have compelled the scholarly Lucilius to change morphology so as better to suggest a Greek-like context.

This sort of linguistic play did not begin with Lucilius. Gellius, in the late second century, offers the earliest ancient explanation of which I am aware for a poet changing Latin gender to effect an intertextual allusion. He cites a fragment of Ennius's *Annales*, which we should recall is the first Latin epic poem written in dactylic hexameter, the meter characterizing Greek epic poetry and one not native to Latin. The Ennian fragment consists of only two words: *äere fulva* ("in the yellow air"). This is one of two passages in ancient Latin where the word *äer* is construed as feminine (I treat the second instance below). Gellius advances two mutually compatible explanations for the peculiarity: Ennius wrote this "not only because Homer says ἠέρα βαθεῖαν, but because the sound seemed, in my opinion, more resonant and pleasant" (Gell. 13.21.14: *non ob id solum, quod Homerus* ἠέρα βαθεῖαν *dicit, sed quod hic sonus, opinor, vocabilior visus et amoenior*). Given the context of Gellius's remark, his principal appeal is to euphony, and so he claims that the sound combination *äere fulva* can be uttered more elegantly than *äere fulvo*. The manner in which he expresses his secondary explanation makes it clear that it has already become part of the scholarly tradition: Ennius also altered the gender under the influence of Homer's use of the phrase "heavy mist" in the feminine (ἠέρα βαθεῖαν), an epic echo that would have been even more clear from the fact that the Greek word becomes uniformly masculine after the fifth century BC.[49] In other words, the change of gender in the development of Greek allows Ennius to allude more unmistakably to his Homeric model. Otto Skutsch, the modern authority on the *Annales*, remarks that this assessment of literary influence is "probably right," a grudging (and uncommon) concession to Gellius's aesthetic judgments.[50] Ennius's practice did not go unnoticed: according to the grammarian

---

[48] Although *chartus* is attested only here, see Prisc. *gramm.* II 169, 6–9.

[49] LSJ cites the feminine of ἀήρ only from Homer, Hesiod, and Anaximenes, noting that it is exclusively masculine beginning with Herodotos. This is a convenient place to note that the extant fragments of Livius Andronicus's "translation" of the *Odyssey* contain no instances of gender play.

[50] Skutsch 1985: 598–599.

Diomedes, the young Vergil of the *Eclogues* also changes gender in clear reference to his own Greek model, the bucolic poet Theocritus.[51]

Construing gender change as a sly nod to Greek models enables us to appreciate the only other certain example in which *äer* appears as feminine. In his treatise *On the God of Socrates*, Apuleius discusses intermediate divine beings that inhabit the space "of intervening air" between earth and the ether that surrounds it (Apul. *Socr.* 6 p. 132: *intersitae äeris*; cf. 6 p. 138). In employing the rare feminine form of *äer*, Apuleius seems to strive for a type of intertextuality analogous to that which Gellius claimed for Ennius. Furthermore, since in this instance Apuleius's text seems originally to have been performed, the declaimer's pronunciation of *intersitae* would have ensured that the noun's gender was explicit to his audience. In the context, Apuleius's narrator is responding to the objection of an imaginary interlocutor by channeling Plato in Latin: "let Plato answer, using my voice to express his own opinion" (*responderit enim Plato pro sententia sua mea voce*). Part of the adoption of the Platonic persona, I suggest, involves Apuleius transferring the archaic gender of the Greek word to *äer*, its Latin cognate. In other words, a Greek tradition, and very likely a lost Greek pre-text, once again lies behind the Latin change of gender.[52]

An ancient explanation for another unusual gender in Ennius adopts similar reasoning. Again, the context in Ennius is lost, but Nonius makes clear the interpretation:

> *LAPIDES et feminino genere dici possunt ut aput Ennium:*
> "*tanto sublatae sunt a<u>gmine tunc lapides*";
> *ad Homeri similitudinem, qui genere feminino lapides posuit.* (Non. p. 211.10–13)[53]

> "Stones" (*lapides*) can be spoken of in the feminine gender as well, as in Ennius:
> "Then the stones were lifted at an increasing rate."
> He imitates Homer, who put "stones" in the feminine.

The noun *lapis* is elsewhere universally masculine in classical Latin except for a single instance in Varro's treatise on farming. This unique use of the feminine in the Varronian corpus, together with its later recurrence in the texts of land surveyors over several centuries, raises suspicion that the feminine form may have a technical meaning in prose.[54] In epic poetry, by contrast, Nonius assumes that Ennius alludes here to Homer's analogous deployment in the feminine of the normally masculine Greek noun λίθος (*Il.* 12.287; *Od.* 19.494). The

---

[51] Verg. *ecl.* 5.38: *pro purpurea . . . narcisso* (following Diom. *gramm.* I 453.36 in opposition to all manuscripts), Theocr. 1.133: ἁ . . . καλὰ νάρκισσος; Klotz 1931: 344, Renehan 1998: 228–229.

[52] On the Greek sources of the treatise, see Harrison in Harrison et al. 2001: 185–189.

[53] See Skutsch 1985: 709 for the emendation *augmine*; he doubts an intentional echo of Homer (Enn. *ann.* 567 Skutsch). It is worth noting that the thorough study of Knauer 1964 does not cite an example of Vergil changing a noun's gender under Homeric influence.

[54] Varro, *rust.* 3.5.14 (all other uses in Varro are masculine); for the *Gromatici* see Josephson 1950: 157–158.

Iliad passage, famously describing stones in a siege that fly as thickly as snow in a violent storm, would particularly suit Ennius's epic. Whatever the precise allusion, however, it should be noted that the type of literary echo imagined here is more complex than it was with *äer*. In the case of *lapis*/λίθος, the imitation stems not from changing the gender of a loan word (ἀήρ), but from switching genders between two words that are related only semantically and not etymologically.[55]

The next example finds Lucretius employing an unusual gender in response to a Homeric intertext. Amidst his account of how all plants and animals have their ultimate origins in the earth, Lucretius interjects with an impossible counterexample:

> *haud, ut opinor, enim mortalia saecla superne*
> *aurea de caelo demisit funis in arva.* (Lucr. 2.1153–1154)

> For I hardly think that a golden rope (*aurea . . . funis*) brought living
> beings down onto the fields from above.

Outside the exegetical tradition, the feminine form of *funis* ("rope") appears to occur only here.[56] In contrast with the two cases from Ennius discussed above, this time a fully surviving context allows us to evaluate Lucretius's unusual choice more securely. First, it is necessary to exclude the possibility that the poet chose the feminine gender for metrical reasons: while the masculine form *aureus* could certainly not be substituted for *aurea* in the line's current formation, Gellius long ago pointed out the minimal change that Lucretius would have needed to make to remedy this difficulty (e.g., *aureus e caelo*; Gell. 13.21.21). In spite of this common-sense demonstration, however, we need not continue to follow Gellius's discussion and agree with his contention that the choice of gender simply promoted euphony (about which see above). Rather, modern scholars generally agree that Lucretius offers here a clear reminiscence of Homer, in this case of the "golden rope" mentioned at *Iliad* 8.19 (as also rendered by a phrase in the feminine gender, σειρὴν χρυσείην). The *Iliad* passage, which has Zeus whimsically imagining a golden rope that connects the earth to Olympus, came to have an afterlife in the later philosophical tradition as offering an "allegorical interpretation of the heavenly origin of life."[57] By altering the expected gender of the Latin *funis*, Lucretius silently makes explicit the allusion to the feminine rope of the Greek tradition, and thereby recalls Homer's role as "general" of a philosophical army that Plato explicitly challenges in his own citation of the *Iliad* passage (*Tht.* 153c). Lucretius, following this Platonic tradi-

---

[55] Neither Maltby 1991 nor ThLL indicate that the Romans linked the words etymologically.

[56] ThLL vol. VI, 1 1594.33–48 (M. Leumann). I discount the probably late chapter title at Cato *agr.* 72, since everywhere in Cato's text the word is masculine. Radke 1956: 82–83 offers cogent reasons (in addition to Gellius's explicit testimony) for not construing *aurea* with *arva*.

[57] Bailey 1947: 2.981, who does not mention the *Theaetetus* passage; Radke 1956.

tion of questioning the value of Homer's text as philosophy, describes with sar-
casm (*haud, ut opinor*) Zeus's hypothetical invention. In so doing, Lucretius
corrects a philosophical tradition that arose from Homer without needing to
mention it explicitly. Life arose from the earth, the materialist Lucretius maintains, not from the sky, a false interpretation to which the poet has offered a
clear allusion with the feminine, and therefore Greek, golden rope.

Following the leads of Gellius and Nonius, modern scholars have attempted
similar explanations for other passages containing abnormal gender, but with
limited success. I shall review some of these attempts in the next chapter. For
now, I would like to conclude by examining one final instance of unusual gender that had already received attention in antiquity. This passage involves a rare
instance in which Greek practice is represented as influencing the choice of
gender not in poetry, but in a piece of Latin prose. Here there begin to emerge
clues concerning why gender change tends to be restricted to the province of
poets: as with the other prose example from Gaius Gracchus, the anomaly is
thought to originate from a perceived archaic usage.

Roman scholars saw in the recognizably archaic language of Roman law an
attempt by the framers analogous to that of the poets, to forge authority by
reaching back to an early stage in the development of Latin itself. On two occasions the sources cite Varro for quoting old laws that attribute an uncustomary
masculine gender to the normally feminine word for sheep (*ovis*, cognate with
the English "ewe").[58] The first example comes from Aulus Gellius:

> *quando . . . nunc quoque a magistratibus populi Romani more maiorum multa dicitur*
> *vel minima vel suprema, observari solet ut oves genere virili appellentur; atque ita M.*
> *Varro verba haec legitima, quibus minima multa diceretur, concepit: "M. Terentio,*
> *quando citatus neque respondit neque excusatus est, ego ei unum ovem multam dico";*
> *ac nisi eo genere diceretur, negaverunt iustam videri multam.* (Gell. 11.1.4)

> When even now a fine is levied by Roman magistrates according to ancestral custom
> (*more maiorum*), regardless of whether it is for the minimum or maximum value, the
> customary practice is to name sheep in the male gender. Marcus Varro has recorded
> the following legal formula by which a minimal fine is levied: "I fine Marcus Teren-
> tius one sheep (*unum ovem*) since, summoned, he has neither responded nor been
> acquitted." If this gender were not used, they declared that the fine not be considered
> legal.

The masculine gender for *ovis* seems not to be attested again until Latin translations from the Old Testament (ThLL vol. IX, 2 1192.24–38 [K. Plepelits]). Gellius attributes the odd gender here to a practice that had been inherited from the
ancestors (*more maiorum*). This attribution receives additional support from
Festus's reference to the masculine gender of *ovis* occurring in the pontifical

---

[58] Wright 1917: 33–45 offers details about *ovis* as an epicene noun.

books, apparently among a list of which animals are appropriate for sacrifice (Fest. p. 286: *in commentariis sacrorum pontificalium*). Nonius, the only other witness to the phrasing of the law quoted in Gellius, brings our discussion full circle. He adds the surprising explanation that Varro saw this gender change as influenced by the Greek text of Homer, where the generic term for sheep is universally masculine (πολλοὶ ὄϊες; Non. p. 216.25–30). The historical improbability that Homeric diction could have influenced the language of a law in archaic Rome is beside the point here. What is significant is the interlocking influences that Nonius imagines to be at work during an early stage in Latin's development. Archaic legal practice, grammatical forms of the earliest Greek poets, and fluid gender in Latin all commingle neatly in this single example.

While looking back to Greek precedent clearly offers a useful explanatory principle for fluid Latin genders, the approach does not come near to explaining every exception. Nevertheless, I think that this approach comes close to a truth. I would like to adjust this explanatory model slightly to pursue an alternative that has been the subtext of many of the ancient explanations catalogued above. Rather than harking back simply to a literary model, these poets intend to recall a *shared linguistic heritage* with Greek. Both languages, in other words, are conceived of as arising from an ur-moment in which the genders of nouns were self-evident. Such a state of self-evident gender existed for Varro's "firstnamers" encountered in chapter 1. One instance in which ancient discussions indicate a shared antiquity between Greek and Latin gender is in Lucretius's account of the golden rope sent down to earth. As already noted, the Latin word *funis* occurs in the feminine only in Lucretius, as an indisputable Homeric reminiscence. The grammatical tradition adds an unexpected dimension to this seemingly straightforward instance of literary allusion. Priscian sees the mixture of feminine and masculine forms for *funis*, along with other third-declension nouns terminating in -*nis*, as the product of a choice of the earliest speakers of Latin (*vetustissimi*). These ancient shapers of Latin relied upon their own authority to confound genders, and then to choose those most fitting. Their choice depended not on a difference in meaning, however, but on the speaker's authority alone.[59] With the further development of the language, usage forced these nouns to be restricted to a single gender. As a result, everyday speakers are not to follow the ancient authorities in these matters of ambiguous gender (see, e.g., *gramm.* II 160.10–18; 169.6–8, 19–20). Not simply have archaic speech habits influenced the varied genders employed for individual nouns—as we saw, for example, with *crux*—but Priscian perceives the entire phenomenon of fluid gender as belonging to the earliest stages of the language.

---

[59] Contrast Farrell 2001: 28: "For the Latin speaker an authentic and unmediated connection between nature and culture is unattainable"; the grammarians, at least, could posit just such a time of "unmediated connection."

This hypothesis accords well with an aspect of Vergil's status complementary with his authority on gender usage. As early as Quintilian, commentators on the poet repeatedly remark on his perceived passion for, and expertise in, antiquarian matters (*inst.* 1.7.18: *amantissimus vetustatis*).[60] Other literary scholars of the first century of our era attribute similar erudition to Vergil, emending his text to allow a more archaic lexicon and syntax or to fit recent antiquarian researches into myth and ritual.[61] Unsurprisingly, ancient exegesis also recognizes the poet's willingness to change grammatical gender to match a Homeric model, for example by placing *clipeus*, the normally masculine word for "shield," into the neuter form *clipeum* (Serv. *Aen.* 9.706).[62] Vergil's reputation for erudition, bordering at times on omniscience, presents a model for the late Roman grammarian that it would be foolish not to heed, especially given the fact that the earliest Roman authors had all but been eclipsed even in the schools by Vergil's popularity.[63] But the issue acknowledged at the outset of this chapter still remains: Vergil nowhere makes explicit to his readers how to interpret a noun of unusual gender. So let's abandon the conjectures of antiquity and turn for final inspiration to the perspective of a German poet writing in the early twentieth century.

EXPLANATION 8: FLUID LANGUAGE

In a letter written to Nanny Wunderly-Volkart in the year 1920, travel in the sunny clime of Italy inspired the forty-four-year-old Rainer Maria Rilke to comment on grammatical gender. To appreciate this letter fully, it is necessary to recall a peculiarity frequently mentioned in discussions of Indo-European grammatical gender. In most Romance languages the word for sun is masculine, while that for moon is feminine (as in Rilke's French examples of *le soleil*, *la lune*), whereas in German the opposite holds true: the sun is feminine and the moon masculine (*die Sonne*, *der Mond*). And so on to Rilke:

> . . . *ich denke immer im Sinne von le soleil und la lune, und das Umgekehrte in unserer*
> *Sprache ist mir konträr, so daß ich immer machen möchte "der" große "Sonn . . ." und*

[60] Horsfall 1991 assesses the accuracy of this conception (43 n. 85 offers a host of ancient testimonia).

[61] Zetzel 1981: 31–36 (Hyginus), 49–51 (Probus); cf. the absurd claim at Pomp. *gramm.* V 232.30–38 that the final *-o* found in Latin first-person singular verbs arises from Vergil's imitation of Greek quantities.

[62] Hardie 1994: 221–222 recognizes the allusion, but does not mention the gender change; cf. Knauer 1964: 411. For the frequent fluctuations of gender for *clipeus/-um* see ThLL vol. III 1351.23–32 (H. Hoppe).

[63] Zetzel 1981: 27–28. One finds the same respect for Vergilian authority in historical works as well; Ps. Aur. Vict. *orig.* 1.1–5 offers an intriguing example.

*die Möndin! . . . so geht es einem oft, daß man mit dem äußerlichen Benehmen der
Sprache uneins ist und ihr Innerstes meint, oder eine innerste Sprache . . .*

I always imagine that, as in French, the sun is *masculine* and the moon *feminine*; the
opposite phenomenon in our language doesn't make sense to me. I would always
prefer to speak of the great *masculine* sun ("'der' große 'Sonn . . .'") and the *feminine*
moon ("die Möndin")! . . . It frequently happens that we disagree with the external
manifestation of our language and intend what is most intimate (*Innerstes*), or a most
intimate speech.[64]

I wish to suggest that Rilke's intuitive sense of what sex must be assigned to
non-animate objects, and an analogous willingness to violate grammatical
rules in quest of a deeper, poetic truth, seeking what Rilke here calls "*eine innerste Sprache*," is what drives Roman poets to violate gender rules. A rough
parallel for Rilke's notion that the gender of inanimate objects may follow some
sort of instinctual "rule" can be found in a tendency detectable in the variable
gender of the French word for "love," *l'amour*.[65] The story of French "love" is
complex. The word was regularly feminine until the sixteenth century, from
which point French grammarians attempted to bring the noun into line with
Latin practice, so that the masculine took over when the word referred to the
male god of love (Cupid) or to the love that Christians feel for their own god. In
contemporary French, the standard distinction has resulted in a split, with the
singular form being regularly masculine, but the plural commonly feminine.
Nevertheless—perhaps as an appeal to archaism, or perhaps as an appeal to the
allegedly "feminine" nature of romantic love, or perhaps these two are the
same—the word occasionally makes an appearance in the feminine singular.
The standard users of this non-standard feminine singular are, however, poets.

Some other examples in modern European poetry outside of French are
worth citing for the manner in which poets play on grammatical gender. Presumably considerations analogous to those offered here by Rilke help drive
these poetic innovations. For example, the erotic ode to the moon by Goethe
("An Luna") begins by addressing the moon as "sister" ("Schwester von dem
ersten Licht"), despite the moon's masculine gender; Foscolo speaks of a feminine tree with the archaic noun *arbore* (*arbore amica*), apparently to avoid the
standard, and masculine, Italian noun *albero* ("Dei Sepolcri"); Alberti varies
Spanish gender in order to mirror his varying relationship with the sea ("El
Mar. La Mar").[66] None of these instances, however, truly parallel the radical
nature of much of the poetic practice in Latin. Rather than being manufactured

---

[64] Rilke 1977: 1.143 (*Brief* 48), cited in Bussmann 1995: 114. Heinrich Heine's poetic cycle *Die
Nordsee* I, 3 (*Sonnenuntergang*) contains an analogous resistance to German's native genders; see
Yaguello 1978: 107.

[65] My discussion of *l'amour* follows Grevisse 1969: 196–198.

[66] Lunelli 1969: 170–171 cites the Goethe and Foscolo examples; I am grateful to Claudia
Fernández for the Alberti reference.

as either an inspired innovation, or perhaps even out of apparent willfulness, these modern examples exploit already existing grammatical and lexical forms or employ well-established poetic motifs. Indeed, even Rilke's seemingly passionate objection to the alleged nonsense of German gender has its limits. In the very letter that voices his dissatisfaction, the pressure of usage forbids him simply to write the blatantly incorrect forms of "*der große Sonne*" and "*die Mond.*" Instead, he resorts to putting his masculine sun in scare quotes and to adding a suffix ("*-in*") in order to render the noun "*Mond*" unmistakably and unerringly feminine. It would appear that his "*Innerstes*" does not extend so far as to allow him to break grammatical rules. The poets of the Republic, by contrast, exhibit no such scruples.

Despite the convincing examples discussed in the previous section, in which Ennius and Lucretius change grammatical gender so as to allude to a specific Homeric intertext, not all examples of Latin gender play can be resolved so readily. Rather, I would maintain that when Roman poets echo Greek precedent they do not simply try to place themselves in intertextual competition with Greek models. As Dubuisson points out, the reigning assumption among ancient grammarians was not that Latin and Greek had significant differences but that they were inherently alike.[67] One manifestation of this assumption is the theory that Latin was in fact a dialect of Greek or, in its less extreme form, the notion that Greek and Latin share a number of traits, a phenomenon that may indicate origins from a shared proto-language.[68] In either case, what often needed explanation for the grammarians were not the places where the two languages resembled one another; the existence of a shared general grammar and even vocabulary is the main principle upon which they based their researches. Rather, what required explanation were the deviations.[69]

A common sub-genre of the Roman grammatical tradition provides a clear instance of this point put into action. The similar origins of Latin and Greek explain the need for the existence of *idiomata*—lists of Latin words and constructions that offer deviations from analogous Greek diction in apparently insignificant details such as grammatical gender or associated syntax. Charisius introduces one such list with the following explanation:

> *cum ab omni sermone Graeco Latina lingua pendere videatur, quaedam inveniuntur vel licentia ab antiquis vel proprietate linguae Latinae dicta praeter consuetudinem Graecorum, quae idiomata appellantur.* (Char. *gramm.* 380.21–24 B. Cf. Diom. *gramm.* I 311. 3–6; Macr. *exc. gramm.* V 599.5–10, 631.7–19)

---

[67] Dubuisson 1984: 63–64.

[68] Latin as Greek dialect: Gabba 1963; Fögen 2000: 49–51. Varro's views are inconsistent, but he seems to have adopted a middle position between autochthony and Greek dialect (Cavazza 1981: 88–97).

[69] Dubuisson 1984: 64.

> Although the Latin language seems to depend entirely on Greek speech, it is possible
> to find certain expressions spoken contrary to Greek usage on account of either the
> permissiveness of the ancients or the inherent nature of the Latin language. These
> expressions are called *idiomata*.

Upon encountering statements such as this, it becomes clear how O'Hara's description of the importance of etymology to poetic production in Vergil applies equally well to poetic manipulation of gender. Both tropes involve "the story of the origin and development of a word, and poets play with details of the story in a way that may be compared with the way they play with myths."[70] Part of that story includes instances of the historical intersections and deviations of the Latin and Greek languages.

And what, at last, can be said about the basic plot of this "story" of Latin grammatical gender? Otto Skutsch remarks on gender fluctuation in Ennius as follows: "There are . . . so many instances of uncommon gender . . . that they are best explained as being due to a state of the language still somewhat fluid."[71] This assertion—and it can only be an assertion since, as we have seen, such claims cannot be proven—prompts three observations.

First, a belief in the archaic existence of fluid gender categories echoes an already-mentioned remark of Festus, who insists that uncertain genders in archaic Rome, for which he provides several examples from both poetry and prose, "should be accepted, since they offer witness not to error but to ancient practice" (Fest. p. 286: *quae non ut vitia, sed ut antiquam consuetudinem testantia, debemus accipere*). In fact, features analogous to Festus's "ancient practice" characterize an aspect of the poet's craft that can be traced to its Indo-European roots. In a discussion of features of Indo-European poetry such as archaic vocabulary, obscure word order, and complex metaphor, West remarks that these verbal devices

> . . . were part and parcel of the Indo-European poet's stock-in-trade, of what gave
> him his claim to special status. His obscurities were not necessarily perceived as
> faults; what is not fully understood may seem more impressive than what is. In some
> branches of the tradition the poet seems to have positively gloried in his mastery of
> a language beyond common comprehension. (West 2007: 77)

Manipulation of gender becomes for the Roman poets a part of this "mastery" by reaching back to an imagined time of mysteriously fluid gender. Second, as I demonstrated in chapter 1, the Roman grammatical tradition tended to attribute a semantic status to instances of masculine and feminine gender. The tradition depends, either implicitly or explicitly, on the story that, at the creation of the Latin language, gender was thought to correspond to some quality in the signified that would identify it with biological sex. Third, I would now like to

---

[70] O'Hara 1996: 58.
[71] Skutsch 1985: 66–67.

speculate that, when Vergil and other classical poets emulate predecessors such as Homer, they too are hoping to recall this era when genders of nouns had an inherent instability.

GENDER FLUIDITY AND THE (HETERO)SEXING OF THE WORLD

So let us continue to pursue the hypothesis that genders were thought to be elastic and adaptable to a specific rhetorical context by the skilled speaker and, in particular, by the poet. I would like to give three demonstrations of how this hypothesis works in practice before turning to discuss some of its broader implications.

The first illustration of a poet making a non-traditional gender choice, while straightforward, depends on the principle of personification that will inform my subsequent examples. The Latin word for "sky," *caelum*, is neuter. In four passages of Republican Latin, however, the noun is unambiguously construed in the masculine as *caelus*.[72] Two such examples are in Ennius's *Annales*, and one of the fragments surviving explains clearly the apparent anomaly:

> . . . *Saturno*
> *quem Caelus genuit.* (Enn. *ann.* 23–24 Skutsch)

> . . . for Saturn,
> whom Caelus begat.

The verb *genuit* is familiar from the previous chapter: Varro defines grammatical gender, which for him includes only the masculine and feminine, as those forms that "give birth" (*generant*; Varro frg. 245 Funaioli). The appearance of this verb helps clarify the reason for the masculine gender of "Caelus" in the fragment. In the words of the Christian apologist Tertullian: "Saturn castrated Sky while he was asleep—we read of Sky in the masculine gender (*Caelus*), since how could he be a father unless masculine?"[73] The actions of Sky as a sexual being, in other words, eventually set in motion the establishment of Jupiter as supreme deity in the Olympic pantheon. And so it is natural, in every sense of the word, that Ennius make this great progenitor's gender masculine. This may seem a trite observation, but it is key to note that in making the shift from neuter to masculine Ennius emphatically identifies grammatical gender, like Varro, with sexual generation, and hence with biological sex.

---

[72] Including Enn. *frg. var.* 60, *Ann.* 559 Skutsch, and Lucr. 2.1097 (*caelos*), the latter two of which I treat below. Among other instances, Vitr. 4.5.1 is anomalous ("hardly sound," Skutsch 1985: 183), and for Petronius see Adams 2013: 421–422.

[73] Tert. *nat.* 2.12.10: *Saturnus quidem Caelu<m castra>vit dormientem—legimus Caelum genere masculino: ceterum <quomodo> pater nisi masculinus?*

Three additional details are worth mentioning. First, despite the apparently transparent explanation for variable gender in this instance, the Latin exegetical tradition feels compelled to cite a rule to underscore it: "we have written 'father Caelus' to designate the deity, since no god belongs to the neuter gender" (Serv. Auct. *Aen.* 5.801). Second, as the grammarians also recognized, every extant occurrence of the noun in the plural occurs in the masculine (*caeli*), which "bears witness to an original masculine gender."[74] If Ennius too were aware of the historical basis for this distinction, he would recall through his gender slippage not simply the mythical connotations but also the originary force of an archaic masculine Sky. This possibility appears even stronger when we consider that the poet, an early if not native speaker of Greek, would have had in mind the invariable masculine gender of Sky's Greek equivalent, Οὐρανός. As with the allusions discussed in the previous section, however, an influence of the Greek gender does not necessarily indicate direct literary imitation, but rather a sense of the Latin poet reaching back to the origins of language. Finally, this interpretation of masculine *caelus* provides insight into the other fragment of the *Annales* where *caelus* is undoubtedly masculine—*fortis Romani sunt quamquam caelus profundus* (Enn. *ann.* 559 Skutsch: "The Romans are brave despite the deep sky"). Skutsch conjectures that the earlier uses of *Caelus* to denote a male god facilitates this rare appearance of *caelus* as masculine in "the ordinary sense."[75] And yet another interpretation presents itself, one more in keeping with the discussion of this chapter: the gender emphasizes further the admirable nature of Roman bravery by stressing human emotional stature when faced with the forces of elemental, primordial nature.[76]

Clear indications that the personification of nature can change grammatical gender appear elsewhere in Latin poetry. Poets such as Ennius and Catullus are attested as making feminine the masculine noun *arcus* ("rainbow") in order to, as one ancient source notes, "refer to its origin" as the female divinity Iris (Serv. *Aen.* 5.610: *referentes ad originem*).[77] Another example brings us down to earth, to a personification among Roman flora. As mentioned in the previous chapter, names of trees in classical Latin are predominantly feminine, as in *arbor*, the generic word meaning "tree," despite the fact that this word's descendants in the Romance languages are almost universally masculine.[78] Ennius violates this

---

[74] Skutsch 1985: 183; compare Char. *gramm.* 91.14–15 B (*caelum hoc . . . etiam masculine veteres dixerunt*). For the masculine plural, see ThLL vol. III 79.20–39 (W. Bannier).

[75] Skutsch 1985: 183.

[76] The interpretation holds if we read Baehrens's *tamquam*. Of the remaining sixteen examples of *caelus* in the *Annales* in only one case is the gender unambiguously neuter (205 Skutsch). The occurrence at *ann.* 27 Skutsch is likely masculine if Atlas is indeed the subject of the verb (an "inescapable" conclusion, according to Skutsch 1985: 186).

[77] Cf. Prisc. *gramm.* II 259.5 (*apud veteres*), Skutsch 1985: 562–563.

[78] Tree names: full list at NW 931–937; Bögel 1966 notes that all five examples of *arbor* masculine at ThLL vol. II 419.61–63 (W. Bannier) are in fact ambiguous.

tendency toward the feminine when he twice describes the cypress with masculine adjectives, and in such a way that the result argues against the reason for the gender change being the avoidance of homoioteleuton—*longi . . . cupressi/ stant rectis foliis* (*ann.* 223 Skutsch) and *rectos . . . cupressos* (*ann.* 511 Skutsch). The supposition that Ennius intends to recall in each instance the young boy of myth named Cypressus, whose endless grief prompted his metamorphosis into the tree of mourning, is supported by two of the words Ennius uses in describing these trees in the first fragment—the adjective *longus* is not used regularly of trees in classical Latin, but of people, and the verb *stare*, while not unusual for trees, assists in anthropomorphizing the cypresses.[79] In the second fragment, Gellius notes that *rectos* gives a *firmior . . . et viridior sonus* ("stronger and more vigorous sound") than the expected *rectas*, again in probable allusion to a male personification. More generally, Priscian claims that both the masculine and feminine forms of the cypress were acceptable, but only to the earliest Latin speakers (*vetustissimi*; *gramm.* II 169.6–20). Although this interpretation of masculine *cypressus* must remain uncertain, Servius makes explicit an analogous claim for Vergil's use of the noun *crocus* in the *Georgics*: "he uses the masculine here poetically, referring to the boy who is said to have turned into this flower."[80] As with *Caelus*, the perceived archaic flavor of fluid gender enables the noun to retain a mythical resonance, and change to the masculine gender marks the original male behind the natural object.

Visual evidence indicates that this tendency to equate gender and sex constitutes a feature of Roman culture that extends beyond the literary realm. Representations of deities and abstract concepts always depict the subject's sex as reflecting their name's grammatical gender. The feminine noun *clementia*, for example, appears on coins as the female *Clementia*, whereas the tutelary divinity of the *genius*, a masculine noun, is consistently figured as a man across a range of media, and so forth.[81] Outside the elite realm of textual and visual representations, similar phenomena appear in the extant epigraphic material, indicating that the willingness to personify based on grammatical gender does not represent simply a trope of the educated elite.[82] In two extant epitaphs, a rock is either speaker or addressee. To alleviate the dissonance of a neuter subject (*saxum*) addressing the passerby, the author of an inscription found in Rome and traditionally dated to the first century BC changes the nominal form into the masculine diminutive *saxsolus*:[83]

---

[79] *Longi*: Skutsch 1985: 400–401.

[80] Serv. *georg.* 4.182: *hic poetice masculino, referens se ad puerum, qui in hunc florem dicitur esse conversus.*

[81] Clementia: Hölscher 1986: 3.1.295–299, 3.2.230; Genius: Romeo 1997: 8.1.599–607, 8.2.372–377.

[82] Further epigraphic examples in Adams 2013: 422.

[83] Massaro 1998: 194–196 sees the gender influenced by Greek πέτρος.

adulescens, tametsi properas, / hic te saxsolus rogat ut se / aspicias, deinde ut quod scriptust / legas. hic sunt ossa Maeci Luci sita / Philotimi vasculari. hoc ego voleba[m] / nescius ni esses. Vale. (ILS 7703 = CLE 848)

Young man, even though you're in a hurry, this little stone asks you to look and read what is written. Here are the bones of the whitesmith Lucius Maecius Philotimus. I just wanted you to know this. Goodbye.

Another example, from the next century, finds the tombstone addressed in the masculine form of the vocative: "Now receive me gladly, stone" (*nunc recipe me, saxe, libens; ILS* 1980). These are two of the clearest examples of personification actively causing the gender of a noun to change, but dozens of others can be added to the list. The colorfully direct language of the freedmen at Trimalchio's dinner party, for example, provides a particularly rich source, with neuter words such as "fate" (*fatum*) and "death" (*letum*) being personified and, accordingly, transformed into their masculine equivalents (*fatus, letus*).[84] These personifications from apparently sub-standard Latin further support the notion of an innate Roman desire to anthropomorphize the world and its concepts.

The mentions of death and burial lead to the third and final type of literary example to be discussed in this chapter. This instance leaves the realm of learned mythology to concentrate on how changing a gender successfully calls attention to a human being's relationship with the natural world; in contrast with the examples above, this type of gender change does not attempt to make direct, positivist correspondences between gender and nature. The word for "dust" (*pulvis*) is masculine without exception in Latin prose writers up to the fifth century.[85] In poetry, however, five examples of the feminine form of *pulvis* occur: two from the works of Ennius, three in the Augustan poet Propertius (1.22.6; 2.13.35; 4.9.31).[86] Renehan has pointed out that in the first two of these Propertian examples *pulvis* is meant to recall the earth that covers a human corpse and he suggests that the change to the feminine form is influenced by the well-known conception of Earth as feminine. This change to the feminine form, a form by this time unprosaic and archaic-sounding, also allows Propertius to suggest the conservative style of Latin grave epigrams.[87] Further support for Renehan's claim can be found in the analogous use that poets make of the noun *cinis* ("ash"). At Catullus 68.90, in a passage that scholars have claimed influenced Propertius here, the poet adorns his lament for the destruction of Troy with the collocation *acerba cinis* ("untimely ash"). Like *pulvis*, this word *cinis* is masculine in every classical prose writer, but can be feminine in poetry

---

[84] Heraeus 1937: 131–138; Adams 2013: 420–424.

[85] Feminine (perhaps neuter?) at Cael. Aurel. *chron.* 2.1.33, but masculine with apparently the same meaning at 4.2.16.

[86] I discount Enn. *ann.* 264 (see Skutsch 1985: 443–444) and Sil. 14.507. Propertius also has the masculine four times; 1.17.23, 1.19.6, and 22 (all in context of death); 4.2.40.

[87] Renehan 1998: 221–223. I treat Prop. 4.9.31 in the next chapter.

in the context of death.[88] Later evidence, however, shows the feminine taking hold outside poetry in both technical treatises and colloquial language.[89] It is worth noting that another word for "earth" or "dirt" experiences a no less surprising development. *Humus, -i,* while masculine in early Latin and with clear masculine morphology, becomes feminine, once again no doubt on account of its association with the feminine earth.[90]

I would like further to speculate that the archaic atmosphere associated with fluid gender informs the two usages of feminine *pulvis* in Ennius, one occupying an epic context, the other a tragic. A fragment from the *Annales* describes dust that arises during the carnage of battle, and so it would be simple to posit a context of death for its occurrence (*pulvis fulva*; *Ann.* 315). More significantly, however, in a fragment from an unidentified tragedy Ennius describes dust as mixing together with the sky:

> *crassa pulvis oritur, omnem pervolat caeli fretum.* (Enn. *trag.* fg. 387 Jocelyn)
>
> The dust rises up thickly, and flies through the whole passageway of the sky.

This isolated line provides a rare occasion of two unusual genders occurring in a single verse. Alongside the feminine form of *pulvis* stands the unusually masculine *fretus,* and *fretus* receives its unusual gender while juxtaposed with the similarly fluid sky (*caelum* or *Caelus?*).[91] Context for the fragment is unknown, as is the title and subject of the play in which it appeared. Perhaps, however, a grammatical peculiarity of Latin poetry can help offer illumination. Modern grammarians agree in locating the origins of the Latin dative case not in the idea of someone or something being the object of motion ("he went *to* the door") but of being the recipient of an action ("he gave the dog *to* his friend"). One apparent exception to this dichotomy is a poeticism such as *it clamor <u>caelo</u>* ("the shout goes *to* the sky"; Verg. *Aen.* 5.451). The explanation of this exception is to see the sky as the personified recipient of the action: "the dative *caelo* pictures the sky as something sentient which is affected by the shout."[92] Combining this grammatical observation with the present chapter's discussion can create, if not a complete context for the fragment, then possibly a subtext. By explicitly and unusually creating a contrast between masculine and feminine genders—female dust in the male atmosphere—the renewed mixing of Earth and Sky as sentient and sexual beings recalls the last time that Earth and Sky

---

[88] For the Catullan parallel, see Fedeli 1980: 501, who does not note the analogous variations of *cinis* and *pulvis*. The only exception to feminine *cinis* in poetry not used in the context of death is Lucr. 4.926.

[89] Lunelli 1969: 93.

[90] For *humus* as an exception see Char. *gramm.* 19.19 B, *Ars anonyma Bernensis* VIII 129.8. For its development see Garcia de Diego López 1945: 142–143.

[91] ThLL vol. VI, 1 1311.52–55 (H. Rubenbauer) lists only six possible instances of the masculine *fretus*.

[92] Woodcock 1959: 39–40.

commingled, namely during the internecine violence and cosmic turmoil of mythical creation.[93]

COGNITIVE MODELS FOR NOUN CLASSIFICATION

Modern comparative evidence offers a final perspective on the role that personification plays in helping to explain the existence of fluid Latin genders. As part of a study of how language can reveal the ways in which the mind organizes thought, George Lakoff has examined the various factors that cause speakers to categorize nouns into preexistent classes in ways that at first may seem contrary to "rules" of grammar. In the case of Latin, we have already seen several instances of such nouns, as demonstrated most clearly perhaps by tree names, where native speakers attribute the production of their feminine grammatical gender to a perceived "female" aspect of trees, despite the strictly masculine morphology of the nouns that describe them (Prisc. *gramm.* II 154.7–14). Lakoff's examples that are most relevant to a study of fluid gender in Latin derive from field research conducted in 1963 by Dixon on the four-part noun classification in Dyirbal, an indigenous language of Australia.[94] One common factor that can drive speakers to assign a word to a seemingly counterintuitive noun class Lakoff terms the "myth-and-belief principle": "If some noun has characteristic X (on the basis of which its class membership would be expected to be decided) but is, through belief or myth, connected with characteristic Y, then generally it will belong to the class corresponding to Y and not to that corresponding to X."[95] For example, Dyirbal speakers normally assign non-human animals of either sex to the noun class occupied by male human beings. Among the exceptions are crickets; since folklore refers to these creatures as "old ladies," they transcend their expected class and join the grouping that includes female human beings. The tendency for myth to categorize the world overtakes, and in fact becomes assimilated with, grammatical categories, with the result that new groupings are created based on shared semantic features in the daily, lived world. Another Dyirbal example recalls Latin practice. An observer unfamiliar with Dyirbal culture would likely classify the word for "rainbow" in class IV, whose members include the wind and other natural phenomena. Since, however, rainbows exist in the world of myth as male entities, they are assigned a class with "human males." We recall the opposite phenomenon occurring in Latin, whereby the masculine noun for rainbow, *arcus*, occasionally attracts feminine modifiers as a result of associations with the goddess of the rainbow,

[93] Ernout 1956: 119–120, followed by Skutsch 1985: 443–444, maintains convincingly that Nonius (p. 217.9) is incorrect in construing the feminine adjective *vasta* as modifying *pulvis* at Enn. *ann.* 264 Skutsch. As a result, its gender there must remain uncertain.

[94] Lakoff 1987: 92–104; Dixon 1982: 178–183.

[95] Dixon 1982: 179.

Iris. In both cases, myth has the capacity to refashion language successfully, in opposition to the systemic pressure exerted by the rules of grammar.

The Dyirbal case also offers a model for understanding possible connections that could have been made by a poet choosing a Latin gender. As the previous sections make clear, the reassignment of gender cannot be predicted—instances exist, for example, where a feminine "dust" may resonate poetically, but where the poet chose not to exploit this possibility, retaining instead the standard masculine gender. At the same time, however, reassignment of gender is not simply a random act of poetic license, much less one having no significance. I have traced several instances of non-standard gender assignment in which ancient critics believe that the poet has chosen to adopt archaic conventions or has opted to follow a cultural model based on myth or folklore. Lakoff supplies a paradigm for understanding the workings of this type of cultural model by positing what he calls a "radial structure," by which a central concept (e.g., "long and thin" as a category) generates extensions of meaning. Although the trajectory of a spear, for instance, describes an arc, speakers assign the concept of this type of trajectory to the "long and thin" category since this adequately describes the spear itself rather than its course. By similar association the category of "long and thin" includes the word denoting a home run in baseball; it is the baseball bat that determines membership in the category.[96] Noun assignment, it is clear, occurs not in accordance with a set of preconceived and predictable rules, but with an eye to culture-bound conventions that must be learned individually. Lakoff gives as an example of radial structure from 1980s America the various subcategories of the word "mother." He notes that the term "mother" as applied to a woman has (had?) at the basis of one of its central cognitive models not the biological notion of parenting but the social notion of "nurturing." In opposition to this structuring idea of "nurture" are generated variants that in some way limit the idea of nurturing—terms such as "working mother" and "surrogate mother" imply with their adjective and noun-qualifier a definition of "mother" that reaches outside the central model of mother-as-nurturer. At the same time, the creation of these variations serves to reinforce the "mother-as-nurturer" model.[97] American English has changed in the few decades since Lakoff used this example—the recent popularity of the radial term "stay-at-home mom," where the qualifier now in fact emphasizes rather than assumes the nurturing model, would seem to indicate that the cognitive model of "mother as nurturer" has undergone another shift.[98] And it is in fact the very slipperiness and instability of these radial structures that help shed light on the Roman sample. A culture-determined view of how categories are

---

[96] These examples are from Japanese (Lakoff 1987: 104–109).

[97] Lakoff 1987: 80–84.

[98] Contrast the now outdated statement in Lakoff 1986: 39: "We have no term *housewife mother*—we don't need one since that is taken to be the norm."

redeployed over time helps us imagine the ways in which Roman grammarians sketched the development of *humus, -i* ("earth"): originally, as attested by instances in early Latin, the masculine morphology (nominative in *-us*, genitive in *-i*) accords with the anticipated masculine gender but, as time progresses, a new cognitive model for understanding *humus* develops—as, I would suggest, a mythic model equating earth with feminine nurture—and accordingly speakers violate the apparent rules of grammatical morphology in order to align the word with cultural conventions, thereby assigning a feminine gender to the noun. What seems, then, an androgynous and anomalous noun to later critics in fact finds its justification in a worldview accessible to Latin speakers of an earlier period.

As Dyirbal continues to die as a native spoken language, and as recent generations of its speakers have become influenced by English linguistic structures, the original four complex categories of Dyirbal noun classification have broken down into three comparatively straightforward groups: 1) human males and nonhuman animates; 2) human females; 3) everything else.[99] And as younger speakers adopt this new system, traditional speakers keep to the old categories, causing dissonance between generations of native speakers concerning where to classify exceptions (such as crickets and rainbows). Interestingly for our purposes, just as in Latin the notion of antiquity (*vetustas*) constitutes a mysterious but powerful criterion for determining contemporary linguistic usage, similarly one of the last principles of categorization to be lost in the process of language decay in Dyirbal is the connection with myth and folklore. These extralinguistic cultural beliefs were able, early on, to exert influence over linguistic categories, and over the course of time they have remained among the final features of this traditional society to retain a hold on the language.

CONCLUSION

The many explanations offered in antiquity for linguistic gender change possess different levels of credibility, but even the less persuasive attempts at explanation have the signal advantage of seeking to appreciate sympathetically a practice that early Roman poets could have access to and that ancient scholars felt compelled to catalogue and, at times, to justify. While it remains impossible to predict whether a Latin poet of the Republican period will vary a noun's gender at any particular moment, it is nevertheless important to have ways of explaining why their choices make some kind of literary and cultural sense whenever they do choose to alter a gender. It is safe, I think, to assume at least one explanatory principle. Roman scholars believed that the poets upon whom they concentrate could change a noun's expected gender in order to demonstrate

[99] Lakoff 1987: 96–98.

access to a special poetic language, one steeped in mythical and folkloric associations. In a similar way, readers of Latin poetry were expected to distinguish at the level of diction a difference between poetic and "unpoetic" vocabulary, a distinction that tended to assimilate, particularly for epic poetry, archaic and poetic registers.[100] In the case of grammatical gender, the ability to fluctuate has special ties to an archaic time when gender could be read as a transparent reflection of biological sex. After Vergil, this poetic practice tends to vanish from our records, giving the impression that gender—and therefore concepts of sexual division—ceased, at a point, to be fluid and began to reify into fixed categories.

Despite the helpful analogies that arise from comparing Dyirbal noun classification, it is necessary in closing to stress a crucial difference. While traditional Dyirbal had a complex four-part classification that has been deteriorating in quotidian use with exposure to other languages, for Latin, it is the Roman scholarly tradition that acts to consistently transform the three- to five-part system of grammatical gender into a dual system characterized by the two "real" genders—the sexually "generative" genders of masculine and feminine. What I will offer in the next two stages of this book is an examination of how the reification of these categories helps effect a dichotomy of male and female outside the realm of poetry and language. As early as the beginning of the fourth century AD, there is already clear evidence of the calcification of gender boundaries, in both observable usage and public attitudes. The early Christian apologist Arnobius writes sarcastically about the willfulness with which non-Christians could use gender: "we see you denoting, without any distinction, masculine things as feminine and feminine as masculine and using neuters in every which way" (*nat.* 1.59: *atqui vos conspicimus et res masculinas <feminine> et femineas masculine et quas esse dicitis neutras et illo et hoc modo sine ulla discretione depromere*). Arnobius, who is clearly consulting the Roman grammatical tradition for the examples he deploys throughout this passage, no longer shares with his contemporary scholars wonder or awe at these variations but simply redefines as errors those cases of gender fluctuation that Festus assured us were free from fault.[101] This emergent system of rigidly assigned gender, presaging the development of a literally heterosexual worldview, will be employed in chapters 4 and 5 to explain anomalous elements in the history of Roman culture. These are: 1) the process by which the androgynous gods of archaic Italy, real or imagined, became replaced by a pantheon that is distinctly and discreetly male and female; and 2) the transformation of the figure of the hermaphrodite from an object of divine awe during the Roman Republic into an object of mockery under the empire, as the hermaphrodite comes to be reinterpreted as an aberration of what had now become recognized as the natural way of organizing the world.

---

[100] Axelson 1945, esp. 25–45, and more generally Clackson and Horrocks 2007: 174–181.
[101] For Arnobius's sources, see McCracken 1947.

Chapter 3

Poetic Play with Sex and Gender

> "Renehan observes that 'a literary genre can determine gender.' Deliberate literary variation . . . is a large topic waiting to be studied."
>
> —Adams 2013: 388

INTRODUCTION

The previous chapter focused primarily on reconstructing how ancient grammarians and commentators made sense of the practice of the poets who had preceded them. I posited that these scholars deemed select poets to possess both the ability and the authority to speak a special language, a possession that afforded them access to the earliest stages of Latin or its imagined ancestor. My principal interest lies in how this poetic language treated the phenomenon of grammatical gender. Since this poetic knowledge was seen to hark back to the earliest stages of culture, the ways in which poets manipulated gender often could be explained by exploring the mythical and folkloric associations of the affected word. Despite the frequent occurrence of fluctuating genders in the Republican period, however, the poets themselves offer no direct information concerning their intentions; like the ancient scholars, modern scholars too must rely solely upon interpretation of the texts before them. I would like therefore to ponder in more detail the ramifications of the conclusions offered in the previous discussion before moving on to the promised treatment of how grammatical gender also affects Roman perceptions of gods and hermaphrodites.

In this chapter I will examine selected instances of grammatical gender-bending that occur in extant poetic texts, for most of which instances scholars both ancient and modern have largely chosen not to offer explanations. The passages chosen are meant to demonstrate the potential range of approaches that the poets could apply to the manipulation of grammatical gender. Each passage will receive consideration based on the model hypothesized in the previous chapter. From these test cases there will emerge a consistent method that a reader may adopt in approaching those instances of fluid grammatical gender that are not considered here.

Fluctuating Latin gender has driven interpreters to wild speculation since the earliest days of Roman scholarship, some instances of which received attention in the previous chapter. To illustrate the difficulties of trying to recover all possible ramifications of grammatical gender, I preface my own speculations with a passage from Servius that demonstrates the lengths to which one ancient scholar could go when it came to interpreting this trope. In book 10 of the *Aeneid*, Turnus has been lamenting how he had been duped by the gods into abandoning his troops at a key moment of battle. After wondering aloud what the gods have in store for him and whether he will see his camp again, his thoughts turn to his fellow soldiers: "'what about that band of men who have followed me in arms?'" (10.672: "*quid **manus illa virum**, qui me meaque arma secuti?*"). This apparently straightforward query prompts an unusual observation in the exegetical tradition concerning the juxtaposition of the feminine singular pair *manus illa* ("that band") with the masculine plural noun *virum* ("of men"):

> *syllepsis per genus: nam a manu, id est multitudine, ad viros, <u>a feminino ad masculinum</u>, transitum fecit.* (Serv. *Aen.* 10.672, with additions from Serv. Auct. underlined)

> [This is an example of] an incongruous construction in gender. For Vergil has created a transition from *manus* (that is, "a group") to *viros* ("men"); [in other words] from the feminine to the masculine [gender].

It is unclear why the scholiast chose to comment on this particular juxtaposition of contrasting genders.[1] The use of the feminine noun *manus* to describe a group of male human beings would have been a common occurrence in daily speech no less than in elevated poetry. At the same time, however, and as happens not infrequently, the Servian commentators record the alleged oddity without drawing an explicit inference from it. I see no means of making any intelligent sense of this note, much less of rescuing it as a refined literary observation that could reveal something of Vergil's poetic technique. Nevertheless, this note does make two points very clear. It illustrates well the sensitivity that ancient readers such as Servius could display concerning the manipulation of grammatical gender, and therefore the potential that this manipulation could have in determining a text's meaning or in enhancing an appreciation of its poetic qualities.

In the spirit of Servius, I will examine a group of passages displaying anomalous uses of grammatical gender in order to present a set of test cases for the reconstructions of the previous two chapters. After a brief excursus on visual material, I shall turn to selected textual examples, the majority of which have not been considered before in this context.

ISSUES IN VISUAL PERSONIFICATION *OR* CAN THE MOTHERLAND BE A MAN?

It has long been noted that the presence of grammatical gender in a language contributes "to the purposes of animation, sexualization and personification in

---

[1] I thank James Adams, Nicholas Horsfall, and James McKeown for opinions on this curious passage.

literature" in ways that genderless languages are less readily able to achieve.[2] Since, therefore, personification—literally "person-making"—is a function of grammatical gender, it follows that the sex of the personified noun both in literature and in the real world should match that noun's gender. Turning from the textual to the material evidence from the Roman period reveals few challenges to the corresponding claim that when a Roman visual artist depicts a personification, visible sex and grammatical gender will match.[3] Most abstract concepts in Latin (and Greek), for example, are expressed through feminine nouns; accordingly depictions of such abstract notions as "fidelity" (Fides) and "justice" (Iustitia) unexceptionally portray females.[4] That the correspondence is not accidental is confirmed by the fact that those few concepts that possess grammatically masculine gender, such as "high rank" (Honos) or "year" (Annus), are invariably figured as males in their visual depictions.

Negative indications support this tendency to match gendered nouns with representations exhibiting the corresponding sex. Roman Jakobson cites a particularly lucid example of how this association is exhibited as much in daily life as in literature and the plastic arts: "the widespread Russian superstition that a fallen knife presages a male guest and a fallen fork a female one is determined by the masculine gender of [the Russian word for] 'knife' and the feminine of [the Russian word for] 'fork.' "[5] When the sexual equivalence of these two categories of word and thing becomes disrupted, however, native speakers experience difficulty in accepting the association. Jakobson cites examples of Russian artists, authors, and readers who express emotions from bafflement to dismay when trying to comprehend representations made by non-native speakers that do not agree with their native language's system of grammatical gender. He records, for example, the bafflement of a Russian child upon encountering male representations of Death in translations of German folk tales ("death" is feminine in Russian). Conversely, Jakobson notes the "despair" experienced by a translator rendering Pasternak's collection *My Sister Life* into Czech, where the word for "life" is masculine. How can a masculine noun be a sister?

All evidence indicates that an analogous resistance to crossing boundaries existed in Roman visual culture. Indeed, apparent exceptions to this rule of sex matching gender are easily accounted for. Most recall a theme from earlier chapters: the intrusion of Greek models. Numismatic depictions of the Roman senate provide an unambiguous example. The Latin designation *senatus* is a masculine noun, and so it is unsurprising that the historian Dio Cassius de-

[2] Fodor 1959: 206.

[3] This survey is based on my own reading, combined with a perusal of the relevant entries in LIMC. For classical Greek art see Shapiro 1993: 27, who cites as the sole exception *limos* ("famine"), a noun that is, interestingly, of variable gender (Stafford 1998: 51).

[4] The reason why abstracts tend to be feminine in gender has yet to receive satisfactory explanation; discussions in Yaguello 1978: 91–113, Stafford 1998: 52–53, Paxson 1998.

[5] Jakobson 1959: 237, from which I take the other examples in this paragraph.

scribes the typical anthropomorphized senate as a crowned old man clothed in senatorial dress (68.5.1), a description that corresponds with numerous coin types as well as with depictions of the senate's male *Genius*.[6] Not infrequently, however, on coins minted in the Greek East the senate is personified as a woman; a particularly telling instance features the accompanying inscription *SACRA SINATUS* [*sic*] ("sacred [feminine] senate"), which may indicate through the misspelling of *senatus* and the mistaken gender of the noun that the author was not fluent in Latin.[7] Regardless of the precise reason for the alternative orthography, however, it seems clear that in this representation the author of the inscription is influenced by the Greek word used to describe the senate, σύγκλητος [βουλή]; since this Greek form is grammatically feminine, the artist accordingly depicts the senate as a woman, adding to this personification a Latin label that describes what he has depicted without consideration or understanding of the rules for Latin gender agreement.[8] An analogous inconsistency occurs in the western half of the empire on the so-called cosmological mosaic from Emerita (Mérida), Spain. Here the depiction of a young man labeled with the feminine noun "Aet[ernitas]" ("Eternity") arises from the interference of an original Greek personification of Αἰών ("Age"), which is a masculine noun. In other words, the artist (or, more likely, his source) represents Aeternitas as if he were in fact depicting the masculine Greek equivalent. This type of mismatch between Latin label and visual personification occurs elsewhere on the same mosaic: the sky god is depicted as an old bearded male, an image that conflicts with the label identifying him as "Caelum," a Latin neuter noun. As we saw in the previous chapter, just as Ennius, in personifying the sky in his *Annales*, makes the god Caelum masculine in part by influence of the masculine noun that describes the Greek deity (Οὐρανός), so too do the Greek sources of the mosaicist in Emerita account for what is only an apparent case of dissonance between neuter noun and male personification.[9]

The personification of neuter nouns presents a special challenge for the visual artist. In classical Greek art, such personifications are rare and, on the two certain occasions that they do occur, for Kratos ("Strength") and Geras ("Old Age"), the artist has chosen to represent the figures as male.[10] A third figure on the Emerita mosaic offers another apparently Roman example, with the only certain depiction of Chaos in the Greek and Roman world.[11] Although *chaos* is a neuter noun in both Greek and Latin, the artist has resolved the problem of

[6] Talbert 1984: 217; for the *Genius Senatus*, see Canciani 1994.

[7] SNG France 1928 (Cilicia, AD 249–251).

[8] Forni 1953: 61 with nn. 1–2 lists at least twenty-four numismatic examples of the female senate. I thank Bert Smith for calling my attention to this phenomenon; for an intriguing parallel at Aphrodisias, see R. R. R. Smith 2013: 87.

[9] For the artist's Greek sources see Tran 1994: 135; Dunbabin 1999: 150 discusses *Aeternitas*.

[10] Shapiro 1993: 27; Stafford 1998: 52.

[11] Fernández Castro 1986.

the sex-less label in the same way as his Greek counterpart, by portraying the deity as a bearded and veiled figure with the features of an old man.[12] A similar appropriation of masculine qualities occurs in a passage of literature that involves the description of an artwork. In one of his verse fables, Phaedrus describes a statue of the grammatically neuter Tempus ("Time"). In the course of this poem, Tempus seems to attract associated words in the masculine, thereby personifying the neuter Time as male (5.8.2–3: *calvus... quem*). Yet again, Greek sources lie behind the incongruity: Phaedrus's fable refers here to a Hellenistic statue by Lysippos of Opportunity (that is, "Key Time") whose name is rendered in Greek texts by the masculine noun καῖρος.[13] In this instance, it would seem that the Greek masculine gender of the name that graced the artistic original has reached out into a passage of Latin literature to affect the corresponding Latin noun's gender. Visualizing the male statue being described, Phaedrus understandably employs masculine descriptors.

Returning to the visual record that is extant, the transformation of neuter gender into male appearance provides an artistic solution for the only other two Latin examples of this phenomenon that I have discovered: in a single representation of Ingenium ("Inborn Talent") from the third- to fourth-century Nonnus mosaic found at Trier and in a variety of depictions of Saeculum.[14] A representation of Saeculum, the divinized concept that normally represents the span of a single human life, appears on the Emerita mosaic as a bearded male, and scholars again attribute the sex of the personification to a corresponding masculine Greek noun.[15] The male type of Saeculum as it appears on Roman coinage seems, however, to arise from a different set of considerations. These numismatic representations, depicting sometimes individuals of either sex and sometimes groups of people, are accompanied by legends that obscure the noun's gender through abbreviation (*SAEC*) or by occurring in oblique cases (*SAECVLO*), although the near-universal occurrence of *saeculum* as neuter in literature should cause us to assume that neuter is also the gender here.[16] In these instances, I would suggest that the concept "Saeculum" does not appear as a personification in the most literal sense. Rather, *saeculum* belongs to a special class of nouns, those that denote periods of time or distinct epochs. Parallels from coins for this class are plentiful, in which men are engaged in activities

---

[12] *Chaos* appears in the masculine in Latin only once, at Vet. Lat. *Luc.* 16.26 (rendered more literally by Jerome *ad loc.* with the neuter *chasma*): ThLL vol. III 990.48–49 (H. Hoppe).

[13] Statue: Morena 1990: 921–923. Later Latin references render Καῖρος with the feminine noun *occasio* (ThLL vol. IX, 2 332.2–7 [R. Teßmer]) and, accordingly, depictions regularly become female (Panofsky 1939: 71–72). I thank John Henderson for the reference to Phaedrus.

[14] Ingenium (only partially preserved): Balty 1990.

[15] López Monteagudo 1997, who also lists numismatic representations.

[16] The masculine form *saeculus* appears once in the *Regula magistri* of the sixth century (90.87; cf. 87.15), where it has developed the specifically Christian sense of "the secular world"; Bozzi and Grilli 1995: 2.422 cite late-antique parallels.

appropriate to a period of time, but are accompanied by legends with nouns other than in the masculine, such as *TEMP[ORIS] FELICITAS* or *SAECVLI FELICITAS* ("Richness of the era," where *felicitas* is feminine).[17] The visual illustration, in other words, represents not a personification of an individual deity or concept but a scene that befits the time period indicated. As a result, the sex and number of the participants have no direct correlation with the gender and number of the Latin caption.

The clearest example of how a visual representation may present a tableau of activity rather than a specific personification occurs in the numerous depictions of the seasons of the year. Latin grammar from the beginning provides complications for this imagery, since the commonest words for each season span all three genders—*ver* ("spring") is neuter, *aestas* ("summer") and *hiems* ("winter") feminine, and *autumnus* masculine. To complicate matters further, the nouns do not correspond in gender to their corresponding Greek designations. Perhaps as a means of maintaining consistency between sex and gender, the earliest Greek depictions show all the seasons as female, in correspondence with the grammatically feminine noun denoting "season," ὥρα (Latin *Hora*).[18] Roman artists adopt this convention until the time of Hadrian in the second century AD, when males, particularly as winged young boys, begin to appear interchangeably with the previously standard female representations. A thorough study of the subject concludes that the Romans "did not conceive of the Seasons in terms of personified powers, and apparently felt that representation of Seasons by human figures was . . . not determined by the real nature of the Seasons."[19] It seems clear that in this case we have another instance where replication of grammatical gender carries less importance than the representation of those activities deemed appropriate to a specific period of time.

The above evidence for how grammatical gender affects a visual personification is consistent with our findings concerning the personification of gender in literature. When visual representations are accompanied by labels in Latin that may appear incongruent, interference from the corresponding Greek names offers the most likely explanation. Alternatively, for personifications relating to time, one should consider the possibility that the representation depicts activities connected with the time period rather than specific entities. Before returning to Latin poetry, let us consider a remark that treats metaphorical personification in such a way as to seem to pose a problem for identifying grammatical gender with sex in the world.

[17] E.g., Bastien 1992: vol. 3, pl. 118 (Probus) and pl. 143 (Diocletian); Hanfmann 1951: 1.168–178.

[18] See Morena 1990 for a good discussion; Hanfmann 1951: 1.173 with n. 193.

[19] Hanfmann 1951: 1.171–173, 214–215 (quotation from 173). The phenomenon has geographic variation: of thirteen mosaics from fourth-century Britain or later, only two figure males (where all are putti), with one possible male representation of Autumn (Ling 1983: 16–18).

In the epigraph to chapter 1, I quoted from Sterne's *Tristram Shandy* the joke that Switzerland "can in no construction be godfather" to the French king's child on account of that country's feminine grammatical gender. I asserted there that, analogously, it would have been unthinkable for an ancient artist to portray the personified city of Rome as a man. This assertion does indeed receive unanimous support from all the visual depictions of Rome and its empire known to me. There does exist, however, a significant and, so far as I am aware, unique textual example in which the Latin grammatical gender of a state conflicts with the sexual characteristics of its corresponding personification. The context within which this apparent exception is discussed, however, in fact underscores the fixity of the rule.

In the third book of Cicero's mature rhetorical work *On the Orator*, the interlocutor Marcus Licinius Crassus has been asked to give an account of oratorical adornment. As part of his response, Crassus includes a discussion of the various categories of metaphor, stressing the sensual impact that this figure can have on the hearer, even when the metaphor resides in a single word. His examples of the latter include the "rumble of the sea" and the "sweetness of speech" (*murmur maris . . . dulcitudo orationis*; *de orat.* 3.161). On account of the audience's natural, innate attraction to metaphor, Crassus advises the speaker to avoid excess in using a metaphor that is overly exuberant, or that does not constitute a true resemblance. The worst abuse, however, involves not taking properly into account metaphor's greatest asset, its ability to make a vivid impression on the senses. Crassus accordingly gives the following advice:[20]

> *fugienda est omnis turpitudo earum rerum ad quas eorum animos qui audiunt, trahet similitudo. nolo dici morte Africani "castratam" esse rem publicam, nolo "stercus Curiae" dici Glauciam; quamvis sit simile, tamen est in utroque deformis cogitatio similitudinis.* (Cic. *de orat.* 3.163–164)

> Avoid any ugliness in those elements of the comparison that are intended to influence the minds of the audience. I don't want to hear that the state (*rem publicam*) was "castrated" as a result of Africanus's death, or that Glaucia is the "excrement of the senate house." Although [the things being compared] may include similar elements, in both cases contemplating (*cogitatio*) the comparison is offensive.

The distasteful element of the second comparison is clear. Compelling an audience member to contemplate a Roman senator as a piece of excrement—along with perhaps the accompanying image of the personified senate house producing that excrement—is indeed likely to prove damaging to the dignity, and therefore to the persuasive ability, of the speaker.

It is the figure of the castrated republic, however, that attracts special interest. Neither Cicero nor Quintilian (who cites the same examples at *inst.* 8.6.15)

---

[20] Innes 1988: 318 notes that this proscription applies to oratory, and not literature more generally.

makes explicit what is objectionable in this metaphor. The personification of the Roman state is not uncommon in Cicero's orations—one need only cite the famous instances of prosopopoeia of *Patria* in the first speech delivered against Catiline (*Cat.* 1.18, 27–28). Furthermore, the body of this anthropomorphized republic becomes subject to all matter of metaphorical abuses in the Ciceronian corpus, as it is beset with deadly wounds or subjected to radical surgery.[21] Rather, part of the distaste that Cicero finds in this comparison can be paralleled from the metaphor equating Glaucia with senatorial excrement: with a little thought (*cogitatio*) on the hearer's part, Scipio can quite readily appear in the imagination as a piece of bloody genitalia. But what kind of genitalia? Following the numerous arguments found throughout this book that the Romans necessarily equate grammatical gender with biological sex, a literal reading of this metaphor would require understanding the castration of a female *res publica*. And yet while the verb *castro* is twice attested in the elder Pliny for the removal of the uterus from female animals, context makes clear that this type of female castration was exceptional.[22] Rather, I would claim that Crassus's revulsion at the metaphor stems precisely from this misunderstanding on the speaker's part of the significance of grammatical gender, which results in the incongruous image of removing male genitals from a female personification.[23] Far from contradicting our findings, therefore, this passage from *On the Orator* in fact emphatically supports them. It offers compelling evidence that not recognizing the equation of sex and gender in a rhetorical context can invite ridicule and thereby reduce a speaker's authority in the eyes of his audience.

GRAMMATICAL GENDER AS AN ARCHAIZING MOTIF

Cicero's interlocutor Crassus advises care in the use of grammatical gender in a public context since insufficient attention can bring a charge of "ugliness." This concern to maintain the dignity of the oratorical persona pervades rhetorical tracts from antiquity. Their authors continually advise the Roman politician, when speaking among both his peers in the senate and the people in assembly, to avoid excess in imagery, solecisms of grammar, and other misplaced instances of empty erudition. "Leave preciosity to the poets" sounds the not unfamiliar warning. And so I turn now to a small selection of examples of Roman poets employing grammatical gender in non-standard ways; in ways, in other words, that would have invited ridicule if used by a public speaker. I analyze each of the instances below in accordance with the model that I have adopted in the previous two chapters. My discussion will treat different poetic genres

---

[21] Walters 2011.

[22] ThLL vol. III 547.30–32 (G. Goetz) cites only Plin. *nat.* 8.68 and 209 (of camels and sows).

[23] Mankin 2011: 250 cites for this interpretation Harless 1816: 566 ("*res publica . . . castrari non potest, h.e. genus maris nec habere nec amittere*").

from the Republican period, the very era, as later grammarians recognize, when poetic play with sex and gender reached its peak.

Plautus: From Colloquialism to Archaism

The comedies of the playwright Plautus, one of the earliest Latin writers surviving in more than fragments, offer our first two instances, from the beginning of the second century BC. I begin with an intriguing counterexample, in which a literary text alters expected grammatical gender not to create a more elevated tone, but to match the idiomatic expectations of an addressee. In Plautus's *Stichus*, the two slaves Sangarinus and Stichus are preparing a celebration at which wine features prominently. In a rupture of dramatic illusion, Sangarinus turns to one of the stage musicians, commanding him to put down his pipes and have a drink. After some initial reluctance the piper accedes to the request, whereupon Sangarinus continues: "OK, piper. Since you've drunk, put the pipes back to your lips" (Plaut. *Stich.* 723–723a: *age, / tibicen, quando bibisti, refer ad labeas tibias*). This is the only passage in Plautus where the feminine plural *labeae* occurs for the noun "lips." Later attested uses of the form indicate clearly that the feminine grammatical gender, in contrast with the neuter plural *labia*, represents popular speech. As a result, the explanation offered by Adams for the gender used here seems correct: "Plautus presumably chose the form to mark the switch to casual speech outside the dramatic dialogue, or to characterise the addressee."[24] The source of the humor seems clear. The audience, accustomed to a different speech register from a comic character, would have laughed at hearing the drunken Sangarinus "forget" his presence on stage and devolve into everyday speech.

In Plautus's *Poenulus*, by contrast, the alteration of grammatical gender adds grandeur to the stage action. In this play, a Carthaginian character named Hanno has just rediscovered his two daughters after years of separation. In order to ensure a successful reunion, he utters a prayer to Jupiter that begins as follows:

> *Iuppiter, qui genu' colis alisque hominum, per quem vivimu' vitalem aevom, quem penes spes vitae sunt hominum omnium, da . . .* (Plaut. *Poen.* 1187–1188)

> Oh Jupiter, you who cherish and nourish the human race, [and] through whom we live our span of life (*vivimu' vitalem aevom*), [and] with whom reside life's hopes for every human being, grant me . . .

This short invocation has unmistakable archaizing characteristics. The varied repetition of relative clauses in asyndeton to describe the province of the deity's powers characterizes the earliest extant Greek prayers (*qui . . . per quem . . .*

---

[24] Adams 2013: 399, who provides details on *labeae* and related terms.

quem penes).[25] The archaizing effect is enhanced by the use of the phrase *vivimu' vitalem aevom*, in which the verb and adjective derive from the same root (approximately, "we live our living age"). Etymological figures such as this convey a serious tone in the "long verses" of Plautus and are recognized by scholars since antiquity as redolent of sacred texts from the earliest periods of Rome.[26] In further keeping with this solemn tone, I would suggest, Plautus uses a rare non-standard gender to convey the notion of "lifespan." He seems here to employ the masculine form of a theoretical noun *aevus*—the gender being indicated by the accompanying adjective *vitalem*—instead of the regularly neuter *aevum*. The alteration is unlikely to be accidental. Modern researchers now consider that the rare masculine form in fact reflects the noun's original gender, which was replaced by the neuter over time, perhaps by analogy with the neuter Latin noun *tempus* ("time").[27] Whatever the linguistic reasons for the change to neuter by the classical period, Plautus's use of the masculine noun in the phrase *vitalem aevom* would have already sounded unusual, and the change strongly suggests that the playwright is making a further attempt to conjure an archaic mood by evoking cultural memories of an original, by now lost, gender.

One additional observation connects this passage of Plautus with a phenomenon discussed in the previous chapter. The Greek word cognate with *aevus / aevum* is the noun αἰών. This word first appears in Homer in the masculine gender, where it has the meaning that Plautus assigns to *aevus* here, namely "lifetime, life" (LSJ s.v., A I). If Norden is correct in seeing traces of a Greek original in Hanno's prayer, Plautus's imitation of Greek models would predate by approximately one generation the literary trope credited by ancient scholars to Ennius, Lucretius, and Vergil, by which the use of a non-standard gender in Latin harks back to the earliest stages of Latinity and thereby endows the Roman author with a particularly forceful poetic authority.[28] In the case of this occurrence in Plautus, the archaic flavor helps to portray effectively for his audience the somber and serious tone of the hopeful father Hanno.

Considering these connotations of the rare masculine gender of *aevum*, it is not altogether surprising to find the form applied in a didactic context by Lucretius over a century later than the Plautine usage. On two occasions, the form of its associated adjective makes clear that the poet uses the noun in the archaic masculine, and these two Lucretian examples constitute the only remaining instances of that gender known from Latin authors of the classical period.[29] On

[25] Norden 1913: 168–176.

[26] Haffter 1934: 10–43; LHS 38–40.

[27] Vaan 2008: 29 (this evidence makes it improbable that the Plautine and Lucretian uses are feminine); Adams 2013: 392–419 provides a full discussion of non-standard genders in Plautus.

[28] Norden 1913: 172; for Plautus's Greek sources for this play see Arnott 1959, Gratwick 1982: 101–103.

[29] ThLL vol. I 1164.47–49 (J. G. Kempf), who cites two Christian examples, to which add CIL 12.2130 = CE 762, and CIL 12.2127 (by conjecture).

both occasions, the noun is used in a prepositional phrase not to indicate the years in a person's life, but to designate the age of the known physical universe: while atoms must by definition exist "for all time" (2.561: *aevum . . . per omnem*), the human soul does not have an equivalent capacity (3.605: *non omnem . . . per aevum*).[30] In the same way that Hanno's use of the archaic gender lends an air of sanctity to his prayer to Jupiter, Lucretius's knowing artistry bestows poetic authority upon his own poem. The poet's knowledge strengthens his ability to make an assured and persuasive statement about something over which he would normally have no certain knowledge: what can and cannot exist over the entire span of creation.

Wombs

A second example in which archaic usage informs poetic practice involves the treatment of the noun *alvus, -i* ("belly"). Both morphology and declension would dictate that the word be masculine and, accordingly, a number of early authors such as Plautus, Accius, and Cato the Elder treat it as such. By the first century BC, however, the seemingly counterintuitive conception of *alvus* as possessing the feminine gender comes to dominate and be accepted as the norm. In contrast with many of the instances previously encountered, most recently that of **aevus*, the earliest behavior of the Latin word *alvus* seems certainly independent of a Greek model since none of its commonest equivalents are of the masculine gender (γαστήρ, ἡ; νηδύς, ἡ; σπλάγχνον, τό). Nor does semantics appear to play a role in affecting the gender: the extant occurrences do not suggest, for example, that the feminine form describes a "womb," while the masculine form covers parts of the body not restricted to a particular sex. Regardless of the historical reasons for the noun's behavior, the later grammarians' attempts to explain the transformation from masculine to feminine universally assume that the original form must have been masculine.[31] They cite in support of this assertion both the universally masculine morphology (*ratio*) and the authority of early usage (*auctoritas*).[32] Once again, these scholars assume that poets and other early authorities have access to a special knowledge of the nature of grammatical gender.

Such a conception may explain an oddity in the surviving testimony for the gender of *alvus*. Although, as noted above, the noun is firmly feminine in first century BC prose writers, extant fragments attest that two poets of the middle of the century, the so-called neoterics Helvius Cinna and Licinius Calvus, reverted in their works to the masculine gender—interestingly enough, to de-

---

[30] Bailey 1947: 1.87 ascribes Lucretius's unconventional use of morphology, including variable gender, principally to metrical considerations and less often to a desire to create "an old-world solemnity or dignity."

[31] Evidence in Panayotakis 2010: 446; Adams 2013: 412 doubts the grammarians.

[32] Prisc. *gramm.* II 169.8, 268.16–269.2; cf. Caper *gramm.* VII 107.12, Serv. *Aen.* 2.51.

scribe the female womb (Char. *gramm.* 101.20–26 B). These examples take on even more import if there is any significance in the fact that the majority of changes of gender among the neoterics go in the opposite direction, from masculine to feminine.[33] A hypothesis for explaining this apparent fluidity in gender, one by now familiar, lies ready to hand: Cinna and Calvus have consciously chosen the masculine out of an awareness of its presence in the earliest period of Latin literature. As we shall explore further in discussing the contemporary poet Catullus, the change represents a conscious attempt to participate in the neoteric pleasures of recherché knowledge. Awareness of the masculine womb ascribes a mark of authority to this famously learned group of contemporary poets.

Dust (Again)

The analysis of poetic attitudes toward fluid gender prompts a reconsideration of the previous chapter's discussion of the grammatical gender of *pulvis* ("dust"). There are five instances in Latin poetry where this noun occurs in the non-standard feminine gender, and I followed Renehan's suggestions in arguing that in four of these cases it was the association of dust with death and the personified female Earth that prompted poets to change the gender of *pulvis* to feminine (Enn. *Ann.* 315, *trag.* frg. 387; Prop. 1.22.6, 2.13.35). It was also posited that the appearance of fluidity lent these passages an archaizing tone, a conclusion in keeping with the present discussion. The final instance of feminine *pulvis* was not treated. This example, like two of the others, occurs in Propertius, in his fourth and final book of elegies. This, the latest datable example of feminine *pulvis* in the classical period, does not at first seem to fit the notion that the gender change intends to portray dust as a part of the mythologized Earth.

Propertius situates his poem—elegy 4.9—in the mythical past, relating the visit of Hercules to Rome, a visit whose narrative culminates in an explanation of the Greek hero's institution of the Ara Maxima. At one point in the narrative Hercules, parched with thirst, desperately approaches the entrance to a sacred grove to request water from the girls that he hears laughing inside. Before the hero makes his request, Propertius describes him as having "dust heaped into his dry beard" (Prop. 4.9.31: *in siccam congestā pulvere barbam*). Two initial considerations prompt the reader to seek literary significance in the unusual use of the feminine form for "dust" here: first, the masculine form of the phrase (*congestō pulvere*) scans identically with that form preserved in the manuscripts, and so Propertius does not change the gender here simply as a concession to meter; second, Propertius does use the noun *pulvis* in its standard masculine gender on four different occasions elsewhere in his corpus, including in book 4 (1.17.23, 1.19.6 and 22, 4.2.40), a fact that further prompts the reader to

[33] Lunelli 1969: 101.

ascribe significance to any deviation here. The verbal construction of the ablative absolute (*congestā pulvere*) offers an initial clue to interpretation, since at its most literal level—"with dust heaped into his beard"—it suggests that Hercules has intentionally gathered the dust and deposited it into his facial hair.[34] There is only one explanation for why someone in the Roman world, begging for relief from thirst, would throw dust into his beard, and that is to put on public display his internal feelings of grief and mourning as a way of gaining sympathy from onlookers.[35] If one adopts this interpretation—and no equally satisfying reason for Hercules's behavior has been suggested—then once again the Roman poet, as in the other Ennian and Propertian examples of feminine *pulvis*, associates the gender change of this noun with a nexus of ideas: mourning, dirt, and the female personification of Earth.

But perhaps two more points can be made for this poem in particular. First, the earlier three instances of feminine *pulvis* in Propertius have been ascribed to conscious imitation of the poet Ennius.[36] Although it is not possible to prove this claim, it does seem likely that the gender change of 4.9.31, even without the associations with Earth, would be understood as contributing to the poem an archaizing and epic flavor (cf. Fest. p. 150, p. 286). And indeed, a touch of archaizing here befits Propertius's fourth book, a book that programmatically professes to "sing of rites and festivals and the ancient names of [Rome's] places."[37] In this particular poem, the story of Hercules establishing the Ara Maxima offers the book's first example of the " 'classic' type of *aition*," and so adding an archaic touch to this foundation story would be thematically satisfying.[38] It is perhaps also not incidental that the commonest Greek equivalents of *pulvis* are of the feminine gender (κόνις, κονία), although if Propertius alludes to a specific Greek intertext here, it is no longer extant. Second, learned humor may also inform the gender change. After dirtying his face, Hercules tries to persuade the girls to admit him into the grove by referring to his own experience in woman's clothing when under the sway of Omphale, even going to the extreme of exclaiming "I was a girl equipped with calloused hands!" (4.9.50).[39] With transvestism being a central theme of the poem, what, then, are we to think of the grammatically transgendered dust, arising as it does from an earth explicitly personified as female and fertile (4.9.22: *terra . . . feta*)? As suggested

---

[34] So Camps 1965: 140, who nevertheless concludes that "this can hardly be meant."

[35] See, e.g., Stat. *Theb.* 6.32, Comm. *instr.* 2.8.11, for dust in the beard as a sign of mourning. For this interpretation, see Rothstein 1898: 2.294–295, followed by ThLL vol. X, 2 2631.45–57 (F. Spoth); contra Hutchinson 2006: 212, who oddly claims that "dust in the beard . . . does not suggest mourning."

[36] Tränkle 1960: 30–31.

[37] Prop. 4.1.69: "*sacra diesque canam et cognomina prisca locorum.*" For the notion that this verse offers a programmatic statement for the entire book see Welch 2005: 26–27 and, for complications of this idea, Hutchinson 2006: 59–61.

[38] Hutchinson 2006: 205.

[39] On divine transvestism as a central theme of the poem see Janan 2001: 142–145.

above with the neoteric use of *alvus*, Propertius here appears to manipulate gender change to allude learnedly to a lost past—and perhaps in this case the change also adds a humorous touch as it echoes the fluid status of Hercules's own gender.

Female Spiders

The last instance in which I shall consider fluid gender as an archaizing motif is drawn from Vergil. A passage from his *Georgics* uses grammatical gender to travel into the distant past, and this time to a past where myth and language intermingle in an even more coherent way than in Propertius. The Vergilian use here contrasts with the several examples of the same poet's manipulation of gender in the *Aeneid* discussed in the last chapter, for example in making Aeneas's mother the male Caucasus (4.366–367) or in the imagery of the feminine city (*urbs*) being "widowed" (8.571). In the former case, Dido equated the masculine grammatical gender of an inanimate feature of the landscape with an imagined male sexuality, while in the latter an understanding of the significance of grammatical gender in personification added greater complexity to a metaphor. Ancient exegetes both noted and explained the poet's manipulation of gender in each of these cases. In the passage I shall discuss next, however, while they recognize an anomalous use of gender they offer no explanation.

In the fourth book of his *Georgics*, Vergil recounts how to ward off the various insects that can threaten the honeycombs of bees (4.241–247). The list of pests concludes with the following image:

> *invisa Minervae*
> *laxos in foribus suspendit aranea cassis.* (Verg. *georg.* 4.246–247)

> The spider (*aranea*), hateful to Minerva, hangs her snares loosely at the entrance [to the hive].

In his commentary, Servius accuses Vergil of nodding in using the feminine form of the noun to describe the spider (Serv. *georg.* 4.247: *Vergilius quidem confundit*). The "ancestors" (*maiores*), he observes, employed the masculine to denote the insect (*araneus*) while reserving the feminine form for its web (*aranea*). It is worth noting that the distinction Servius draws does not accurately represent the situation in Latin, but does describe well the Greek tendency, by which the masculine (ἀράχνης) normally describes the animal, the feminine (ἀράχνη) its web.[40] Although Servius refrains from explaining Vergil's alleged confusion, the remainder of his note (along with that of Servius Auctus) offers a helpful hint: through the phrase "hateful to Minerva" the poet alludes to the tale of the girl Arachne, who was turned into a spider after beating the goddess

---

[40] For the Latin evidence see ThLL vol. I 394.15–25 (E. Bickel).

in a weaving contest. The alteration of the gender, we can now see, plays an essential role in this allusion to the Greek myth, one that would have been less palpable if the spider were masculine. As the learned reader ponders the unusual form *aranea*, and perhaps considers its formal connection to the Greek name *Arachne*, the significance of the reference to Minerva should become evident.[41] Simply through a change in grammatical gender, Vergil calls up a mythical story. This sort of manipulation of a gender category recalls the classification system of the Dyirbal, in which the power of mythic connections compels speakers to transcend the accepted man-made categories of gender and morphology. Ultimately, the example from the *Georgics* serves to conjure up once again Vergil's nearly mystical familiarity with the relationship between language and the world, where grammatical gender conforms not to rules but to the exigencies of the poetic moment. Here, however, his cleverness seems to have escaped even the sensitized perception of his ancient commentators.

GRAMMATICAL GENDER AS A LITERARY TROPE IN CATULLUS

Of those Latin poets whose work survives in more than fragments, Catullus deserves special notice. While the instances of unusual grammatical gender of the types that have so far received attention—two sexes for tree bark, for instance—are not proportionately as high as in Vergil, nor nearly as well noted in the grammatical and exegetical tradition, Catullus nevertheless stands out by his innovations in the use of grammatical gender as a literary device. He likely signals his interest in this trope as early as the programmatic poem that opens modern editions of his poetry (Catull. 1). Scholars have demonstrated the many ways in which this seemingly straightforward dedication to Cornelius Nepos alludes through its vocabulary, imagery, and conversational tone to poetic principles and literary antecedents from the Hellenistic period of Greek literature.[42] The meter of the poem plays an analogous, though less overt, role. The opening two syllables of each verse (the "basis" of the hendecasyllabic line) tend to appear as a spondee in Latin poetry preceding and following Catullus.[43] By varying Latin practice in the first four lines of the poem (where there appear, in sequence, spondee, trochee, spondee, iamb), Catullus advertises his facility in imitating Greek measures, rather than yielding to the less flexible quantities available in Latin. It is within a learned, craftsmanlike context such as this that the reader can most readily accept as true the indication from Servius, already mentioned several times in this book, that the poet alters the gender of the

---

[41] Thomas 1988: 2.192 detects a similar allusion in the use of *aranea* at Catull. 68.49.
[42] Syndikus 1984: 1.71–78 provides an overview.
[43] Müller 1894: 178; Thomson 1998: 195–196. Compare Horace's deploying nine different Greek meters in the first nine poems of his three-book collection of *Odes*.

Latin word *pumex* ("pumice") into an otherwise unattested feminine form: like his variations upon the expected metrical "basis," the odd gender provides a learned allusion to the Greek word for pumice, which is indeed feminine.[44] Through the simple change of gender, Catullus signals the division of poetic sympathies that he displays elsewhere, as he imports Greek practice into a Latin idiom. It is time now to turn from this famous example in order to investigate other ways in which grammatical gender functions within Catullus's poetic vision.

Feminine Locks

The first example finds Catullus this time pointing explicitly, rather than covertly, to Greek precedence in his play with gender.[45] In an unusually direct citation of his literary inspiration, the poet advertises his poem 66 as a translation that he has made from the Greek poet Callimachus (Catull. 65.15–16). Both the original and the translation feature a first-person narration by a lock of hair that has been dedicated to Ptolemy III of Egypt by his wife Berenice. It is the grammatical gender of this lock that attracts attention. In the approximately thirty lines that survive from the Callimachean original, the lock consistently uses nouns and adjectives of the masculine gender to refer to himself (e.g., 8: βόστρυχος; 47, 62: πλόκαμος). Yet the "male" lock refers in his narrative to the companion tresses that remain on Berenice's head with a female designation, and in the feminine gender, as "sisterly locks" (51: κόμαι . . . ἀδελφεαί); this inconsistency indicates that Callimachus did not attach any particular significance to the grammatical gender of the queen's hair. In Catullus, by contrast, both the narrating lock and these "sister locks" (51: *comae . . . sorores*) consistently possess the feminine gender, both in the corresponding passage and throughout the poem (8: *caesaries*; 51, 93: *coma*; and all associated pronouns and adjectives).[46]

Several points indicate that Catullus did not alter the grammatical gender of his narrator without reflection. To begin with, in describing the princess's locks Catullus avoids two masculine nouns commonly used to describe hair, *crinis* and *capillus*.[47] This omission is especially remarkable when one considers that extant evidence indicates that the common Latin name for the constellation celebrated in this poem uses the masculine form *Crinis Berenices* ("The Lock of

---

[44] Serv. *Aen.* 12.587; Klotz 1931: 342, followed by Wiseman 1979: 166–171.

[45] I thank John Henderson and Rachel Geer for helpful advice on Catullus 66 (see too Geer 2011).

[46] First noted, to my knowledge, by Koenen 1993: 94–95.

[47] In his corpus, Catullus uses *capillus* twice, *crinis* three times, *coma* four (but of human hair only once, in 66). *Coma* is the noun favored by most poets; details at ThLL vol. III 314 (R. Meister).

Berenice").[48] However, when the Catullan lock comes to talk of hair generally—in her mock lament of the sad fate that has befallen her and her "sister locks" with the invention of iron (scissors)—she uses, naturally it would seem, the masculine *crines* to refer to the collective notion of all human hair and the fate it shares (66.47). Second, for two of the three feminine nouns that he chooses to describe the lock Catullus adopts meanings unique to this poem. The first word used, *caesaries* (8), "always refers to a head of hair" everywhere else in Latin, and only here to a single lock.[49] The same phenomenon occurs at the close of the poem (93) with the feminine noun *coma* describing the one lock even though throughout Latinity the word normally designates full tresses.[50] In other words, a native speaker of Latin would have noted how Catullus calls attention to the special efforts that he has made to transform the gender of Callimachus's male πλόκαμος. Finally, a peculiarity near the beginning of Catullus's translation also centers on his altering the grammatical gender that appears in the parent text. Early in his poem, Callimachus writes that Berenice dedicated her lock "to all the gods," using the masculine form of the noun θεός (8: πᾶσιν . . . θεοῖς). Catullus alters the phrase in two ways; of interest here is the unambiguous use of the feminine: "to many of the goddesses" (*multis . . . dearum*). The change from the formulaic Greek phrasing to the odd use of the Latin partitive genitive has defied precise interpretation or convincing emendation.[51] What is beyond doubt, however, is that the unusual construction allows Catullus to indicate the gender of the deities addressed, a specificity that would be lost had he used the expected construction of adjective with noun (e.g., *multis diis*). Furthermore, the change accords with Roman ritual, whereby sacrificial offerings normally possess the same sex as that of the deity or deities to which they are presented.[52] In the Roman system, a "female" lock represents the expected sex of an offering to female deities. Such a correspondence is not required in Greek ritual, and as a result the relationship is not found in Catullus's Greek model.

It is difficult to decide on the reasons for Catullus's playfulness here—and we cannot preclude that it is simply that, playfulness. One possible explanation, however, recalls the transformation of the noun *pulvis* ("dust") from the masculine to the rare feminine gender in order to recall its relationship with feminine Earth. Analogously, it seems "natural," perhaps even respectful, that the lock of

[48] All four references to the constellation in ThLL, beginning with the Elder Pliny, use only this name: ThLL vol. II 1924.5–8 (O. Hey). The Greeks too favored the masculine form Πλόκαμος (Boll and Gundel 1916–1924: 956–959). The commonly used *Coma Berenices* is a later coinage influenced, seemingly, by Catullus's poem.

[49] Fordyce 1961: 330.

[50] ThLL vol. III 1746.39–41 (A. Leissner). Despite textual problems at Catull. 66.93, the lock unquestionably refers to itself as a *coma*.

[51] For the rare use of the genitive here, see Horsfall 2008: 319.

[52] Arnob. *nat.* 7.19; Capdeville 1971: 302–311.

the princess Berenice should match the sex of its bearer. On a thematic level, moreover, modern scholars have claimed to detect in the lock's narration a more feminine tone and a more stereotypically feminine set of concerns than can be found in the Callimachean original.[53] Perhaps in Catullus's eyes transforming the noun that describes the narrator into the feminine gender, and hence the female sex, makes the narrator's tone less dissonant. However one may explain this change, it clearly represents a move by the poet to introduce a feminine element where there was none in the original, an element that a learned reader, noticing the care that Catullus takes to avoid common masculine nouns describing hair, would surely have noted.

Masculine Trees

The next two examples, from Catullus poems 62 and 63, differ from those that have preceded by offering instances in which the evidence of the poet's manuscripts gives modern readers a choice concerning which grammatical gender to assign a given noun. It is a well-established principle of textual criticism that, in the course of transmitting texts over the centuries, scribes tend to simplify when confronted with unusual and difficult grammar or syntax. A poet's use of a non-standard grammatical gender would provide clear motivation for a scribe to alter, either intentionally or not, the text before him in order to read a gender with which he would be more familiar. In each of the two cases from Catullus considered next, I shall argue that opting for the non-standard gender enriches a reader's experience of the poem.

The textual issue in the first example involves features of the natural world. The poet employs a comparison that imagines for plants a human-like ability to couple and procreate sexually. Poem 62 of Catullus takes the form of a marriage hymn sung by two choruses, one of young women and another of young men, who await the arrival of the new bride at her wedding feast. The poet provides few particulars regarding the precise occasion: there is no mention of the names of the parties involved or of a specific setting. And yet the piece seems more than a simple exercise in generic composition. Just as Catullus's programmatic poem hinted that part of the poet's achievement would involve a successful hybridization of Greek and Roman poetic elements, so too does this poem provide "a fanciful composite picture within which Greek and Roman motifs are combined."[54]

After an introductory set of strophes in which the sex-divided choruses set the stage for their verse competition (1–19), three paired stanzas follow in

---

[53] Van Sickle 1968: 499–500 and, more generally, the bibliography and critique of Gutzwiller 1992: 360–361, 374.

[54] Fordyce 1961: 254; further details in Fraenkel 1955: 6–8, Goud 1995: 30–32. Syndikus 1984: 2.50–59 argues for principally Greek inspiration.

which the chorus of boys responds with confidence to the concerns expressed by the girls over the future bride's impending loss of virginity (20–59).[55] The poem's structure reflects the principal dichotomy that underlies every ancient wedding, that between male groom and female bride. Alongside each axis align contrasting pairs: the approach of evening arouses sympathetic fear in the maidens, but pleasant anticipation in the young men; the girls lament the bride's separation from her mother, while the boys celebrate the imminent union of bride and groom; and so on.[56]

The poem's final strophe, sung by the maidens, is justly admired. The female chorus compares the virgin bride to an unplucked flower, admired by all until the day that she loses her "chaste bloom" (*castum . . . florem*; 46). The male chorus responds by retaining the horticultural imagery, but the boys move the setting from a hidden, walled-off garden to the vineyard, where the training of a grape plant upon a tree contributes to the health and generative productivity of the vine. The sexual overtones of the imagery are obvious; equally obvious for an ancient reader, I would claim, is how grammatical gender reinforces those overtones:

> *Ut vidua in nudo vitis quae nascitur arvo,*
> *numquam se extollit, numquam mitem educat uvam,*
> *sed tenerum prono deflectens pondere corpus*
> *iam iam contingit summum radice flagellum*
> *hanc nulli agricolae, nulli coluere iuvenci;*
> <u>*at si forte eadem est ulmo coniuncta marito*</u> [variant reading: *marita*]
> *multi illam agricolae, multi coluere iuvenci;*
> *sic virgo, dum innupta manet, dum inculta senescit;* . . . (Catull. 62.49–56)[57]

Just as the vine that arises unattached (*vidua*) in the bare field never grows fully, never produces a ripe grape, but gets closer and closer to touching its own root with the tips of its tendrils, bending down its frail body from the stooping weight—no farmers, no young bulls (*iuvenci*) have cared for her (*hanc*). But *if perhaps that same vine is wedded to an elm*, many farmers, many bulls have cared for that [vine] (*illam*). So too the virgin, so long as she remains untouched and uncared for, grows old. . . .

The double entendres contained in these lines are underscored by the use of grammatical gender, which personifies the components of the simile and endows them with biological sex. The lonely and tender vine is feminine, and "she" (53, 55: *hanc, illam*) comes to be the object of concern to the (male) farmers and young bulls (the very word describing which, *iuvenci*, echoes the noun denoting the young men of the chorus, the *iuvenes* [1, 6]). What particularly draws our interest is the suggested solution to this vine's plight: "marriage" to

---

[55] Textual lacunae blur details; I accept the reconstruction of Goud 1995.

[56] Syndikus 1984: 2.59–75 offers a full account of the various types of responsion.

[57] For the reading *innupta* in line 56 for the transmitted *intacta*, see Goud 1995: 26 n. 9.

an elm tree. Catullus clearly wishes the reader to continue personifying the elements of his simile since he chooses a technique of viticulture that involves training the vine to a living tree, as opposed to the alternative means in antiquity of attaching the vine to a lifeless stake.[58] The comparison of the joined vine and tree to the imminent union of bride and groom is complicated, however, by a disputed reading in the text; the textual issue arises with the final word of line 54, where the two manuscript traditions differ in one letter:[59]

| [vitis] est ulmo coniuncta | marita | T |
| | marito | V |

"[The vine] is joined with/to the elm in marriage"

Before evaluating each of these readings, a brief background on the training of grape vines is in order.

The metaphor of "marrying" vine to elm occurs frequently in Latin prose and poetry of all periods, with a Vergilian commentator tracing its origins to the idiom of farmers themselves (Serv. Auct. *georg.* 1.2: *hoc autem rustici maritare dicunt*). In extant instances of the metaphor, moreover, the vine and elm play consistent roles, with the tree being the "husband" and the vine, partly in its role as the future bearer of fruit, being the "bride."[60] This standard conception immediately renders unlikely one interpretation of the reading transmitted by the manuscript T: reading *maritā* as a nominative adjective modifying the "married" vine contradicts the normal understanding of the tree being the part of the pair that is "wed"; more subjectively, the nominative form also creates, in union with the nominative adjective *coniuncta*, an "unattractive tautology and unattractive homoeoteleuton."[61] Grammatical reasons render unlikely the other possible interpretation of the reading of T, as an ablative adjective modifying *ulmo* (*maritā*). Although this reading accords with the conception of the tree as "husband," nowhere in Latin is the adjective *coniuncta* construed with a bare ablative; rather, the dative is the expected construction.[62]

The alternative provided by the manuscripts is V's *maritō*, which also has two possible interpretations. Taking the word as a masculine noun in apposition to the elm ("as a husband") resolves the issue of noun/adjective agreement: since the noun *ulmus* is normally feminine, the expected adjectival form would

---

[58] Syndikus 1984: 2.72–73.

[59] Poem 62 is the only poem of Catullus with testimony independent of V; see Thomson 1997: 23–24.

[60] ThLL vol. VIII 402.80–403.8 (O. Hey); the only exception I know of is the late Brev. Expos. Verg. *georg.* 1.2 (*proprie . . . vites ulmis maritantur*). Cf. Catull. 61.97–106, with Della Corte 1976: 79–80.

[61] Trappes-Lomax 2007: 157, who unnecessarily accepts Heinsius's conjecture *maritae*; Thomson 1997: 369 also notes that Catullus avoids short *a* at line end.

[62] Trappes-Lomax 2007: 157.

be *maritae*.[63] While this certainly settles one grammatical issue, the apposition is stylistically awkward and, more significantly, in parallel occurrences of this viticultural metaphor *maritus* always acts as adjective and never as an appositive noun.[64] This leaves one final interpretation, that of understanding *marito* as an adjective in agreement with *ulmo* (literally, "the vine is joined to her wedded-husband elm"). This choice has several points in its favor. First, in sense, the construction matches the notion of the tree being the imagined "male" in this metaphorical union. Second, the use of the adjectival form for *marito*, rather than the noun, is consistent with other extant instances of the metaphor. Finally, there is no syntactical objection to the construction, since the verb *coniungo* would be construed with the expected complement in the dative.[65]

Only one oddity remains. The noun *ulmus*, like most species names for trees, is strictly of the feminine gender during the classical period.[66] The previous chapter has, however, provided parallels for poets changing the grammatical gender of a plant to match the sex of an imagined personification (*cypressus*, *crocus*). In this particular poem of Catullus, the marriage of the two plants offers a particularly Roman metaphor since the training of vines on living trees represents a practice that is normally, if not exclusively, Roman.[67] In changing gender, then, Catullus achieves two particular effects. First, he creates yet another explicit expression of the dichotomy of male vs. female upon which the theme, structure, and occasion of the surrounding poem rests. Second, in creating a personified nature that he divides into sexual categories he once again shows his learnedness by alluding to an early, pre-literary past. Although the reading *marito* has been defended by scholars in the past, seeing it in the context of other poetic changes of gender helps the modern reader understand the manner in which the adoption of this technique lends to Catullus an aura of poetic authority.

Changing the Sex of Flint

According to Aldo Lunelli, the majority of changes in standard grammatical gender made by the Roman neoteric poets with whom Catullus associated move in the direction of masculine to feminine. This statistical fact, he suggests, stems from an unconscious tendency for these poets to align themselves with a refined, feminine-leaning ideology.[68] While this assertion is ultimately unprov-

---

[63] So, e.g., Quinn 1973: 281.

[64] E.g., Quint. *inst.* 8.3.8; Plin. *nat.* 14.10; Apul. *apol.* 88.

[65] ThLL vol. IV 335.11–29 (O. Probst).

[66] The only exception I know is from the third-century (?) treatise on cattle Garg. Mart. *cur. boum* 7 (*ulmi vernaculi radicem*).

[67] Courtney 1985: 87, building upon Fraenkel 1955: 8.

[68] Lunelli 1969: 170 ("una tendenza inconscia, il riflesso di un atteggiamento spirituale, la preferenza per ciò che è raffinato e insomma femmineo").

able, a remark made by the third-century AD scholar Porphyry indicates that the claim could have had more resonance among an ancient audience than a modern reader might first imagine. Porphyry has noted an instance of gender change in Herodotos of a similar type to those that Lunelli notes among the neoterics; after citing parallels for the Ionic dialect changing a masculine gender to the feminine, Porphyry surmises that the example before him, far from reflecting a scribal error, in fact provides evidence for the character of the Ionians, since it is typical of Ionians to "enjoy" making masculine nouns feminine (Porph. *ad Od.* p. 288.18–20 Schrader).[69] Porphyry does not supply an explicit account of his reasoning, but it is likely that the stereotype of the "effeminate" Ionian, dating to as early as the fifth-century BC, informs his verdict. What could prompt a speaker to construe the masculine words for "stone" and "column" in the feminine gender, Porphyry seems to be thinking, other than a disposition toward seeing the world through an effeminizing lens? Although their analyses are separated by centuries, for both Lunelli and Porphyry the alteration of a noun's gender is seen to reflect significant societal attitudes that characterize particular groups of language users.

Although Lunelli is the only person to remark explicitly on this phenomenon of grammatical gender, modern scholars have observed other ways in which the Catullan persona subverts typical Roman notions of masculinity. Some more straightforward examples include his adoption of the motif of *servitium amoris* ("being a slave to love") and the reference to the female beloved as *domina* ("female master").[69] The most explicit example of the poet embarking on a pointed journey away from the realm of the masculine forms the subject of Catullus 63. This poem narrates the psychological turmoil of the mythical figure Attis, who castrates himself in order to become part of the sacred retinue of the great mother goddess, Cybele. In clear fashion, the poem illustrates the relationship between physical biology and grammatical gender, as we see Attis's emasculation accompanied by a change in grammatical agreement.

Following his self-castration in line 5, the first adjective used to describe the hitherto masculine Attis is the feminine *citata* (8: "quickened"). For the remainder of the poem, Catullus continues to represent Attis's changed physical sex through attendant adjectives and pronouns that mark him as a figure of uncertain grammatical gender.[70] Other, less overt, features of the poem further demonstrate the figurative unmanning of Attis, as his laments echo those of abandoned heroines of the Greek past and his situation corresponds metaphorically with that of the disempowered member of the male elite during the late Republic.[71] Attis's slippage into the feminine, rather than neuter, gender after castra-

---

[69] Skinner 1997: 142–147.

[70] The extant manuscripts show both genders at various points throughout the poem. For a succinct overview, with bibliography, see Nauta 2005: 92–93.

[71] Heroines: Harrison 2005: 17–19; late Republic: Skinner 1997.

tion also accords well both with Roman invective, where emasculated men are continually represented as at risk of becoming "women," and with Roman law, which refused to accept the existence of a third "sex."[72] In this poem, therefore, Catullus not only demonstrates with perfect clarity the relationship between grammatical gender and biological sex, but he also displays the ways in which grammatical gender can relate to culturally constructed notions of masculinity and femininity. For this reason alone Catullus 63 deserves discussion in this book.

At the risk of adding an element to his poem that Catullus did not intend, I would like to offer a suggestion of how the poet may have pressed Latin grammatical gender even further. At the point when Attis castrates himself with a piece of flint the consensus of the best manuscripts preserves a line of apparent nonsense (Catull. 63.5):

> devolvit iletas acuto sibi pondere silices　　　V

He rolled down *iletas* (?) flints from himself with a sharp weight

Editors normally emend the otherwise unattested form *iletas* to *ipse* ("[Attis] himself") or *il[e]i* ("[the weight] of the groin"). This emendation need not delay us further. For the remainder of the verse, however, the majority of editors since the Renaissance have accepted that Catullus originally wrote something akin to the following:

> devolvit [or devolsit]. . . acutō sibi pondera silice

He rolled off [or tore off] the weights [i.e., his testicles] from himself with a sharp flint

I would like to suggest one small but significant change to this reconstruction. As noted in the previous chapter, the Roman grammarians recognized that the word for flint, *silex*, possessed a gender that wavered between masculine and feminine. Universally appearing as masculine in texts of the Republican period, it is first attested in the feminine in Vergil, whereafter it is construed in both genders through the rest of Latinity, in both prose and poetry.[73] I would suggest that Catullus here anticipates Vergil in exploiting the fluidity in the gender of *silex*, allowing him to foreshadow in his typically clever and learned manner the poem's theme of slippage between genders: he uses for the castration an object whose own potential for gender fluctuation reflects the use to which it is put. Hence I would propose reading *acutā* for the adjectival form *acuto* that is preserved in V. This suggestion has the additional merit of explaining why Catullus made the unusual alteration of having Attis castrate himself with flint in this poem—a means nowhere else mentioned—rather than with the better attested

---

[72] Invective: Corbeill 1996: 143–159; law: Thomas 1992: 85.
[73] NW 985 offer testimonia.

pot shard (*testa*).[74] Presumably, the noun *testa* was not chosen by the poet since its morphology could not provide the same opportunity for fluid gender as the third-declension noun *silex*.

If this reading is accepted, it accords with other poetic uses of unusual gender in the poem already discussed. In addition to manufacturing for Catullus a link with the pre-literary past and thereby establishing his poetic authority, the existence of feminine flint would have an additional, related effect. The alteration would lend an air of archaic solemnity to a mysterious theme: a crazed man from the mythic past undergoes a violent and arcane transformation as a means of getting closer to an understanding of the divine.

When Gender Does Not Mean Sex

The final example from Catullus confronts a different use of grammatical gender from those that have been considered thus far. The preceding chapters have argued that the equation of biological sex with grammatical gender not only forms part of the Roman story about the evolution of language but that it also plays an important role in the establishment of literary authority for the reputedly wise poet. This section has suggested ways in which a self-consciously learned poet such as Catullus playfully flaunted this authority for the amusement of his contemporary readership. I will close this discussion of Catullus by focusing on one poem in which I propose that grammatical gender constitutes an essential theme and for which an understanding of gender allows the reader to appreciate the poet's irony.[75]

At first glance, Catullus 6 seems to have a riddle as its basis, with the narrator presenting at the outset a mystery that he seeks to solve as the poem unfolds. By poem's end, however, the essential question facing the speaker remains unanswered—or at least apparently so. I quote the poem fully in Latin and in translation. Those Latin portions significant to Catullus's play on gender are highlighted in bold.

> *Flavi, **delicias tuas** Catullo,*
> *ni sint illepidae atque inelegantes,*
> *velles dicere nec tacere posses.*
> *verum **nescioquid** febriculosi*
> ***scorti** diligis: hoc pudet fateri.*   5
> *nam te non **viduas** iacere noctes*

---

[74] I know of no independent instance of flint being specified; the inexact reference in Ovid (*fast.* 4.237: *saxo . . . acuto*) clearly derives from Catullus. For the pot shard, see Plin. *nat.* 35.165 (*Samia . . . testa*), Iuv. 6.514, Min. Fel. 22.9, and compare Lucil. fg. 282, Mart. 3.81.3. For knives, see Courtney 1980: 142.

[75] This reading was inspired by a lecture given by Randall McNeill at the 2009 meeting of the American Philological Association (now part of McNeill 2010).

nequiquam tacitum cubile clamat
sertis ac Syrio fragrans olivo,
pulvinusque peraeque et hic et ille
attritus, tremulique quassa lecti 10
argutatio inambulatioque.
nam nil stupra ualet, nihil, tacere.
*cur? non tam latera **effututa** pandas,*
ni tu quid facias ineptiarum.
*quare, **quidquid** habes boni malique,* 15
*dic nobis. volo te ac **tuos amores***
ad caelum lepido vocare versu.

Flavius, you'd want to tell Catullus about your
love (*delicias tuas*)—you wouldn't be able to keep quiet—
except that it is lacking in charm and elegance.
But the fact is that you're cherishing some kind of (*nescioquid*)
a feverish whore (*scorti*) and are ashamed to admit it. 5
Your bed—unable to maintain silence—cries out that
you're not spending companionless (*viduas*) nights:
it smells of garlands and Syrian oil,
while your pillow is evenly rumpled on both sides
and your bed trembles and shakes 10
like a shrieking, pacing District Attorney.[76]
It's not possible to be quiet about all this sex; not at all.
Why so? You wouldn't be limping like that from
your over-fucked (*effututa*) flanks unless you were doing
something frivolous. And so, whatever (*quidquid*) you've got, 15
good or bad, tell us. I want to praise to the heavens you and
your lover (*tuos amores*) in clever verse.

The entire poem involves a teasing of the addressee, Flavius. The speaker knows that Flavius is sleeping with someone since, regardless of how furtive his friend may try to be, the poet finds signs of activity everywhere, both in Flavius's bedroom and on his body. The poem possesses a structural resemblance to Catullus's abuse of Gellius in poem 80, where the poet also evokes visible evidence to explain his friend's uncustomarily pale appearance and haggard condition.[77] One significant difference between the two poems, however, lies in their respective endings. At the conclusion of the epigram about Gellius, the reader learns precisely what Gellius is doing in lieu of sleep and the name of the person with whom he is doing it. Not so with Flavius.

---

[76] I follow Thomson 1998: 222–223 for the rhetorical nuances of *argutatio inambulatioque*.
[77] See Kroll 1959: 12–13 for the type outside Catullus.

Without exception, commentators tacitly assume that Flavius's reticence stems from the shame that he feels about an unnamable "girlfriend."[78] Nothing in the text of the poem, however, justifies such an assumption. I would maintain that the teasing nature of the poem increases if we pay attention to the grammatical genders that Catullus assigns to Flavius's presumed lover. The first mention of the lover occurs in the poem's opening line, where the names of Flavius and Catullus bracket the words *delicias tuas* ("your love"). This noun/adjective combination is visibly of the feminine gender, as is its corresponding adjective *illepidae* ("lacking in charm") on the next line, but that need have no more consequence for identifying the sex of the person signified than the fact that the noun is also plural in number. Just as no commentator has suggested from the plural that Catullus is accusing his friend of having multiple lovers, so too there is no need to assume from these same words that the beloved is a female, since the term *deliciae* may apply equally well to a male without a change of grammatical gender.[79] A different perspective is immediately provided by lines 4–5, as the poet now uses two neuter words, a noun and pronoun, to describe the beloved: *nescioquid . . . scorti* ("some kind of a whore"). The neuter noun *scortum* ranks among the most abusive terms to use of a prostitute. As a result, the addition of the comparatively tender verb *diligis* ("you cherish") creates a pointed oxymoron, adding further to the mysterious relationship that Flavius is having with his lover.[80] Moreover, unlike less opprobrious terms for prostitute such as *meretrix*, Plautus rarely uses the term *scortum* in his plays to refer to a named character, an anonymity that in the Catullan context echoes the poem's theme of the lover's namelessness.[81] The word also provides no sexual details—beyond an alleged profession—about the person so described since, like *deliciae*, the noun *scortum* can describe either a male or a female.[82]

The next two words to be examined are epithets that derive their significance from semantics rather than from grammatical gender. In line 7, Catullus notes how Flavius's nights are "not companionless"—literally, how his nights are "not widowed" (*non viduas*). On this occasion, word-use casts into doubt the sexual identity of Flavius rather than that of his beloved. While the adjective can refer to both males and females, the word appears substantivized only in the feminine to refer to women (*vidua*, "widow") and, as mentioned above, Catullus's only other use of the adjective in his corpus describes an "unmarried" vine that

---

[78] Quinn 1973: 110; cf. Kroll 1959: 13 ("Flavius' Geliebte"); Thomson 1998: 221 (*innamorata*); I know of no exceptions to this assumption.

[79] Many examples included (without division of the sexes) in ThLL vol. V, 1 447.77–448.36 (K. Simbeck); in Catullus alone, contrast 2.1 and 3.4 (male sparrow) with 32.2 (woman).

[80] Adams 1983: 325 notes that in Plautus *scortum* is never the direct object of "verbs such as *amo*," in opposition to *meretrix*, which serves as object six times.

[81] Adams 1983: 325; at Plaut. *Capt.* 69–76, the parasite Ergasilus discusses his nickname *Scortum*.

[82] Adams 1983: 322.

has been personified as a new bride (62.49). More significantly, we have already encountered how Roman commentators are sensitive to the sexual connotations of forms of this word: Servius notes the appropriateness of Vergil describing a city as "widowed" since the noun *urbs* has the feminine gender, and Porphyrio makes a related observation about a use of the adjective in Horace.[83] As a result, a reader thinking along lines similar to these Romans will be further alerted to a potentially inconsistent play with sexuality: if Flavius avoids spending his nights as a "widow," what does this imply about his masculinity?[84] The other epithet under consideration plays with Flavius's sexuality in an analogous manner. Catullus notes that his friend has "over-fucked flanks" (*latera effututa*). Based on parallels elsewhere for verbs compounded of *futuere* ("to fuck"), scholars take this phrase in an extended rather than a strictly literal sense, so that it merely refers to Flavius's flanks as "exhausted by fucking."[85] On a literal level, however, the simplex verb form *futuo* describes in the active voice the action of a man, and only a man, in sexual intercourse, either vaginal or anal.[86] Accordingly, throughout Latinity the passive form of the verb has only women as the grammatical subject—or, occasionally, men who are penetrated by other men.[87] And indeed an example of just such a literally construed passive, built from a compound like *effututa*, occurs elsewhere in Catullus's polymetric poems to describe Ameana "the well-fucked girl" (Catull. 41.1: *Ameana puella defututa*). I would propose that Catullus intends this literal connotation to be available here as well, adding piquancy to the notion that Flavius, no "widow," has been the object of another man's fucking night after night. The literal meanings of the adjective *viduus* and of the participle *effututus* provide clues to the alert reader concerning what precisely Flavius has been doing in his bedroom.

In the final summation of the poem, Catullus directly asks Flavius to tell him "whatever he's got" (*quidquid habes*; 15), once again describing the lover of Flavius with a vague word, this time a pronoun of the neuter gender. In the following line the poet changes the gender one last time, introducing into the poem the first reference to the lover that uses a masculine term, *tuos amores* ("your lover"). As with *deliciae* in the opening line, the masculine plural *amores* would normally refer to only one person, either male or female.[88] Nevertheless, it is tempting to see this final phrase, marking as it does the first use of the masculine to describe the lover, and combined with the double entendres of *viduas*

---

[83] Serv. *Aen.* 8.571; Porph. Hor. *carm.* 4.5.30.

[84] With all commentators, I understand *viduas* as a transferred epithet, from the nights to Flavius.

[85] Catull. 29.13 (*diffututa mentula*); Priap. 26.7 *effututus* (describing Priapus); Adams 1982: 119.

[86] Adams 1982: 118–122, to which this entire discussion of *futuo* is indebted.

[87] Passages such as Mart. 7.70, when a woman adopts sexual behaviors identified as masculine, affirm the rule. This category also likely explains the use of *fututum* at Mart. 11.7.13.

[88] Catullus, for example, uses the term for both females (10.1, 45.1, 64.27) and males (15.1, 21.4 and, apparently, 40.7).

and *effututa*, as constituting Catullus's sly hint to Flavius that the poet, despite feigning the need to know, does in fact understand the situation. Flavius's lover is a man, and the relationship is one in which Flavius plays the passive, submissive role. This is the kind of information that a young elite male of the late Republic would not wish to become public. Once the actual situation is realized, Flavius's reticence no longer remains a mystery.

This interpretation of poem 6 depends upon the reconstruction of the previous two chapters concerning the significance of grammatical gender to Roman scholars and poets. And yet despite my confidence in this reconstruction, it remains difficult for me to imagine—in particular since my native language, English, does not have a full system of grammatical gender—how this play with gender in poem 6 would have been processed by Catullus's original Roman readers. Nevertheless, I do think that Catullus lets us know with the final line of the poem how he would characterize the most careful of these readers. The "clever verse" (*lepido . . . versu*) with which Catullus promises to celebrate Flavius's love affair in the final line is of course poem 6 itself, which is now part of the "clever new little book" (*lepidum novum libellum*) that he had promised in the opening verse of his dedicatory poem to Cornelius Nepos.[89] That book is, if Servius is accurate, polished with a type of "dry pumice" that itself plays with an odd gender whose significance is left to the reader to interpret. Catullus's ancient readers, if *lepidi* themselves, will have been conditioned by this introductory example to be sensitive to the grammatical revelations that unfold during the course of poem 6.

The revelation of Flavius's lover through play with grammatical gender finds a possible parallel in Ovid's *Metamorphoses*. This is my only consideration of Ovid's epic in this book, which may occasion surprise since Ovid has been known since antiquity for being, to paraphrase Quintilian, excessively enamored of his own cleverness and since the entirety of the *Metamorphoses* treats "change" from a seemingly endless variety of angles.[90] Nevertheless, I have discovered in the *Metamorphoses* no manipulation of grammatical gender of the kind found in Vergil and his predecessors, perhaps because of the prevailing anxiety over Vergilian authority outlined in the previous chapter. But on one occasion at least Ovid does seem to avail himself of a type of grammatical play that may offer a parallel for Catullus's practice in poem 6.

In book 14 of the *Metamorphoses*, the shape-shifting god Vertumnus transforms himself into an old woman in order to approach the virginal Pomona and convince her of the sincere affections that Vertumnus feels for her. After entering Pomona's garden, Vertumnus gives her kisses "such as a true old woman would never have given" (14.658–659: *qualia numquam / **vera** dedisset **anus***).

---

[89] For the word *lepidus* and its congeners evoking in Catullus's day an atmosphere of eroticism, literature, and social performance, see Krostenko 2001: 233–290, especially 266–267 n. 85.

[90] Quint. *inst.* 10.1.88: *nimium amator ingenii sui.*

The pairing of the noun and adjective *vera . . . anus* ("true old woman"), while grammatically correct and not in itself unusual, hints from the dissimilar terminations (*-a / -us*) at what they describe: Vertumnus may seem an old woman but he is in no way a "true" one: and just as masculine and feminine reside in the same body, so the term designating Vertumnus-as-old-woman seems to contain both masculine and feminine forms. Moreover, part of this false old woman's subsequent seduction rhetoric recalls the analogous attempts by the chorus of youths in Catullus 62 when "she" compares the future bride to a vine and the groom to the tree upon which she relies. Perhaps not accidentally the metaphorical groom in Ovid appears, like the god, as a seemingly transgendered body (*ulmus . . . speciosa*; 661), and one to whom Vertumnus insists that the vine must be a "bride" (*nupta*; 666). Ovid here seems unwilling to change the standard gender of a noun, in this case *ulmus*, in the way that Catullus had. As a result, the shape-shifter is exposed, to the learned reader at any rate, by the grammar of his exposition.

SHEDDING SNAKES

The various forms that the poetic manipulation of grammatical genders adopts in the poetry of Catullus reveal a learned poet exploiting to the fullest an inherited poetic trope by extending its practice in ways apparently not attempted by figures such as Ennius and Vergil, poets working in the more sober genre of epic. In contrast, my final pair of examples returns to the preoccupations of the previous two chapters: how notions of grammatical gender tie in with the origins of a language that reflects the natural world, and how those notions connect grammatical gender with human sexuality.

Snakes have mythical associations with shifting sexes. A particularly memorable tale, dating back to Hesiod, involves the famous Theban seer Teiresias.[91] As a young man, Teiresias was wandering in the mountains when he came upon a male and female snake mating. Separating the two (and, in some versions, killing the female), he is suddenly transformed into a woman. Several years later he comes upon a similar sight, which provokes a similar response from the now transgendered seer. On this occasion he is restored to his masculine form. A less overt example of snakes effecting a sex change occurs in book 4 of *On the Nature of Things*. Lucretius is listing examples of the many objects in nature that give off bodies, among which he includes snakes while molting:

> *et item cum lubrica serpens*
> *exuit in spinis vestem; nam saepe videmus*
> *illorum spoliis vepres volitantibus auctas.* (Lucr. 4.60–62)

[91] Hesiod apud Apollod. *Bibl.* 3.6.7; for a full discussion of sources, see Buslepp 1916–1924: 180–182.

... and also when the slick serpent (*lubrica serpens*)
doffs its covering onto thorns. For we often see
brambles covered with their (*illorum*) windblown spoils.

This short passage contains two oddities of grammatical gender. First, with the shedding of her skin, the feminine "slick serpent" (*lubrica serpens*) transforms into the masculine plural ("their"; *illorum*), as Lucretius presents the image of several discarded skins draping the bramble bushes. The noun *serpens* is recorded in the Roman grammarians as a noun that may have either gender, a fact that could have eased the transition here from feminine to masculine.[92] Of noteworthy significance, however, is the fact that Lucretius himself uses the masculine—and not the feminine—in describing a *serpens* in the very next book of his epic (5.33: *asper . . . serpens*), which raises the suspicion that some poetic intent lies behind his calling attention to the fluidity of gender here. The second uncommon gender in the passage rests among the brambles (*vepres*), which Lucretius employs here in the feminine. This rarer gender drew the attention of the ancient commentators; Servius, for example, contrasts the Lucretian passage with Vergil's use of the more standard masculine.[93] In the context of Lucretius's poem, however, these grammatical changes have a point. The example of snakes shedding their skins is one of the analogies he employs in arguing that physical bodies are continuously emitting material films, replicas of themselves that, among other phenomena, touch our eyes and ears so as to facilitate sight and hearing. With the shedding of her skin, the female serpent turns into a new form, signified by the male gender. Its former, feminine self in turn feminizes the brambles to which the snakeskin adheres. It is fitting that fluid genders from the natural world, in which the grammarians postulated a true understanding of gender, should be the site of Lucretius's analogy about the constantly changing and shifting universe.

CONCLUSION: BACK TO VARRO

This survey of poetic exploitation of grammatical gender ends, fittingly, with Marcus Terentius Varro, the Roman scholar whose linguistic theories began the investigation into the origins of grammatical gender. His influence over the subsequent grammatical tradition came to be immense, and no less notable was his influence over how later Roman grammarians and exegetes from antiquity were to interpret cases of unusual grammatical gender. In addition to being a formidable and influential scholar, Varro also composed literary works in which, intriguingly, he "not infrequently admits genders that had otherwise

---

[92] Bailey 1947: 3.1187; for the variable gender of *serpens*, NW 923–924.
[93] Serv. Auct. *georg.* 3.444 (cf. Non. p. 231.17–19); the main MSS. of Lucretius are divided here between *auctas* and *auctos*. Full account of ancient testimonia in NW 1006–1007.

been eliminated by the classical period."[94] Among his works are included 150 books of *Menippean Satires*, literary essays in prose and verse that cover a wide variety of topics. Of the approximately 600 fragments of these satires that survive, few consist of more than a couple lines, usually of tantalizingly mysterious content. One of these is cited by Nonius in the context of the noun *tibia* ("flute"). This word normally occurs in the feminine gender, as one would expect from an inanimate first-declension noun whose nominative singular ends in *-a*. Nonius cites as the sole known exception to the noun's feminine gender a line from Varro's Menippean satire entitled *Modius*, where the noun appears in the masculine:

> †*quaero meas lubidines ad tibias bilinguos.* (Non. p. 229.19–20 = Varro.
> *Men.* 309)

The fragment is difficult to translate: "I seek(?) my pleasures to the tune of(?) double-tongued flutes." The interpretation creates similar difficulties. Cèbe reconstructs from its eighteen surviving fragments that this particular satire was set at a banquet and involved a dialogue concerning the propriety of knowing one's limits, particularly in dining and dress.[95] One other element inextricably associated with the Roman banquet in texts from the period is excessive sexual activity.[96] As a result, scholars have been tempted to see some type of obscenity hiding in the image of a (feminine) flute having a masculine adjective that describes two tongues, but attempts to determine the precise sense have met with varied success.[97]

Telling parallels, however, exist from the periods both before and after Varro composed these lines. The first occurs in a comedy of Plautus, an author and genre to which Varro devoted a great deal of scholarly attention.[98] In one play, the slave Pseudolus is returning drunken from a banquet, and includes the following in his list of the true pleasures of life:

> . . . *ubi amans complexust amantem, ubi ad labra labella adiungit, ubi*
> *alter alterum bilingui manifesto inter se prehendunt.* (Plaut. *Pseud.* 1259–1260)

> . . . when lovers have embraced, join lips to lips, and clasp each other
> openly with double tongues (*bilingui*).

---

[94] Adams 2013: 395, with a list of examples.

[95] Cèbe 1987: 1337–1340.

[96] Corbeill 1996: 128–173.

[97] ThLL vol. II 1986.49 (M. Ihm) simply notes "*obscurum, inesse videtur obscaenitas.*" Cèbe 1987: 1353–1355 critically reviews other interpretations. A reader for the Press suggests that Nonius misconstrued Varro's text and that *bilinguos* in fact modifies *lubidines*. This is a tempting alternative; if correct, my interpretation about gender fluidity still holds, since *lubidines* is also universally feminine in gender.

[98] Rawson 1985: 273–278.

The description shares with Varro the adjective *bilinguis* ("double-tongued"; presumably a noun such as "kiss" is to be supplied in the *Pseudolus* passage), and the Plautine quotation occurs in the similar context of a luxurious banquet. A second analogous reference occurs in Ovid's *Art of Love*. As in Varro, the context has the poet lecturing on propriety, in this case on how an aging boy should work to cultivate intellectual attributes when his physical charms are on the wane. Ovid concludes his remarks with the following couplet: "Do not neglect cultivating the breast through the liberal arts and learning to be proficient with two tongues" (*nec levis ingenuas pectus coluisse per artes / cura sit et linguas edidicisse duas*; Ov. *ars* 2.121–122). Both aspects of the advice bristle with double entendre, but it is the second recommendation that provides the parallel: in encouraging his young pupils to learn double-tongued skills as they age, Ovid describes "the activity he is recommending in terms of the outcome it is intended to procure."[99] Seeing the same allusion in both these erotic contexts offers the most satisfying explanation for the "double tongues" of Varro's fragment: the speaker finds his pleasure in French kissing (or, perhaps more graphically, he finds the best form of sexual fulfillment to happen while simultaneously French kissing).[100]

And yet Varro's mode of presenting this sexual allusion differs from the other two examples cited in its exploitation of fluid grammatical gender. In his case, the mingling of masculine adjective and feminine noun intends to provide a match for the male and female partners who commingle in this singular act. Once again, grammatical gender recalls biological sex, and in this instance brings to mind explicitly erotic human activity. This same Varro, you will recall, derived the Latin word for grammatical gender, *genus*, from the verb describing sexual reproduction, *genero* (Varro frg. 245 Funaioli). It is fitting then to end here, with masculine and feminine genders—and sexes—battling it out.

[99] Houghton 2009: 281, who compares Tibull. 1.8.37, Ov. *am.* 2.5.57–58.
[100] Krenkel 2002: 551–552 provides additional parallels.

Chapter 4

Androgynous Gods in Archaic Rome

In the midst of a reasoned dispute over the superiority of monotheism to polytheism, the fourth-century Christian apologist Arnobius uses Cicero as an authority to deny that divinities possess sexual characteristics. As a supplement to Cicero's arguments, Arnobius confronts the masculine grammatical gender of *deus* ("God"):

> *ac ne tamen et nobis inconsideratus aliquis calumniam moveat, tamquam deum quem colimus marem esse credamus, ea scilicet causa, quod eum cum loquimur pronuntiamus genere masculino, intellegat non sexum sed usu et familiaritate sermonis appellationem eius et significantiam promi. non enim deus mas est, sed nomen eius generis masculini est, quod idem vos dicere religione in vestra non quitis. nam consuestis in precibus "sive tu deus es sive dea" dicere, quae dubitationis exceptio dare vos diis sexum diiunctione ex ipsa declarat.* (Arnob. *nat.* 3.8)

> And yet no one should thoughtlessly rebuke us [Christians] for thinking that the god we worship is male just because we use the masculine gender when we speak of him. Understand that it is not the sex of God that is being expressed but a name and designation that has arisen through common, everyday speech. For "God" is not male, but the noun naming "God" is of the masculine gender. You [pagans] are unable to make this distinction in your religion. For you have the custom of saying in prayers "whether you are a god or a goddess," an expression of doubt that makes clear from the alternative provided that you attribute sex to your gods.

In professedly—and passionately—espousing Christian doctrine in his treatise *Against the Pagans*, Arnobius presents himself as a man who converted late in life to a religion whose tenets he does not yet completely comprehend. Indeed, one of the few anecdotes circulating about his life in antiquity claims that the local bishop had requested that Arnobius compose this treatise as a way of demonstrating the seriousness of his conversion to a faith that he had previously acquired a reputation for attacking.[101] As a result of this status as a late and only partially formed convert, Arnobius's references to the principles of paganism, even when couched in ridicule and vehement denial, provide an excellent

---

[101] Hier. *chron. a. Abr.* 2343. For his limited knowledge of Judaeo-Christian traditions, see McCracken 1949: 1.24–28.

source for reconstructing ideas about divinity in the pre-Christian Roman world.

With this status of the author in mind, three particular points of the passage quoted stand out in light of the previous chapters. First, the fact that Arnobius feels compelled to deny that grammatical gender equates with biological sex indicates that the equation of these two categories, a tenet analyzed in the first chapter, remained a common tendency in his day. Second, the entire context surrounding this excerpt attests that the polytheistic world of pre-Christian Rome abounded in gods readily identifiable as male and female; the distinction between "goddess" and "god," in other words, extends beyond the simple consequences of personification. Rather, the grammatical gender of a deity implicates the god's sex with the ways in which worshippers perceive that deity's function. Third and most strikingly, Arnobius concludes with the assertion that something about the language and thought of pre-Christians necessitates that they must conceive of a god's sex as inseparable from the grammatical gender of the name describing it. To his contemporary non-Christians, he seems to be saying, a divine appellation such as the grammatically masculine *Messor* can be conceived of as embodying only the traits that characterize a male while, conversely, the feminine name *Maia* carries with it inseparably female connotations.

In the immediate context of this quotation, Arnobius faults pagans for populating the world with deities having sexual characteristics, and with gods who in turn populate the heavens with successive generations of descendants. This rampant heterosexualization of the archaic Roman world also describes the theme of the rest of this book. In this chapter I will make a link between Latin linguistics and Roman theology. In the previous three chapters I traced how scholars and grammarians perceive in the development of their language an early period when masculine and feminine genders could fluctuate, and how certain mantic poets could manipulate this flux to create effects that resonate with poetic authority. In an analogous fashion, there exist indications that these same scholars hypothesized not simply that Rome's gods possessed sexual characteristics, as Arnobius notes and as any student of mythology can attest, but that those sexual characteristics, like the archaic gender of *äer*, could in many cases be decidedly fluid.

INTRODUCTION

In choosing to discuss gender in human language before considering the sexual characteristics of the gods, I have taken my cue once again from the Roman Republican scholar Varro. In organizing his paired treatises on the archaeology of human and divine institutions (*Antiquitates rerum humanarum et divinarum*), Varro deliberately chose to discuss the activity of human beings before that of the gods. His justification is as follows: "Just as the painter precedes the painting and the craftsman precedes the building, so too do organized communities come into existence before their institutions."[1] In a similar way, I shall argue that the conception that a god possesses sex depends upon the preexistence of a human language that could categorize these gods in the abstract as masculine and feminine in gender and only then, through an association that makes Arnobius oddly uncomfortable, as male and female in sex. As a result, my conclusions in the first chapter about the essence of Latin grammatical gender form a necessary prelude to understanding how the earliest Romans named their gods. The Latin-speaking worshipper accepts the tendency to equate grammatical gender with biological sex and, in the process, creates a series of androgynous gods.

Before proceeding further, let me review the main points that I have made in the previous three chapters about the scholarly interpretation and poetic practice regarding grammatical gender in Latin. The theories of Roman grammarians and of ancient commentators on Latin poetic texts see fluctuation of gender as determined by three factors: first, that biological sex and linguistic gender originally shared analogous if not identical categories; second, that the assignment of these categories to a given signified—or, in the case of gods, to a given divine power—depends upon the perceived function of that signified in the real world; and, third, that this assignment takes place in an early, prehistoric time to which careful study can provide some access.

NAMING GODS

As a number of scholars of ancient religion have postulated, it seems intuitive that a human being would conceive of a divinity as existing first as an abstract power and only afterward as a distinct personality—and perhaps, eventually, as one possessing human traits.[2] Of equal importance is the fact that some Romans thought so too: Varro writes that the early Romans worshipped their gods without images for the first 170 years of the city's existence.[3] This claim has been much debated, and yet the claim's historicity is not so important here as the fact that Varro could conceive of a time when the gods were not in possession of physical bodies.[4] Indeed, one scholar even posits as a reason for aniconic worship "a conscious effort to prevent men from attributing sex to the gods."[5]

---

[1] Aug. *civ.* 6.4 (Varro frg. 5 Cardauns): *sicut prior est . . . pictor quam tabula picta, prior faber quam aedificium, ita priores sunt civitates quam ea quae a civitatibus instituta sunt*; for the sentiment, see Cardauns 1976: 139.

[2] E.g., Usener 1896: 4–5, 75–76; Bertholet 1934: 4–5; West 2007: 134–138. Beard, North, and Price 1998: 2.1–4 offer a brief critique of applying the model too rigidly to Rome.

[3] Aug. *civ.* 4.31 (Varro frg. 18 Cardauns): *dicit etiam [Varro] antiquos Romanos plus annos centum et septuaginta deos sine simulacro coluisse.*

[4] On the scholarly debate see Cardauns 1976: 146–148.

[5] Taylor 1967: 311.

Whatever the cause, the hypothetical development is clear. Varro imagines that there occurred a process in which the essence of being divine grew from a set of amorphous and disembodied abstractions into a pantheon of individualized beings endowed with distinguishing anthropomorphic characteristics. In attempting to reconstruct a narrative of this process I will be making extensive use of an invaluable treatise on the naming of the gods by Hermann Usener (1896), who hypothesizes how, in the creation of divine personality, it is language that plays the most crucial role. Nouns and naming determine how a given god comes to be understood by its worshippers.

Realization of the power that language has in shaping conceptions of the world that exist outside language proves particularly helpful in discussing the special set of indigenous Roman gods normally referred to in our ancient sources as the *indigetes*.[6] These gods are best—and in numerous cases exclusively—known to us from the Christian apologists who detail their activities in order to mock them. Partly as a result of our reliance on these tendentious sources, many scholars believe that the role of the *indigetes* in Roman religious expression was minimal, although even contemporary skeptics such as Seneca acknowledge their relevance to ritual practice.[7] Indeed, a careful consideration of their functions encourages a more general application of a recent reassessment of those *indigetes* associated with marriage ritual: "These archaic names are evidence . . . of the importance which [the pagans] attached to simple but essential human acts, as necessary to the perpetuation of the race as eating and drinking to the individual human beings."[8] The phrasing of this characterization is telling since there did in fact exist divinities whose sphere of influence encompassed the very acts of eating and drinking, acts clearly reflected in the gods' names, *Victa* and *Potua*.

A particularly vivid sense of the ubiquity and day-to-day usefulness of these *indigetes* is conveyed in Augustine's discussion of a Roman wedding night:

> *domum est ducenda quae nubit; adhibetur et deus **Domiducus**; ut in domo sit, adhibetur deus **Domitius**; ut maneat cum viro, additur dea **Manturna**. . . . et certe si adest **Virgin**ensis dea ut **virgin**i zona solvatur, si adest deus **Subigus** ut viro **subig**atur, si . . .* (Aug. *civ.* 6.9)

> The bride must be **led home**, and for this the god **Home-leader** (*Domiducus*) is used; so that she **be** at **home**, there's the god **Home**body (*Domitius*); so that she **stay** with her husband, there's also the goddess **Stay-where-you-are** (*Manturna*); . . . and surely if **Virgin**ensis is there to remove her **virgin**al belt and Missionary (*Subigus*) to put her beneath her husband, and if . . .

[6] Peter 1890–1894 remains essential; recent notable discussions include Scheid 2003 [1999], Perfigli 2004.

[7] Sen. frg. 39 (apud Aug. *civ.* 6.10).

[8] Treggiari 1994: 326.

After the ceremony, the god Domiducus ("Home-leader") leads the bride home, Domitius ("Homebody") and Manturna ("Stay-where-you-are") keep the bride there, Virginiensis unbinds her clothing, Subigus ("Missionary") helps the groom initiate the sex act, and so on (Augustine continues by debating in increasingly intimate details the need for the husband to petition deities such as Prema, "the Presser"). These so-called "specialty gods," for whom Peter lists the names of more than 140—and nobody doubts that there are more—are in fact mostly little more than names to us.[9] This fact, however, is precisely to my point here, especially since our sources indicate that these divinities were not much more than names to most Romans. As the passage from Augustine indicates, these gods have names that are, to use Usener's formulation, "conceptually transparent," so that Domiducus, for example, does literally signify a divine "home-leader."[10] That transparent concept, moreover, "often draws its origin from something whose importance is socially recognized," with examples ranging from Robigo, the god of wheat rust, to Statilinus, who helps the infant to stand erect.[11] The portions marked in bold type in the Augustine quotation above show unequivocally that the Romans were aware of the ability to etymologize these appellations, as Varro (Augustine's source here) demonstrates clearly how name and function correspond for each of these deities.

The notion that a name allows access to the underlying characteristics of the god or person so named appears widespread among traditional societies, and ancient Roman culture provides no exception.[12] In fact, the Roman grammarians saw conceptual transparency as a defining characteristic not only of proper names but of all nouns perceived as originally belonging to the Latin language. Consider Varro's etymology of the Latin word for "name" (*nomen*), which is also the commonest word for "noun":[13]

> res **novae** in usum quom additae erant, quibus ea<s> **novissent, nomina** ponebant. (*ling.* 6.60)

As **new** things (*novae*) had come into use, [the first Latin speakers] would add **names/nouns** (*nomina*) by which they might **know** (*novissent*) them.

Applying Varro's phrasing to the *indigetes*, it is their "name" (the *nomen*) that allows the worshipper to "recognize" (*nosco*) the features of each of the divinities and thereby know when best to address them in prayers and petitions. In the case of *indigetes*, the worshipper was helped in this pursuit of knowledge by the so-called *indigitamenta*. This contested term includes within its semantic

---

[9] Peter 1890–1894: 187–233; compare the list at Radke 1979: 55–363.

[10] Usener 1896: 73–79, a section entitled "Begrifflich Durchsichtige Götternamen."

[11] Perfigli 2004: 25 ("il teonimo trae spesso origine da qualcosa la cui importanza è socialmente riconosciuta"; her entire book treats this issue).

[12] Corbeill 1996: 57–98.

[13] The actual etymology of *nomen* is disputed; see Vaan 2008: 412–413.

range a set of texts, kept in the pontifical books but no longer extant, that provided indications of which of the many gods available are the appropriate ones to call on for a given ritual. In preparation for the wedding night, for example, the priests would have been able to enlighten celebrants on the names of the gods appropriate for the ritual, from Domiducus to Pertunda, and at which point each was to be entreated. These lists also likely included indications of which precise name a petitioner should use in addressing a deity.[14] As Servius notes in commenting on the appearance of the river god Tiber to Aeneas in a dream, petitions directed to Rome's river required that he be addressed in the form *Tiberinus* rather than with the more prosaic address *Tiberis* or the poetic *Thybris*; otherwise, the wrong appellative could render the prayer unsuccessful.[15] The most recent thorough analysis of the content and use of the *indigitamenta* notes that these lists arise from a conception that "praying to a divinity requires a formalism and precision guaranteed by etymological investigation."[16] The *knowing* that one acquires from *nouns* emerges as central to Roman ritual and ritual language.

NAMES AND SEX

We may now move from a glimpse at the way that contemporary Romans understood and used the various names of their gods to a hypothetical reconstruction of the considerations that they took into account in first applying these names. Just as in their government the Romans pursued a generous policy of extending citizenship to annexed peoples, so too did those gods not indigenous to their worship often receive a systematic welcome into the Roman pantheon. Not surprisingly, considering their great number and diverse spheres of unrelated activity, the mix resulted in deities at Rome who exercised functions that were relatively fluid and non-hierarchical. This contrasts, for example, with Greek treatment of gods, where the hierarchy of individual deities and the assignment of specific duties adopted more rigid forms, and included placing the various gods in precise genealogical relationships such as parent and child, or brother and sister.[17] At Rome, there arises as a corollary of this tendency away from genealogical classification the fact that the majority of Latin names tend clearly to reflect function. In addition, those divine names that are likely to be the earliest linguistically often indicate through morphology their status as masculine or feminine (e.g., *Parca* is unambiguously feminine, *Genius* mascu-

---

[14]Serv. *georg.* 1.21 (Varro frg. 87 Cardauns, who offers notes and other testimony); full discussion in Perfigli 2004: 219–265.

[15]Serv. *Aen.* 8.31; Perfigli 2004: 186–188.

[16]Perfigli 2004: 249 ("Pregare la divinità richiede un formalismo ed una precisione che l'indagine etimologica può garantire").

[17]Beard, North, Price 1998: 1.61–72; Rüpke 2007: 16–17.

line). As a result, the process of applying a name entailed not only a consideration of the divinity's sphere of influence but also of the grammatical gender of the signified that would mark that divinity. Needless to say, this decision about gender determines the assignment of the god's biological sex.

Not infrequently in the naming process the gender of a god's name corresponds with the customary sex of the person who performs an analogous function in the human sphere.[18] Clear examples of such correlations include the deities connected with childbirth, all of whom, like the Roman midwife and mother, are female.[19] These include: Nona ("Ninth") and Decima ("Tenth"), who represent the standard number of months of gestation; Lucina, who brings the newborn into the "light" of existence (*lux*); and Rumina, the goddess of suckling (from *rumis*, "nipple").[20] If we can believe Augustine, however, such associations of sex are not always rigidly applied, with the result that a given divine sex may seem to border on the irrational. In continuing his description of the ritual of the wedding night, for example, Augustine sarcastically wonders about why the deity presiding over penetration of the bride by the groom, Pertunda ("Borer"), has the feminine gender:

> *dea Pertunda ibi quid facit? erubescat, eat foras; agat aliquid et maritus. . . . sed forte ideo toleratur quia dea dicitur esse, non deus. nam si masculus crederetur et Pertundus vocaretur, . . . contra eum pro uxoris pudicitia posceret maritus auxilium . . .* (Aug. *civ.* 6.9)

> What's the goddess Pertunda doing there? She should be ashamed and leave the room—the husband has to do something too! . . . But maybe she's tolerated because she is said to be a goddess and not a god. For if she were considered masculine and called "Pertundus" [a name not otherwise attested], the husband would seek help against him in order to defend his wife's chastity.

Augustine's point is not unfamiliar. As is the case with the commonest vulgar Latin words for genitalia, by which the female term is masculine (*cunnus*), and the male feminine (*mentula*), exceptions not infrequently disrupt what otherwise can appear to be a rational and coherent system. One might compare the common nouns *uxor* ("wife") and *soror* ("sister"), two nouns that baffled Roman grammarians: their meaning requires that they be feminine despite the clear masculine morphology (due to the suffix *-or*).

By a logic analogous to that of identifying a specific divine sex with human roles, if the function of the deity is perceived as performing a duty capable of being executed by *either* a man or a woman, then the naming logic permits the

---

[18] Perfigli 2004: 93, 104–106, 119–138, *passim*.

[19] Similarly, the Etruscan deities of love, birth, and education appear as exclusively female in visual representations (Cristofani 1997: 214, 216).

[20] Augustine *civ.* 7.11 attests to a male Ruminus, whose sex prompts satiric rationalizations; cf. Frazer 1929: 367 on "the absurdity of assuming a male deity to give suck."

god to be addressed as a member of either or both sexes. Augustine in fact goes on to acknowledge this tendency by immediately footnoting his discussion of Pertunda with the remark that the male deity Priapus, the ithyphallic god of fertility, joins that goddess in presiding over events. With this addition, the initial sexual penetration of the bride has divine witnesses that are both male and female. And outside the context of marriage ritual, sex differentiation continues to have representational value. Varro provides a clear example of how observation of the natural world determines the assignment of sexual function. In his explanation of the divinity of the earth, he posits a dual force (*geminam vim*), the feminine *Tellus* and the masculine *Tellumo*. For this couple, the male deity produces seed whereas the female receives and nourishes that seed.[21]

Further evidence of the significance of a deity's sex can be found in two areas of Roman civilization in which the issue receives open recognition: the comic stage and cult practice. Names for gods that were unambiguously neuter presented a problem for the Roman petitioner. As we saw in chapter 2, the neuter word for sky, *caelum*, transforms in deified form into the masculine and male noun *Caelus*, presumably in part by association with the male equivalent in the Greek pantheon, Οὐρανός. By contrast Plautus, in bringing on stage in his *Cistellaria* the otherwise unattested deification Auxilium ("Aid"), allows the neuter form to remain and exploits it for apparent comic effect since "the neuter gender is foreign to deity."[22] In several other passages as well the playwright identifies, again presumably for humorous ends, male characters on stage with feminine personifications such as Salus ("Health") or Victoria ("Victory").[23] Firmly male and female gods, with corresponding masculine and feminine names, have become the expectation. This expectation continues in the rules of ritual sacrifice. In contrast with Greek custom, for an animal offering in the Roman world to meet with success, the sex of the victim normally needed to match that of the divine recipient, with a female goddess receiving female offerings, and a male male.[24] This constitutes but one of several ways in which the sacrificant chose an offering in accordance with known characteristics of the god being honored. Dark animals, for example, regularly are offered to chthonic deities, while those having colors reminiscent of flames go to divinities that govern fire.[25] A god's sexual status, then, is tied up with understanding fully that god's

---

[21] Aug. *civ.*7.23 (Varro frg. 265 Cardauns): *una eademque terra habet geminam vim, et masculinam, quod semina producat, et femininam, quod recipiat atque nutriat; inde a vi feminae dictam esse Tellurem, a masculi Tellumonem.* For the antiquity of the pair see Weinstock 1934: 800–802.

[22] Axtell 1907: 71 on Plaut. *Cist.* 149–202; see too Feeney 1998: 90. It is worth nothing, however, that the god gives his name only in the dative (154) and refers to himself in the masculine (153; cf. the neuter at 200), thereby leaving his gender in fact ambiguous.

[23] Axtell 1907: 70.

[24] Arnob. *nat.* 7.19; Capdeville 1971: 302–311.

[25] Wissowa 1912: 412–416.

relevance to ritual observance and not, as in the Greek world, with situating him or her in a mythical genealogy.

So what then does one do when in the position of applying a name to a divinity? There is some intriguing but controversial evidence that the earliest Indo-European divine powers were most naturally categorized in the neuter gender. Analogous figures from Greece and Rome that fall into this class include Hesiod's originary Chaos (τὸ Χάος), and the Latin term *numen*, which is also universally neuter. In fact, even the English word "God" appears to derive from a proto-Germanic neuter noun.[26] When gods do come to be perceived as beings having sex, their names accordingly tend to be assigned to animate genders, namely, the masculine and feminine. Gender imbalance is, however, apparent from the beginning. Among the earliest Indo-European deities known to us, the most important sex was male. For example, most of the goddesses mentioned in Vedic hymns normally have no personality, and possess names that are transparently the feminine form of a male counterpart who is already known.[27] Alternatively, sexed deities may arise directly from powers formerly classed as inanimate and therefore belonging to neither gender. The noun that forms the basis of one of the most well-known Roman divinities, for example, originally seems to have had no sex. Linguists concur with near unanimity that the name of the archetypal female goddess of Roman antiquity, Venus, derived from a noun (*venus*) denoting the abstract qualities of physical charm or grace. That noun, however, initially was classified as neuter and so originally had no gender and, as a result, no sex.[28] Her later, feminine, grammatical gender deserves credit for the female attributes by which the goddess is now recognized. A similar development seems to have occurred for the neuter Latin word for boundary, *termen*, where a change in morphology accompanied its development into the masculine god Terminus.[29] A single divine power could also be associated with both sexes. The Sanskrit stem *dyáu-*, a stem cognate with the names of the hyper-masculine heads of the Greek and Roman pantheon—Zeus and Jupiter—appears capable of having both masculine and feminine manifestations.[30]

DIVINE ANDROGYNY IN ROME

All this about the earliest gods, however, must ultimately remain speculation—albeit learned speculation—and throughout this book my interests have lain

---

[26]Further discussion and examples in Kretschmer 1924: 102–103; West 2007: 120–121, 134–138.

[27]Usener 1896: 29–32, who posits that there were only two, maybe three, original Indo-European goddesses. For Greece, see Loraux 1992.

[28]Vaan 2008: 663.

[29]Wagenvoort 1947: 82–83; on the general principle see Kretschmer 1924: 103–104 and cf. **vermen* > *Verminus* (Radke 1979: 315).

[30]Kretschmer 1924: 113–114.

more in Roman conceptions than in historical validity. So let us contrast these guesses about the origins of the earliest European gods with what the Romans are recorded as saying about their own deities. Amidst a critique of the tendency among the Romans to worship an overly broad range of gods, even to the point of welcoming foreign deities into their pantheon, Augustine seems to attribute to Varro a surprising and, at first glance, glaringly inaccurate assertion:

> *sub hoc tot deorum praesidio, quos numerare quis potest, indigenas et alienigenas, caelites terrestres, infernos marinos, fontanos fluviales et, ut Varro dicit, certos atque incertos, in omnibusque generibus deorum, sicut in animalibus, mares et feminas.* (Aug. *civ.* 3.12)

> Who can count how many gods offered protection among so great a number? [There were] the indigenous and the foreign-born, those of the sky and those of the earth, of below ground and of the sea, living in fountains or in rivers, and, as Varro says, the certain and uncertain, and, among each of these types of gods, just as among animals, there are males and females.

This catalogue, for which the original context unfortunately no longer exists, concludes by alluding to the notion that gods are created in the image of their human worshippers and are therefore imagined to occupy male and female bodies.[31] This assertion stands as a marked parallel to a skeptical tradition in Greek thought, expressed most famously in the caustic remark of Xenophanes that, if animals such as horses or oxen could make representations of their gods, they would make them in the likeness of horses and oxen (as quoted in Clem. Al. *Strom.* 5.110). Varro seems to be acknowledging this tradition by accepting it. Of course divine society operates along the same principles as human—how can it be otherwise? In the face of such satirical remarks, therefore, we must assume that Varro made the claim attributed to him by Augustine based upon what he knew about Roman gods, which is far more than we do. That is, both female and male representations of gods naturally coexisted in every category of divinity known to the Romans.

Other ancient evidence supports the claim preserved in Augustine that each type of Roman god could possess both a female and male manifestation. To begin with, such a claim aligns with those masculine/feminine pairings that structure Indo-European society, such as sun/moon, sky/earth, fire/water, day/night.[32] Remnants of the need for this dichotomy persist in the Roman world. In the second book of Vergil's *Aeneid*, the narrator Aeneas describes himself leaving the ruins of Troy under divine guidance. The passage presented ancient

---

[31] Usener 1896: 33 n. 14 attributes to Varro the entire phrase from *certos* through *feminas*; Cardauns 1976: 63 limits the quotation to *certos atque incertos*. Varronian authorship is in any case not essential to my point. For a possible Greek instance of divine androgyny, see Burton 2005.

[32] Yaguello 1978: 106–109, who discusses deviations from these tidy pairings in the daughter languages.

commentators with a conundrum since the phrase describing this guidance—
"with a god in the lead" (*ducente deo*; 2.632)—is in the masculine, whereas the
immediate context mentions only the assistance of Venus, Aeneas's mother. As
a means of explaining the use of the masculine gender to describe a female god,
Servius refers to a school of thought that accords to the gods the ability to manifest themselves in the guise of one or the other sex.[33] He follows this statement
with evidence from literature and the arts that supports the notion that the one
deity Venus was known to embody elements of both sexes. A more widespread
belief in such divine androgyny is further attested by a fragment of Seneca, who
alludes to contemporaries providing the immortals with "mixed sex and opposite types of bodies" (Sen. frg. 31 [Aug. *civ.* 6.10]). Ancient non-literary
sources provide clear examples of this phenomenon in divine couples such as
Liber and Libera, or in *indigetes* such as the deities of purification, Februus and
Februa. Usener has stressed two special characteristics of how the Romans
named their earliest gods: first, the power ascribed by adjectives such as *liber*
and *februus* is relevant to both the male and female deity and, second, these
adjectives are intended to be names that indicate unambiguously the sphere of
activity for the deity so named.[34] To these points may be added a third, already
illustrated by the Roman deities that preside over birth (see the previous section), namely that it is often possible to demonstrate how the sphere of activity
in any given instance determines the sex of these *indigetes*.[35]

And yet, despite the testimony for divine androgyny found among antiquarians such as Varro, Seneca, and Servius, scholars have largely not followed their
lead and gone on to consider in detail the frequency of male/female pairings.[36]
Addressing this gap by reflecting on those names—often of little-known deities—for which the adjectival forms make the pairings transparent, as well as by
using other evidence for divine pairing, I have collected so far from the disparate sources—Christian, antiquarian, and epigraphic—approximately fifty con-
jectural couples. The sheer accumulation of these similar names, and their presence in such a wide range of sources, attests to my mind that single divine
powers having characteristics of both the male and female sex constituted
an active part of the Roman religious imagination. In appendix 1 I have listed

[33] Serv. *Aen.* 2.632: *secundum eos qui dicunt, utriusque sexus participationem habere numina* (cf.
6.64: ἀρσενοθήλεις *esse omnes deos*); for scholarly discussion see Horsfall 2008: 452–453. Despite
Servius's uncertainty, the masculine form *deus* in fact occurs frequently in prose and poetry to refer
to goddesses: ThLL vol. V, 1 890.16–41 (A. Gudeman).

[34] Usener 1896: 33.

[35] Perfigli 2004: 104–116 (on why goddesses are connected with education) and with other examples *passim*.

[36] Bouché-Leclerq 1871: 45–46 conjectures that the *indigitamenta* organized gods in male/
female pairs (contra Peter 1890–1894: 186), whereas Guittard 2002: 48–52 limits true couples to
Liber/Libera and Ceres/Cerus; Latte 1960: 59–60 is less skeptical. Brelich 1949 accumulates much
important ancillary evidence for these pairs in Rome, while Bertholet 1934: 16–18 offers comparative evidence, particularly from Babylonian religion.

those combinations to which our sources allow access. Many of these cases must remain highly speculative, and the listing aims for comprehensiveness rather than certainty. It is important to note, however, in particular for pairs with early attestation such as Liber/Libera, a significant difference that exists between these Roman deities and similar lists that one could make for the Greek gods. These Roman groupings normally do not denote "couples" in the Greek sense—that is, a wedded pair that may constitute part of a much broader genealogical and mythical cycle. The couple Faunus/Fauna make it particularly clear that the relationship between the sexes was not fixed, since ancient sources describe them variously as spouses, siblings, and father/daughter.[37] In fact, to posit a marriage relationship would violate the well-established Roman naming system for humans, where Faunus/Fauna would most naturally be construed as denoting not spouses, but a blood kinship of brother/sister (or father/daughter).[38] It is hardly surprising that the precise relationships can rarely be pinpointed among the myriad divinities that populate Roman religion. Indeed, given the Roman tendency not to probe too deeply into areas beyond knowing, I doubt that these relationships were even considered relevant. Instead, divine designations play a role that is unrelated to mythical narrative. The similar names of deities confirm that the powers of the male and female are thought to be allied, that each deity in a pair was thought to perform analogous functions.

Pairs of Roman divinities govern areas of the social or natural world in which human endeavor is envisioned to require the cooperation of each sex, either individually or in tandem.[39] This concern for the importance of female and male cooperation in the divine realm finds reflection in the human. A key example may be found in the divine offices that the scholar Festus ranks, perhaps not coincidentally, as the two most important priesthoods of early Rome (Fest. p. 185). The chief priest of Jupiter (*flamen Dialis*), a functionary dating back to Rome's mythical origins, shared with his wife, the *flaminica*, both ceremonial obligations and a set of ritual taboos and restrictions. The necessarily mutual cooperation in maintaining the cult that is implied by these similar rules receives further support from the fact that the *flamen* was expected to abdicate should his wife die. These considerations indicate that "the flaminate should be viewed as a single priesthood that required the services of a married couple"; such a status was also likely enjoyed by another long-established priestly pair, the *rex* and *regina sacrorum*.[40]

[37] Holland 2011: 221–224. I agree (*pace* Holland 2011: 217 n. 24) with Wissowa 1912: 26–27 that the terms *pater/mater* do not refer in cult practice to familial relationships among the gods.

[38] Holland 2011, who discusses how gendered names of gods could determine perceptions of "some divine relationships in familial terms" (213).

[39] Bayet 1957: 112.

[40] Schultz 2006: 80–81 (quotation from 81); Delcourt 1966: 69–70 connects the flaminate directly with androgynous divine power.

Further indications of a divine androgynous imagination may be found among classes of deities that arose later than the *indigetes* and other early gods, and where semantically related forms do not allow so readily the identification of divine couples. Anna Clark has recently applied the term "divine qualities" to deified abstract ideas such as Concordia ("Civic Harmony") and Felicitas ("Prosperity"). These qualities, realized as gods, receive temples and cult from the earliest historical periods. Among these divine qualities, the feminine sex and gender dominates, due to the simple fact that abstract nouns tend to be feminine in Latin. Nevertheless, despite the strong feminine bias among these abstractions, a reading through Clark's testimonia reveals an urge to couple them into divine heterosexual pairs, as can be seen in examples such as the joint shrines to masculine Honos and feminine Virtus ("High Rank" and "Courage") or the paired statues on the Capitoline of Bona Fortuna and Bonus Eventus ("Good Luck" and "Good Result") or appearances of the feminine abstraction Fides alongside the masculine Dius Fidius.[41] Finally, we find these pairs even among those deities that we more commonly associate with the traditional Roman pantheon. In addition to the example mentioned earlier, by which the feminine goddess of the Earth, Tellus, has a male consort in the vegetation god Tellumo, Ceres too, the goddess of grain, coexists with a male version, Cerus, who is a demonstrably old Italic god of agriculture.[42]

Rather than continue with lists, we can point toward a conclusion by considering the sexual status of one particular god. That god is Pales, the divinity who presides over the feeding and care of herds. Scholars, modern and ancient alike, consider Pales one of the oldest Roman gods, as indicated in part by the fact that the festival for Pales, the Parilia, is celebrated on April 21, the anniversary of Rome's founding. This deity comes down in the ancient sources as having both a male and female manifestation, and modern scholars have debated which sex fits the evidence best or whether it is necessary to recognize here a deity possessing both sexes simultaneously. Although the attestation of a feminine form of Pales dominates a literary tradition that dates back to Varro's Menippean satires and Vergil's *Georgics*, evidence of a male manifestation has a good claim to derive from ancient festal calendars and perhaps even to be the single original form.[43] To offer a new perspective on this tangled issue, let us

---

[41] Honos and Virtus: Bieber 1945: 25–34; Pease 1955: 694–695 lists the textual evidence. Honos is a very early deity (CIL I².31, with Cic. *leg.* 2.58), to whom female victims can be offered despite his masculine gender (CIL 6.2044 I 5). Bona Fortuna and Bonus Eventus: Plin. *nat.* 36.23; Fides/Dius Fidius: Clark 2007: 64. Bonfante 1981 discusses "the prominence Etruscans gave to couples in their art" (334), both divine and human, and the possible influence on Roman conceptions (328–329); see further Cristofani 1993: 18–20.

[42] Ceres/Cerus: Wissowa 1912: 192 n. 9.

[43] Wissowa 1916–1924b: 1277–1278; further evidence at Radke 1979: 243. Dumézil has provided different arguments for considering the male Pales an Etruscan borrowing (e.g., 1956a: 239–240; 1962; summation at 1970: 380–385). For recent bibliography see Prescendi 2002–2010.

return to names and naming and take a closer look at the grammatical morphology of the word *Pales*. Like the majority of those Latin nouns having ambiguous gender—close parallels have been discussed above, such as *pulvis, finis, cinis*—the name *Pales* is declined in the third declension. As is well known, nouns of the second declension with the nominative ending *-us* are normally masculine, while those of the first, with nominative endings in *-a*, are typically feminine. A speaker may, however, construct counterparts of the opposing gender for either class of words by substituting the endings of the contrasting declension: by this practice a male friend, *amicus*, corresponds to *amica*, a female friend, or the sister of Clodius is designated as Clodia. Such a corresponding change in morphology is not possible for a third-declension noun like *Pales*. What then happens if one wishes to change the gender of the name *Pales*, and thereby the sex of the god to whom that name corresponds? It is, I think, significant that the Roman worshipper feels no qualms about using the one morphological form to signify both sexes. As a result, we are led to believe—and grammarians such as Varro apparently *do* believe—that in the case of Pales, just as the two genders coexist in the same word, so too do the two sexes coexist within the single sphere covered by the deity. Although I believe that we can best resolve the ambiguity of the ancient evidence if we accept that Pales was originally androgynous, it is unnecessary to my argument that such a status in fact be historically accurate. The key point is that the clear willingness of independent sources from antiquity to be content with Pales's varying gender— whether in the early stages of the god's development or as a later rationalization—coincides with the general openness that the Romans felt toward divine androgyny.[44]

WHY TWO GODS?

Discussion has reached the point where I must acknowledge the imprecision of the English terms that I have been using to describe the phenomenon under investigation. The adjective "androgynous" or periphrases such as "of dual sex" have been employed to describe simultaneous access to two sexes, regardless of whether those sexes are encompassed by one lexical form (e.g., *Pales*) or by two related but distinct names (e.g., *Februus/Februa*). Two principles justify recognizing analogous processes at work in these two apparently diverse means of expression. First, for the majority of cases of what I call divine androgyny, personification is limited in our sources solely to the indication of a being's gender/

---

[44]For single authors mentioning both sexes, see Varro *Men.* 506 (Gell. 13.23.4; feminine) vs. Varro frg. XIVd Cardauns (Serv. *georg.* 3.1; masculine); Arnob. *nat.* 3.40. For mentions of "Pales" in the plural without details of sex, see Varro *rust.* 2.5.1; Fast. ann. Num. Antiat. Quint. 7. On the perplexing *Fortuna barbata / muliebris* see Champeaux 1982: 293–294.

sex, with additional information about the god rarely available. For example, pairs such as Statanus and Statina, the gods presiding over a child's first attempts to stand, differ principally in the termination that establishes each divinity's sex and gender; beyond this termination we have no reason to suppose that the duties or function or personalities of these two deities differ in any way. As a result, there is no intrinsic difference between dual names such as this and single names such as Pales, for whom masculine and feminine manifestations are treated in the sources as separate entities. Second, I see the sexuality to which these divine powers have access as analogous to the varying grammatical gender of the nouns discussed in chapters 1 and 2: just as poetic context determines whether *pulvis*, for example, is masculine or feminine in a given instance—but never both simultaneously—so too does it seem that the appropriate sex of an androgynous deity is driven by context and that therefore "androgyny" means a choice of one sex or the other, and not the simultaneous possession of both. If we accept these premises about the nature of divine androgyny at Rome, it is now time to attempt to reconstruct what factors help give rise to an androgynous deity such as Pales, or to the related type of androgyny exhibited by other divine pairs.

Antiquity had no shortage of philosophical speculation regarding whether the gods had sexual characteristics and, if so, the possible ways in which these sexual characteristics manifested themselves. Tommasi Moreschini has traced this discourse from the early Stoics on through a blossoming in late-antique Christian texts, and she identifies the belief in divine androgyny as driven by two opposing but reconcilable considerations, of which one makes the divine more accessible to human beings, while the second marks it as distinct from them. In the first case, the possession of sexual identity eliminates one of the many characteristics that otherwise divide gods from human beings—in other words, by giving gods sex, they become more identifiable and therefore more sympathetic to human worshippers. The second consideration holds that, by exhibiting both male and female traits together, divine beings can be seen to transcend human boundaries, since the possession of both sexes offers them a complete version of divine perfection.[45] The tradition of divine androgyny emerges perhaps most famously in certain Gnostic speculations of early Christianity, according to which the Judaeo-Christian creator in the book of *Genesis* must be androgynous since Adam's original body, created in "His" image, produced the woman Eve.[46]

I have been providing throughout this chapter examples of philosophical and theological speculations from outside pre-Christian Rome simply to provide parallels, and to show that the situation suggested above for early Rome does not break radically from currents of ancient thought found in areas rang-

---

[45] Tommasi Moreschini 1998 and 2001.
[46] Pagels 1978: 7–8; 1979: 48–69.

ing from Proto-Indo-European religion to Hellenistic Stoicism to early Christianity. I do not mean to imply, however, that these debates have direct causal connections with the archaic Roman naming practices that I have been outlining. The Roman practices clearly arose out of different and independent considerations. Rather, it seems more likely that the ubiquitous naming practices that saw in grammatical gender a real-world sexual significance helped provide a cultural space in Roman society for these kinds of speculation to develop and find application. This notion of "cultural space," of adapting inherited ideas to a Roman context, can be illustrated for divine sex by a note in Servius's commentary on the *Aeneid*. The Stoics, as is well known, contended that a single divine force rules the universe and that, being incorporeal, it does not and cannot have sexual characteristics.[47] Servius is well aware of this tenet, and in fact he constitutes a not negligible source for reconstructing ancient Stoic theology. Yet despite his awareness of the exclusively numinal nature of the Stoic god, he notes that when human beings conceive of divinity in poetry, the gods, as made manifest in mind, come to possess not just one, but two sexes.[48] In fact, in a paradox that fits his ineffable subject matter, Servius asserts that it is the very fact of their inherent incorporeality that allows the gods to adopt whichever sex befits a particular circumstance:

> *numina utriusque sexus videntur ideo, quia incorporea sunt et quod volunt adsumunt corpus.* (Serv. *Aen.* 7.498)

> Divine powers are seen to be of each sex since they are incorporeal and adopt whatever physique they wish.

This willful donning of sexual identity by the gods resembles the phenomenon discussed in the previous chapters, when archaic Latin speakers and learned poets adopt the grammatical genders deemed appropriate to a particular rhetorical or poetic context. What is at work in Servius is yet another example of a Roman author shaping inherited Greek ideas to fit a new religious context. The necessarily incorporeal god of the Stoics becomes unexpectedly compatible with the multiple, embodied, and sexual gods of the Roman pantheon.

Servius makes explicit elsewhere another element of the divine that develops further the considerations underlying what sex a worshiper should give a god.[49] The more prominent sex adopted, he writes, depends upon which divine nature is required in any given instance:

---

[47] See, for example, Serv. *georg.* 1.5 (*Stoici dicunt non esse nisi unum deum*), *Aen.* 7.146 (*dii . . . incorporei sunt*). Setaioli 2004 and 2008 thoroughly traces the use of Stoic ideas in the Servian tradition.

[48] Tommasi Moreschini 1998 and 2001 outlines this development; for Rome, see Courtney 1993: 66–68 (on Valerius Soranus frg. 2 Blänsdorf). For similar opinions among non-Stoics see Pease 1955: 448, 457.

[49] Setaioli 2004: 11.

sciendum Stoicos dicere unum esse deum cui nomina variantur pro actibus et officiis.
unde etiam duplicis sexus numina esse dicuntur, ut cum in actu sunt, mares sint; femi-
nae, cum patiendi habent naturam. (Serv. *Aen.* 4.638)

It should be acknowledged that the Stoics say that there is one deity to whom various
names are given depending upon its actions and its sphere of duties. As a result, divinities are even said to possess both sexes, so that they are male when in action (*in
actu*) and female when passive (*cum patiendi habent naturam*).

Servius follows this statement of philosophical justification with concrete examples of gods from Roman cult such as Jupiter "the helper" (*Iuppiter iuvans
pater*) and Liber "the liberator" (*Liber a libertate*)—examples, that is, of "active"
roles being attributed to male gods.[50] This dichotomy of active versus passive
spheres, with its attendant identification of activity with the male and passivity
with the female, also appears in Varro, who orders the natural world into analogous sexual categories. In his discussion of sky and earth, he observes that since
the sky acts (*faciat*), it possesses a masculine force, whereas the acted-upon
earth (*patiatur*) necessarily possesses feminine characteristics.[51] These masculine and feminine forces correspond, inevitably, with the male god of sky and
the female god of earth.[52] According to Augustine, our source for this statement, Varro continues from this premise to conjecture that all male divinities
arise from the sky and all female from the earth—as a result, the entire Roman
pantheon divides into an active, male half and a passive, female half. I shall return in my closing remarks to this distinction between active and passive and
to its application as an organizing principle for making sense of the world on
the basis of sex-specific roles.

The preceding chapters can help to clarify more fully the Roman cultural
space into which this kind of philosophical speculation fits, as well as to give
indications of how that space could change over time. The androgynous nouns
of chapters 1 and 2 are imagined in our sources as existing in the same nebulous
prehistory that contains androgynous gods. If we recognize that these two phenomena—one grammatical and one theological—arise from the same cultural
and linguistic context, then further connections can be made, including connections with literature. As noted in chapter 2, an observable phenomenon

---

[50] Pellizzari 2003: 149 discusses Servius's use of Stoicism to justify Roman polytheism.

[51] Aug. *civ.* 7.28 (Varro frg. 263 Cardauns): *ducitur enim [Varro] quadam ratione verisimili, caelum esse quod faciat, terram quae patiatur, et ideo illi masculinam vim tribuit, huic femininam.* Note
that Augustine uses the expected neuter gender (*quod*) for "sky" here; Varro uses both neuter and
masculine forms to refer to the god without apparent distinction (ThLL *Onomasticon* vol. II 26.59–
63 and 66–77 [W. Otto]). On the active/passive division see further Loraux 1992: 14–15, Tommasi
Moreschini 2001: 12–13.

[52] See the contrast at Macr. *Sat.* 1.17.53 between male and hence "hot" Sun (*Sol*) and female,
"moist" Moon (*Luna*). Tommasi Moreschini 2001: 18–23 discusses the development of sex-based
dichotomies in late-antique texts.

brings to an end the attestation of nouns of indiscriminate gender: they more or less cease to have creative poetic resonance with Vergil and his poetry. The dozens of later grammarians who devote the several centuries following Vergil's death to the cataloguing of these nouns represent gender change as belonging to a hallowed and irretrievable past state of the language. In the prose and poetic texts composed after Vergil, by contrast, notions of masculine and feminine come to acquire fixed and irrevocable boundaries, the violation of which is an "error," the Latin terms for which (*culpa, vitium*) can as easily encompass moral faults as grammatical blunders.[53]

A similar development can be observed concerning the perception of androgynous gods. The debate about androgynous deities as part of the lived world that I have been describing is absent from the elite realm of Latin literature, as in fact is any straightforward treatment of Italic religion and cult practice.[54] It is rare to discover in the Hellenized world of Roman literature any traces of the divine androgyny that the Romans communicated with on a daily basis—and, during periods of transition such as the wedding night described by Augustine, even on a minute-by-minute basis.[55] I know of only one example in which a classical poet alludes to native Roman androgyny, and this example in fact provides an explanation for its rarity elsewhere.[56] In one of his lyric poems, Horace includes among a litany of well-known divine abstractions the masculine personification of "Pudor"—a divine manifestation of "Shame" that is otherwise unattested in this gender.[57] Horace has manufactured this god, apparently, because the expected and well-attested female goddess Pudicitia will not fit the meter of this hymn, the *Carmen Saeculare*:

> *iam Fides et Pax et Honos **Pudorque***
> *priscus et neglecta redire Virtus*
>   *audet adparetque beata pleno*
>   *Copia cornu.* (Hor. *carm. saec.* 57–60)

> Now Good Faith, Peace, Honor, and **Shame**
> of old, along with neglected Virtue, all dare
>   to return, and Plenty appears, blessed
>   with full fruits.

---

[53] Varro *ling.* 8.8 (*in culpa*; see ThLL vol. IV 1310.5–15 [W. Schwering]), with Lomanto 1998: 102; Fest. p. 286 (*vitium*).

[54] Axtell 1907: 69–86 treats abstract deities in Roman literature, Fantham 2009 rustic Italic deities.

[55] To cite another instance: contrast the scores of examples of Tutela in inscriptions with her one possible appearance in literature at Petron. 57.2 (Axtell 1907: 40–43; Wissowa 1916–1924e).

[56] Hor. *serm.* 2.6.20 provides the unparalleled *Matutinus* as an epithet of Janus; it is unclear whether a (fabricated?) connection with Matuta is intended (Radke 1979: 209).

[57] Feeney 1998: 89; cf. Ov. *ars* 1.607–608 (*fuge rustice . . . / Pudor*).

Metrical necessity may indeed prompt the substitution of Pudor for Pudicitia here, but an alternative explanation frees the careful craftsman Horace from the charge of creating a deity out of whole cloth simply for the sake of meter. It is perhaps not coincidental that this unique exchange of deities occurs in a poem that is similarly unique in Horace's corpus. The *Carmen Saeculare* was a hymn written for performance at a public festival in 17 BC before a group of contemporary Romans.[58] I suggest that in this Roman ritual context, removed from some of the pressures of the Greek literary tradition, divine androgyny would not be quite so jarring.

CHANGING GODS OUTSIDE OF ROME

This passage from the *Carmen Saeculare* may present a paradoxically rare instance of a Roman poet preserving *Romanitas*. Elsewhere, the adoption of Greek models within the realm of elite Roman literature tends to suppress any reference to the indigenous gods of Italy. This type of cultural transformation has intriguing parallels outside the Roman world. For instance, Pallottino has argued that the Etruscans, a non-Indo-European people, originally possessed only a vague notion about the number and sex of their gods. It has been suggested that this inherent uncertainty is informed by the fact that Etruscan divinities correspond to the life cycles of human beings, animals, and plants and that, as a result of this varied activity, the divine in Etruria possesses a conceptual mobility that can be adapted to suit the circumstances at hand.[59] Once contact with the Greek East had been made, however, modifications to this fluidity became so deep and widespread as to conform to a more recognizably Greek mode of divine organization:

> The influence exerted by Greece was too powerful and too ancient in character . . . not to have left a considerable mark upon Etruscan religious attitudes and manifestations. This is particularly evident in the Etruscan conception of both the individuality and the form of the divine.[60]

The paradigm of Greek anthropomorphism exerted its domination in two distinct areas. First, the seemingly self-consistent powers and attributes of a given Greek god could cause previously unassociated divine powers among the Etruscans to coalesce into one deity. Second, during the process of adaptation

---

[58] See further the discussion of Feeney 1998: 32–38 concerning how other aspects of the poem allude to Roman ritual. Contrast Axtell 1907: 77 on Horace's "mixing of fact and fancy." For a historical example of sexes interchanging, see Suet. *Vit.* 15.4 (Vitellius accepts the cognomen *Concordia*).

[59] Torelli 1986: 198, 207; cf. Pfiffig 1975: 225.

[60] Pallottino 1955: 140.

Greek practice further asserted itself by causing this newly created conception of what had been previously incorporeal divine forces to receive a distinct sex. Pallottino cites as one example Veltha/Veltune/Voltumna, "a god with strange and contrasting attributes, represented at times as a maleficent monster, at others as a vegetation god of uncertain sex, or even as a mighty war god. By a typical process, this local earth spirit . . . is individualized and transformed into a superior divinity, the national god *par excellence*."[61] As ever, systematization creates rigid boundaries in areas where there had previously been adaptability and the potential for change.

Pallottino does not provide in his own discussion an example of a god changing its sex, but a clear case seems to exist for the chief god of war in the Etruscan pantheon, Laran. The proper name *Laran* contains two parts. The first, *lar-*, indicates that the sphere of this deity's duties is war (cf. the Latin *Lars militaris*: Mart. Cap. 1.46, 48), while the suffix *-an* has typically been taken to denote an actor or director within the sphere indicated by the first half of the noun. As a result, *Laran* would mean something like "warrior" or "military leader." In apparent contrast with this etymology, Cristofani has pointed out that all linguistic evidence indicates that the *-an* suffix marks in Etruscan the feminine grammatical gender. Nevertheless, when the Etruscans begin the practice of representing deities visually in the fifth century BC, Greek conventions come to influence native linguistic practice. Once images labeled as Laran began to appear on bronze mirrors, the divinity acquires unambiguous masculine features and associated attributes in apparent imitation of the male Greek god Ares.[62] This is only the most vivid among several examples in which the grammatical gender of an Etruscan divine manifestation seems to have changed to adapt to the more rigid sexual category of its Greek counterpart.[63] Negative evidence also supports this type of sexual transformation. When no clear Greek analog existed for an Etruscan deity, that god could appear on some occasions as female and on others as male. One clear instance is provided by Thalna. This deity is depicted as participating in a wide range of activities; among these, Thalna assists at births in the guise of both sexes.[64] As we conjectured above about Roman practice, it is reasonable to see in Thalna an example of divine sex adapting to the sex of the human being at whose behest that particular god has been summoned.

[61] Pallottino 1955: 141.

[62] For the evidence, see de Grummond 2006: 138–140.

[63] Cristofani 1997: 211, and for visual evidence Simon 1984. Further examples, of varying certainty: Pfiffig 1975: 224–230 (dubious); de Grummond 1991: 14 and fig. 6 (Artumes) and 16 (Lasa); Cristofani 1993 *passim* and 1997: 213 (gods in *-ns*); Rix 1998: 213 n. 12; de Grummond 2006: 148–149 (Cilens?), 157–159 (Alpan, Adhvizr, Leinth, Evan); Simon 2006: 51 with fig. IV.9 (a female Teiresias). Despite Latin evidence (see Hutchinson 2006: 86, 93), the androgynous character of Voltumna in Etruria has been discredited (Cristofani 1997: 209).

[64] Bonfante 1997: 60, with plates 20a–20b; de Grummond 2006: 152–155.

Outside the Greek and Roman tradition, scholars of the religions of ancient Israel have recently argued for a similar type of cultural amnesia in the development of gendered divinities in the ancient Near East. Textual and archaeological evidence indicates that, as the monotheistic belief in a single, male God became widely accepted, Yahweh lost as a consequence his long-standing consort, the Canaanite goddess Asherah.[65] As at Rome, a deity that once represented both the sexes of its human worshippers develops over time into a god with sex-specific traits. In the case of ancient Israel, those traits become identified as masculine and associated with a single, male God.

CHANGING GODS IN ROME I: GENIUS / IUNO

These parallels from Etruria and the ancient Near East provide a perspective from which to consider in greater detail the shifting genders of Roman deities. In her diachronic analysis of the festival of the Parilia, Beard has suggested ways in which ancient speculation about the Roman calendar contributes to a continual redefinition of this festival: as time progresses, the significance ascribed to a particular celebration shifts in order to meet the demands of new social and political contexts.[66] I shall attempt here to trace in an analogous fashion the changing attitudes toward the sexual status of two sets of well-known deities, the pairs Genius/Iuno and Liber/Libera. Each god is well known from both literary and visual traditions, but their complicated biographies have been the subject of inconclusive scholarly debate. I do not, of course, intend in the following two sections to resolve the many difficulties informing this debate. It is possible, however, in light of the context provided by the parallels with Beard's work, to write these biographies so that they correspond with the development of attitudes toward grammatical gender and its use by poets and members of Roman cult.

Several ancient sources derive the name "Genius" from the related verbs *gignere* or *genere* ("to procreate").[67] This etymology recalls those suggested by the ancient grammarians for the Latin noun that describes grammatical gender, *genus*, a noun they traditionally trace to a third synonymous verb, *generare*.[68] Modern scholars agree with these ancient assessments of the origins of the word *genius*, but they commonly divide into two opposing camps concerning whether to construe the inherent verbal notion of "generation" in an active or in a passive sense. One side follows Varro in seeing the god as embodying an active and universal generative force that is "set in charge, with the power of

---

[65] Dever 2005, esp. 196–208, surveys the evidence.

[66] Beard 1987.

[67] Maltby 1991: 256.

[68] *Genius* from *gignere/genere*: ThLL vol. VI, 2 1826.59–65 (V. Bulhart); *genus* from *generare*: ThLL vol. VI, 2 1885.28–35 (O. Hey).

begetting all things" (apud Aug. *civ.* 7.13: "*deus . . . qui praepositus est ac vim habet omnium rerum gignendarum*").[69] In the ancient conceptions of this interpretation, the Genius seems originally to have controlled both male and female procreation equally.[70] The second popular scholarly opinion interprets the root verb *gignere/genere* in a passive sense. By this view, the Genius embodies not active procreative force, but the divine qualities that are "generated within" each human being at birth. This is the set of qualities that allows the antiquarian Censorinus to characterize the Genius as "never straying far, our companion from the time it receives us from the mother's womb to the last day of our life."[71] Most modern scholars follow this explanation, and conceive of the Genius as originally a kind of personal protector, a role that comes to survive in early Christianity in the form of the guardian angel.[72]

The notion of the Genius as a protective spirit particular to an individual also accords with the earliest textual references in the comedies of Plautus. Although all the Plautine uses refer to the Genius of a male character, lexicographical data would suggest that the province of the Genius originally included females as well, both divine and mortal.[73] Furthermore, an event dated to within a generation of the playwright's death seems to concur with these ancient sources in the belief that the divinity governs both sexes from the earliest periods. Cicero records an incident from near the end of the life of Tiberius Sempronius Gracchus, father of the tribunes Tiberius and Gaius Gracchus. Having discovered in his home two snakes, a male and a female, Gracchus consulted the priestly authorities concerning the meaning of this potentially portentous event and was told that if he released the male snake, his wife Cornelia would die, if the female, then he would himself die. Gracchus released the female snake in order to save his wife.[74] Although none of the sources recording this anecdote explicitly identifies these snakes with the Genii of Tiberius and Cornelia, four observations strongly support such a connection. First, echoing most characterizations of the Genius, such as the passage from Censorinus quoted above, the snake has a span of existence in this story that is imagined to match the lifetime of the human to which it corresponds. Second, Censorinus

[69] Varro refers here to the *Genius populi Romani* (Cardauns 1976: 229); see too Varro's contemporary Aufustius apud Paul. Fest. p. 94–95: *ex quo homines gignuntur*; for modern agreement see, e.g., Wissowa 1912: 175, Radke 1979: 138, with bibliographies.

[70] In addition to the passages already cited see, e.g., Laber. *mim.* 54 (Non. p. 119.26–27); Serv. Auct. *Aen.* 12.538. Late sources attest without comment to a neuter *genium* (Char. *gramm.* 33.15–16B, Exc. Bob. *gramm.* I 554.15; cf. Aug. *serm.* 62.6).

[71] Cens. 3.5: *Genius autem ita nobis adsiduus observator adpositus est, ut ne puncto quidem temporis longius abscedat, sed ab utero matris acceptos ad extremum vitae diem comitetur.* Schilling 1979: 417–422 thoroughly discusses the earliest manifestation of the Genius; see too Dumézil 1970: 357–359, Rives 1992: 38–39.

[72] Schilling 1979: 419–420 (guardian angels: 431–441); Rives 1992: 40–42.

[73] ThLL vol. VI, 2 1828.16–32, 1834.72–80 (V. Bulhart); see too Brelich 1949: 13–16.

[74] Cic. *div.* 1.36 (cf. 2.62, Val. Max. 4.6.1); similar account in Plin. *nat.* 7.122.

preserves the opinion that homes of married couples house two Genii—presumably one each for husband and wife (Cens. 3.3)—and this belief accords with the portion of Roman marriage ritual by which the new couple addresses their newly paired Genii (Arnob. 2.67: *cum in matrimonia convenitis, . . . maritorum genios advocatis*). Third, as documented in the visual material surviving from Pompeii, representations of paired snakes in domestic contexts seem to refer to the Genii of the home's master and mistress. Fourth and finally, two sources for the story of Gracchus and Cornelia note that the snakes emerged from the couple's marriage bed, the Latin term for which—*genialis torus*—establishes an explicit etymological connection with the man's and woman's protective Genii (Vir. Ill. 57.4; cf. Plut. *TG* 1.2: ἐπὶ τῆς κλίνης).[75]

If we grant with the majority of scholars that the Genius originally acted as a tutelary deity for both sexes, then a later restriction that develops concerning its domain of influence returns us to the theme of this book. Around the time of the Augustan age the single deity splits along lines of sex, as the female-specific *iuno* begins to appear in texts and visual material, apparently serving "as the functional equivalent of the *genius* of a man."[76] This equivalence appears most clearly in inscriptions such as the following dedication: "to the Genius of Valerius . . . and the Iuno of Valeria . . . and to the Genius of his son . . . and the Iuno of his daughter" (CIL 5.7237).[77] Similarly, a bronze statuette from late second- to early third-century Gaul depicts a female and male having the typical pose and attributes of the male Genius, accompanied by the prominent label *IUNO ET GENIUS*.[78] Genesis amnesia soon sets in, however, as the originally unitary nature of the Genius, equally applicable to each sex, is forgotten. By the middle of the first century AD the split of the duties of the Genius into male and female manifestations comes to be attributed to that familiar repository of wisdom on sex and gender, the nameless and timeless "ancestors" (*maiores*). Seneca records as a given of Roman cult that the ancestors "have given to each individual a Juno and Genius" to act as each person's protective deity.[79] A similar conception may explain the late appearance of the normally masculine spirits of the dead—*di Manes*—in the feminine (see the appendix to this chapter, s.v.). The division of labor that assigns gods according to the sex of worshippers has become the accepted norm.

An analogous, if less spectacular, split seems to occur in the domain of the *Genius loci*. Scholars agree that this aspect of the Genius, which inhabits places

---

[75] Wissowa 1912: 176–177; for the term *genialis* see Dumézil 1970: 359–360.

[76] Rives 1992: 34, with 37–38; Rives attributes the creation of the Iuno to the rise of elite marriage *sine manu*. While plausible, the theory has no bearing on my own discussion.

[77] Several additional examples in ThLL vol. VI, 2 1828.9–16 (V. Bulhart); Rives 1992: 34 mentions "some fifty" epigraphic dedications to a woman's Iuno.

[78] Romeo 1997: 8.2.372, with text at 8.1.601 #11. This is the only example known to me of a naked male Genius.

[79] Sen. *ep.* 110.1: *[maiores nostri] singulis . . . et Genium et Iunonem dederunt.*

of importance to human beings, arose by extension from the original function of the Genius as a spirit protecting individual men and women.[80] With time, however, our sources indicate that this single deity of protection also develops the tendency to divide into a male and female aspect. Epigraphic sources often describe the Genius of a given place as sharing the company of a feminine and female counterpart named Tutela ("Protectress"); it would appear that the two are "frequently named together to give a place full protection."[81] The importance of Tutela ultimately grows so great that by the end of the fourth century Saint Jerome records that she is present throughout the homes and neighborhoods of Rome (*in Is.* 16.57.7). In the visual evidence, we also find apotropaic snakes appearing in pairs both in house shrines and at street crossings, with each snake bearing attributes that seem intended to signify separate sexes.[82]

This apparent move to split the *Genius loci* into a masculine Genius and feminine Tutela in order that it embody separately the qualities of each sex stands in contrast with a much-discussed inscription concerning a particular *Genius loci*, that of the Roman state. The text is preserved in the commentary tradition of Vergil's *Aeneid*:

> *et in Capitolio fuit clipeus consecratus, cui inscriptum erat "genio urbis Romae, sive mas sive femina [est]."* (Serv. Auct. *Aen.* 2.351)

> There was also dedicated on the Capitoline hill a shield bearing the inscription "To the Genius of the city of Rome, whether it is male or female."[83]

Although the commentator does not assign a date to this dedication, he quotes it after a discussion of the sacred books of pontifical law and in the unquestionably antiquarian context of the debate over the original name of the city of Rome. It is likely then that this dedication reflects an early notion that the Genius of Rome, like the Genius of each individual person, originated in a form representing both men and women and hence contained both a female and male aspect.[84] After all, as we have seen in chapter 1, the masculine form of the noun *Genius* would normally not cause the dedicatee of this shield to pause over the god's biological sex unless there existed a well-known tradition concerning the androgynous character of the Genius. This instance of androgyny, like the two sexes inherent in the single divine name "Pales," confirms that the influence of the Genius over the external world originally encompassed the

---

[80] See, e.g., Wissowa 1912: 177–180; Schilling 1979: 428–431; for abundant attestation of the *Genius loci*, see ThLL vol. VI, 2 1835.1–40 (V. Bulhart).

[81] Axtell 1907: 40–43, with quotation from 41.

[82] Boyce 1942 surveys the inconclusive literary and archaeological evidence and attributes paired snakes to a desire for symmetry. Orr 1978: 1572–1575 argues forcefully for identifying the snake as an aspect of the Genius; contra Fröhlich 1991: 56–61.

[83] For formulas of the type *sive deus sive dea* see Guittard 2002.

[84] See CIL 8.21567 (*Genio summ[o] Thasuni et de/o sive deae [nu]/mini sanc[to]*; AD 174) with Guittard 2002: 28.

entire range of human sexual categories.[85] As time goes on, however, the duties of the god are split in order to represent the male and female categories separately.

CHANGING GODS IN ROME II: LIBER/LIBERA

Genius, a single god that originally represented domains of both the male and female, provides one possible narrative by which the perceived sex of a god changed as a result of external pressure from cultural developments in Rome. For my second example I turn to two gods that, by contrast, were originally perceived as acting in consort: Liber and Libera, a pair of deities representing, respectively, the male and female procreative capacities. Over the course of time, however, as Liber's areas of influence become more fully syncretized with those of the Greek god Dionysus, the divine pair no longer shared functions. Instead, the female Libera either came to take on a role in some way subordinate to that of her former equal or she was ignored altogether.

Scholars in antiquity identified the proper name "Liber" with the homonymous Latin adjective meaning "free," thereby allowing them to characterize the god as having the power to "free" human beings from a variety of concerns, ranging from entrapment of the spirit to political oppression.[86] Accepting this ancient association with liberation, many modern scholars have interpreted the Latin name as a calque that derived from epithets associated with the Greek god Dionysus's role as "Releaser" or "Liberator" (e.g., Λύσιος, Ἐλευθέριος). This alleged borrowing from Hellenic precedent has provided evidence for Liber being understood as simply a Roman version of the earlier Greek god.[87] Although the idea of a wholesale borrowing of Greek Dionysus in the form of Italic Liber is not now generally accepted, it is significant to note that even if such a transfer were true, and one could indeed trace Liber's original essence back to Dionysus, we still find innovation among the Romans, as they feel compelled to create a consort for the god, one who possesses an equal level of divinity. Following the pattern discussed earlier in this chapter, that consort, Libera, would imply by her name a range of influence analogous to Liber's and thereby be considered a "new" goddess, one with no correlate in the Greek world.[88]

---

[85] I cannot agree with the contention of Varner 2008: 189 that a late third-century coin of Gallienus as Genius depicts a "deliberate ambivalence of gender." Varner's claim that a crown of towers signifies female divinity can be opposed to the presence of this same attribute in other depictions of Genius; see Romeo 1997: 8.1, nos. 23–25, 28b, etc. I would rather agree with Bastien that the feminizing of Gallienus's features represents a divine trait (1994: 1.135–137).

[86] Full testimony at Maltby 1991: 337.

[87] Wissowa 1916–1924a: 2021–2022; the evidence is fully assessed by Bruhl 1953: 13–29.

[88] Reitzenstein 1893: 216 suggests as an origin for the term *Libera* the alleged Syracusan cult of

There do, though, exist positive indications for considering the Liber/Libera pair as originally having a cult and range of functions independent from those of Dionysus. Six of the Roman calendars extant from antiquity mark the festival for Liber and Libera, the Liberalia, on March 17, a holiday that in the late Republican period seems to have included games.[89] Three facts suggest a strongly Roman character to the festival. First, March 17 also marks a celebration of Mars, the Agonium Martiale, and the priestly books note the importance of a sacrifice to Mars on this day; yet three of the ancient calendars nevertheless refer exclusively to the festival of the Liberalia, with two others referring jointly to the Liberalia and Agonium and a sixth specifying that the day provides honors "for Liber [and] Libera."[90] Literary sources continue this bias toward associating the day principally (if not exclusively) with the pair, referring to the date solely as the occasion for the Liberalia (Cic. *fam.* 12.25.1, *Att.* 9.9.4; *Bell. Hisp.* 31.8). The relegation to secondary status of Mars, Rome's patron god, seems less likely to have been conceded to a celebration that had recognizable Greek origins. Second, extant visual evidence may attest to the festival occurring as early as the fourth century BC. A bronze chest from Praeneste depicts among a group of gods (including the god Mars in a mysterious pose) a bare-chested male figure identified by the caption "LEIBER"; this inscription most likely represents our earliest written reference to the god Liber.[91] Third, the literary evidence for the rites at the Liberalia omits mention of grapes or wine, an indication that the festival's focus was not on the most prominent association of the Greek counterpart Dionysus, an association that otherwise dominates references to Liber during the classical period.[92] The Liberalia, therefore, would seem to have celebrated predominately, if not exclusively, features associated with an indigenous Liber and Libera.

A more significant indicator of the pre-Greek importance of the Liber/Libera pair can be found in the now commonly accepted etymology of the names. Whereas ancient accounts connect the names of the gods to a notion of liberation or release, Devoto derives their stem from the PIE root *$h_1$leud^h* ("increase"); the addition of the suffix -*er(a)* makes the duo into procreating gods of

---

Artemis Λυαία; on our limited knowledge of this cult, see Fischer-Hansen 2009: 214. On the names suggesting a sibling relationship, see Holland 2011: 217.

[89] Scullard 1981: 91–92.

[90] Scullard 1981: 91–92; Wissowa 1904: 168–169 explains the emphasis on Liber as an attempt to avoid confusing the March 17 Agonium with three other Agonia held during the year. Two objections may be made to this argument: first, the composers of the calendars felt no compunction in giving the other three dates the identical name *Agonium*, so it is difficult to see why they would hesitate to add a fourth; second, specifying at March 17 the importance of Mars (e.g., *Agonium Martiale*; Macr. *Sat.* 1.4.15) would eliminate confusion.

[91] CIL 1².563; for image and various interpretations, Bordenache Battaglia and Emiliozzi 1979, 1.1: 52–54, figs. 5a–b; for a possible depiction of the Liberalia see Wiseman 2000: 267.

[92] On wine at the Liberalia, see Bruhl 1953: 25.

increase.[93] It is perhaps this primal function of the god that explains Servius's remark about a peculiar epithet of Liber: the title *pater* ("father") properly attaches to Liber, more so even than to Jupiter himself.[94] These two features of the god—etymology and epithet both implying a role in sexual generation—provide a link to two well known and well established ceremonies attached to Liber and Libera. The first involves a rural celebration described by Varro as taking place throughout Italy, an account of which Augustine preserves in his *City of God* (7.21). This rite included mounting a phallus onto a cart and transporting it openly throughout the countryside and into the cities. The residents of Lavinium, in particular, devoted an entire month to honoring the deity, terminating in a ceremony in which the most respectable matron of the town crowned the phallus with a wreath. Liber and Libera's original status as propagators of fertility in nature receives further support from the fact that they appear frequently in the provinces, particularly of northern Africa, in assimilation with indigenous fertility gods.[95] The generative ritual in the fields also matches the dedication in urban temples of male and female sexual organs to Liber and Libera, respectively, since their names are connected to the notion of men and women being "freed" of their seed during coitus (Aug. *civ.* 6.9).[96] It is difficult not to see in these accounts a preservation of rites rendered to the Italic couple Liber and Libera before a syncretism with Dionysus became fully established.[97] A second probable vestige of the associations of Liber with male procreation returns us to the Liberalia of March 17. Our sources indicate that this was the preferred date chosen by families for a young man's ceremonial rite of passage. On March 17, adolescent boys of the elite remove the striped clothing signifying their boyhood (*toga praetexta*) in exchange for the pure toga of the mature adult male.[98] Some sources refer to this adult garb as the *toga libera*, where the adjective is surely meant to recall the god of sexual increase.[99] It is hardly surprising that the celebration of the god of male potency provides a popular date for the ceremony that ushered young men into puberty.

Despite these probable traces of a native Italic aspect to the divine couple, the assimilation of Liber with features of the Greek god Dionysus and of Libera with assorted female deities can be dated early. In 496 BC, a famine in Italy prompted the Roman senate to consult the Sibylline books—a collection of

---

[93] Devoto 1932: 259–260 ("eccitatore di energie"), followed by, e.g., Bruhl 1953: 22–23, 73, Radke 1979: 176, West 2007: 145, Vaan 2008: 338, all with additional bibliographies.

[94] Serv. *georg.* 2.4; Bruhl 1953: 14 considers *pater* a late development since none of the early dedicatory inscriptions include the epithet; the dozens of later occurrences of *Liber pater*, however, indicate that this may simply be an accident of survival.

[95] Boussaada Ahlem 1992, esp. 1057–1058.

[96] On Libera and theories of female seed see Perfigli 2004: 72–78.

[97] Wissowa 1912: 299, Bruhl 1953: 17–19, Dumézil 1970: 377–378

[98] For the date, see Cic. *Att.* 6.1.12, Ov. *fast.* 3.771–772.

[99] *Toga libera* or similar: Prop. 4.1.132; Ov. *fast.* 3.771, 777; *trist.* 4.10.28.

prophetic texts written in Greek and originating in the context of the Greek god Apollo. There followed the vowing of a temple to Ceres, goddess of grain, in union with Liber and Libera (Dion. Hal. 6.17.2–4). The triad occupying the temple, completed in 493, is clearly modeled on shrines in the Greek world dedicated to Demeter, Dionysus, and Kore (identified with Persephone, daughter of Demeter). As Bruhl points out, the fact that Liber and Libera could step forward to replace the Greek figures indicates that they must already have had well-known roles in the Roman world. As a result, they would have been chosen as approximations, not equivalents, of Dionysus and Persephone.[100] Following this event, our sources with increasing frequency attest to the assimilation of Liber to Dionysus. On the fourth-century *cista* mentioned above, the sole attribute of L(e)iber is a flourishing vine that he holds in his left hand, an unambiguous reference to his associations with wine.[101] By the late third and early second centuries BC, references to Liber and Dionysus in staged drama make it clear that Roman theatergoers recognized many of the traits of these deities as identical, including once again the association with wine.[102]

Coincident with the progressive assimilation of Liber to Dionysus, extant sources hint at a diminishing and altered role for the female Libera. At some time before 202 BC, games in honor of the triad, called simply the Cerealia, began to be celebrated on April 19. Cicero and the only extant calendars datable to the Republic include Libera among the honorands, while later sources make mention only of Ceres and Liber, with Ovid implying that the games at the Cerealia displaced those at the Liberalia.[103] In other words Ceres alone, or in combination with Liber, achieves greater prominence in the annual festal calendar than the Libera/Liber pair. While this impression that Libera suffers a decline attendant upon the rise of Liber's identification with Dionysus may arise from the state of our sources, a passage of Cicero demonstrates that already in his day there was scholarly confusion concerning the role of Libera in the ever-changing Roman pantheon. In the second book of *On the Nature of the Gods*, Cicero's interlocutor, the Stoic Balbus, relates how good deeds can allow human beings to attain divine status after death. His account includes Hercules, the Dioscuri, Asclepius, and Liber. The mention of this last name in the otherwise conventional listing of demigods prompts the speaker to a digression, since there exists no tradition of the Italic god Liber ever having been a human being. Balbus clarifies that he refers by Liber rather to the son of the mortal woman Semele—in other words, to the Dionysus of Greek myth. Liber has now become so strongly associated with Dionysus that Balbus needs to stress that in

[100] Full discussion in Bruhl 1953: 30–45.

[101] Radke 1979: 180, 182–183 offers other early instances of Liber as wine god.

[102] Rousselle 1987.

[103] Libera: Cic. *Verr.* 2.5.36 (cf. 2.5.187 and Cic. *nat.* 2.62), Fast. ann. Num. Antiat. Apr. 19; Liber and Ceres: Ov. *fast.* 3.785–786, Serv. Auct. *georg.* 1.7, Ps. Cypr. *spect.* 4, and cf. Varro *rust.* 1.1.5, Verg. *georg.* 1.7, Plin. *nat.* 3.60.

this example he refers to the Hellenized Liber—that is, Dionysus with his attendant myths, genealogy, and attributes—and not to the Italic deity (2.62). The passage shows a clear awareness among the Romans of not only the existence but also the consequences of Greek–Roman divine syncretism: as posited earlier in the case of the Etruscans, the adoption of a rich Hellenic tradition here threatens to erase details of less celebrated gods native to Roman Italy.

Cicero's Balbus then continues with a topic already broached above. The dissonance of having one divine power possess two genealogies prompts him to offer a new etymology of the names Liber/Libera.

> *quod ex nobis natos liberos appellamus, idcirco Cerere nati nominati sunt Liber et Libera, quod in Libera servant, in Libero non item.* (Cic. *nat.* 2.62)

> Since we call those who are born from us "children" (*liberi*), those born of Ceres were given the names "Liber" and "Libera." This notion remains in the case of Libera, but not of Liber.

Oddly for something written by an adherent of Stoicism, which frequently depends upon word origins for making sense of the world, the second sentence of this passage immediately addresses the slippage between etymology and common practice. The precise relationship between the Latin word for children (*liberi*) and the adjective or proper name *liber/Liber* has indeed long been a subject of uncertainty.[104] And yet, what is odd about Balbus's aside is not so much its diffident conclusion as the fact that the digression arises unprompted from the context of his argument. The aside does, however, reveal a glimpse into contemporary thinking about the divine pair that is relevant to the present discussion. Balbus acknowledges—and his etymology claims to provide proof—that at a prior, unspecified, time Liber and Libera were partners of a sort—in this case, brother and sister as children of Ceres.[105] But Balbus is himself aware of the contemporary status of these two deities, and this awareness prompts reconsideration of the apparent truth behind their names. Liber, unlike Libera, is no longer Ceres's "child." As the literary sources mentioned in the previous paragraph make clear, Liber has, in his Hellenized guise, become Ceres's companion, with Libera fading into the background to play a secondary role as Ceres's daughter. Balbus's assertion receives support from other evidence in the Roman world: coins of the late Republic show Liber and Ceres on obverse and reverse as apparently equal partners (with Libera not depicted). Textual evidence, by contrast, consistently figures Libera as Proserpina, the daughter of Ceres (e.g., Cic. *Verr.* 2.4.106), an identification that dates back to her appearance in the fifth century as the equivalent of Kore and that coincides with Balbus's etymology of the word *liberi*.[106] In fact, the one extant coin from the Re-

---

[104] See most recently Vaan 2008: 338, with bibliography.
[105] For evidence that the cult reflected familial hierarchies, see Holland 2011: 218.
[106] Coins: Crawford 1974: no. 385/3 (78 BC), no. 449/2 and 3 (48 BC). Libera as Proserpina:

publican period that does depict Liber and Libera as apparent equals clearly identifies Liber as Dionysus, and the Italic pair is used as a means of making allusion to contemporary Roman politics.[107] Balbus is correct in his conclusion inasmuch as, ironically, the study of etymology reveals not simply origins but a diachronic truth. The status of Liber and Libera relative to each other has metamorphosed in the course of Roman history. Beginning as equal consorts in charge of the emission of the male and female seed, they develop into gods occupying distinct and unequal provinces. It is the systemic pressure of Rome's adoption of Greek culture that initiates and facilitates this separation.[108]

CONCLUSION

It is clear that the relationship between a god's sphere of influence and its biological sex (and the grammatical gender of its name) developed independently among different cultures, even within related language groups such as Proto-Indo-European. Not infrequently, differences arise regarding what sex is deemed most appropriate to a given function. The tendency for river gods to be masculine in Greek and Latin, for example, contrasts with the dominant feminine rivers in Indian and Persian cultures, while the sun god is identified in different parts of the world as variously male or female or in flux between the two or androgynous.[109] Although certain areas of activity attract divinities of one sex more than the other—female deities tend to preside over the birth and early nurture of both humans and plants, whereas gods of war tend to be male—even here it is not difficult to find exceptions. At Rome alone, consider the male god of earth Tellumo, or Virtus, the female personification of military courage.[110]

Evidence for theonyms in the Roman world has allowed us to posit an explanation for these divergences in the case of Latin by comparing the parallel trajectories for the development of nouns and for that of gods. As gods were being perceived as developing unique personalities, the sex of their personifications evolved in tandem with the grammatical gender of the word used to describe them. It is impossible to reconstruct a chronology for this evolution: whether a

---

Wissowa 1916–1924a: 2029.38–67, who also mentions the uncommon identification with Ariadne, wife of Dionysus and one-time mortal (Ov. *fast.* 3.512; Plin. *nat.* 36.29; Hyg. *fab.* 224), and with other female figures. Holland 2011: 219–221 offers a historical explanation for Libera's identification with Ariadne.

[107] Crawford 1974: no. 386, with pp. 290–291; Frazer 1929, 3: 110.

[108] For an impassioned discussion of Greek culture erasing earlier Roman rites and mythologies, see Dumézil 1956b: 41–43 (on Mater Matuta). Cf. too Radke 1979: 35–36 on the introduction of Greek ideas causing double-naming of archaic gods to be misunderstood; e.g., *Fortuna Iovia*, meaning "Fortuna who acts in the sphere of Jupiter," becoming misconstrued as *Fortuna, filia Iovis*.

[109] Rivers: Bertholet 1934: 10–11, West 2007: 274–275; sun: Bertholet 1934: 12–15.

[110] For tendencies and exceptions, Bertholet 1934: 15; Latte 1960: 58–59.

given word that had been assigned to a divine power came to acquire connotations of "feminine" or "masculine" that over the course of time affected perception of that power's sex, or whether the already present sexual associations of a divine power came to determine that word's grammatical gender. The names listed in the appendix would indicate that the latter represented the more frequent tendency, since here are listed dozens of cases in which the assignment of grammatical gender seems to have been in flux between male and female, presumably dependent upon the task to which the divine power was being put in any given instance. This elasticity in assigning a fixed gender and sex contributes, I would claim, to the much-discussed aspect of Roman prayer ritual by which the worshipper is unwilling to commit to the sex of the god relevant in a given instance. The prayer, consequently, includes an address to a neutral divinity—"whether you are a god or goddess" (e.g., *sive deus sive dea*)—an invocation that does not involve belief in the divinity's androgyny per se, but rather uncertainty over which sex is most relevant to the manifestation of the deity needed at that particular moment.[111]

Our analysis in this chapter has suggested that this initial sexual uncertainty surrounding the gods hardened over time in various ways, in a manner analogous to the development described in chapter 1. Just as nouns with dual gender survive only as poetic reminiscences of an irrecoverable past, so too do the androgynous characteristics of the early gods gradually disappear from the literary record. My intent in this chapter, therefore, has not been to find new evidence about the early nature of gods at Rome—references to scholarly works in the footnotes make clear that this evidence has long been known, and subject to a range of contradictory interpretations. Rather, by identifying a shared tendency between nouns and names, I have attempted to observe patterns in how the sexes of Rome's early gods were perceived. In the process, within the limits of our evidence, I have attempted to draw connections to broader phenomena of evolving grammatical gender. This leads to a typical narrative of de-evolution, exemplified by my sample cases of Liber/Libera and Genius/Iuno, but one in which categories concretize rather than dissolve. Whether this narrative represents historical reality or is the construction of antiquarians and polemicists from antiquity is impossible to discern, but I would continue to assert that for an understanding of Roman attitudes toward sex and gender historical truth is a luxury and not a necessity. Once again, Rome creates a narrative of a mystical lost time—as ubiquitous and polysexual gods join nouns of random gender and the literary practice of wise poets—in order to account for current, divisive, black and white categories. As mentioned above, with the assignment of mutually exclusive realms of active and passive to the sexes of male and female, there occurs a concomitant rise of dichotomous associations that fall to either side of this divide as male/female accrues the associations of dry/wet, reason/emotion,

---

[111] Guittard 2002 provides a careful examination of this formula.

rule/nurture, and so on. These oppositions have been seen by feminist scholars as part of a more general historical tendency to divide the sexes into categories that identify the masculine, and therefore men, with culture, while the feminine, women, become perceived as "being more rooted in, or having more direct affinity with, nature."[112] In the process, cultural divisions become naturalized and there is created a normative view of the separation of the sexes, an invention, so to speak, of heterosexuality.

I would like to conclude then by pairing the remarks of two unlikely comrades, the Christian convert Arnobius with whom this chapter opened and the twentieth-century feminist critic Monique Wittig. In pointing out that his new single God (*Deus*) does not have sex, Arnobius mocks his non-Christian contemporaries for being unable to distinguish between the concepts of linguistic gender and biological sex, to the point of asserting that they do not possess even the ability to conceive of such a distinction. I aimed in this chapter to show why Arnobius could make what at first seems an odd claim: gender and sex do indeed appear to be inseparable in the popular conception of divinity in ancient Rome. Subsequent history has, however, proven Arnobius wrong in his ancillary claim that his God has no sex, as translations of sacred texts and popular conceptions could not but cause readers and worshippers to conceive of the Christian "Him" as male. Wittig, like Arnobius, has called attention in a number of essays and fictional works to the same type of linguistic trap of identifying sex and gender. Although treating twentieth-century concerns, she phrases the issue in ways reminiscent of Arnobius. Just as Arnobius refuses to see his God restricted to one sex, and as contemporary Gnostic speculation takes a similar tack by seeing the supreme divinity as androgynous, Wittig demonstrates in her essay "The Mark of Gender" how grammatical gender "is an ontological impossibility because it tries to accomplish the division of Being."[113] Wittig is here addressing in particular how the sexual specificity of the English third-person pronoun "he" has historically denied women access to expressing ideas that are held to be allegedly universal. Signs of this split, by which the masculine and feminine, the male and the female, "he" and "she," come to have different access to universal ideas, finds earlier form, I suggest, in the Roman world. Roman antiquarians imagined a state of fluid gender, and saw in the gender flux of nouns and gods a sign that both sexes had access to all realms of experience. As time progressed, those realms became sex-specific. Access to the universal had been denied.

[112] Ortner 1974: 73.
[113] Wittig 1985: 6.

APPENDIX TO CHAPTER 4: MALE/FEMALE PAIRS OF DEITIES

Male Name	Ancient Source	Female Name	Ancient Source	Notes	Select Bibliography
1) Peragenor 2) Agonius	1) Tert. *nat.* 2.11 2) Paul. Fest. p.10	Agenoria	Aug. *civ.* 4.11, 16 Osbern A xxviii 45 =a 299	Peter 177–178 says Osbern's *indigetes* derive from Varro—all ancient etymologies derive from *ago/actus*	Radke 58, 252
Bonus Eventus	Plin. *nat.* 36.23 (Praxiteles)	Bona Fortuna	Plin. *nat.* 36.23 (Praxiteles)		Axtell 30–31
Cacus	See Radke	Caca	Serv. *Aen.* 8.190 Lact. *inst.* 1.20.5 Mythogr. 2.153, 3.13.1	Caca betrayed brother to Hercules; Cacus = Caeculus (Radke) Caca: a "forerunner or by-form of Vesta" (Fontenrose)	Radke 75–76 Ogilvie 57–58 Wissowa 161 Fontenrose 339
Cerus		Ceres			Wissowa 192 n. 9
Consus		Ops (Consiva, Opiconsiva)	Fast. frat. Arv. Aug. 25 (Opiconsiva) Varro *ling.* 5.64; 6.21	Varro identifies as Sabine gods of harvest	Axtell 22–23 Wissowa 203–204 Radke 239–240 (dubious)
Dius Fidius	Act. fratr. Arv. 48	Dea Dia	Act. fratr. Arv. 48	Dea Dia attested only here	Usener 33 Radke 104, 110
Dius Fidius Cf. Fisos		Fides	Enn. trag. frg. 350 Joc.; cf. Cic. *off.* 3.104	Fides > Fidius, in part because of proximity on Capitoline and because *flamen dialis* leads her sacrifice (Wissowa)—Fisos (Umbrian): see Pighi 235–239, Radke 128–129	Wissowa 133–134 Axtell 20–21 (dubious)

Male Name	Ancient Source	Female Name	Ancient Source	Notes	Select Bibliography
Domiducus	Aug. *civ.* 6.9	Domiduca	Mart. Cap. 2.149 Osbern D iii 23; d 204		Perfigli 158, 160–161
Domitius	Aug. *civ.* 6.9	Manturna	Aug. *civ.* 6.9	Both attested in Augustine only, with parallel tasks	
Erine patre	CIL I² 392= Vetter 1: 228b	Erinia	CIL I² 392= Vetter 1: 228b		Radke 113
Fabulinus	Non. p. 532 (Varro)	Fabula		According to Radke, from different stems	Radke 116
Faunus	Varro *ling.* 7.36	Fauna	Varro *ling.* 7.36		Radke 119–121 Holland 221–224
Faunus [Fatuus]		[Fauna] Fatua	Gavius Bassus ap. Lact. *inst.* 1.22; *passim*	Sources variously identify as siblings or consorts	Radke 117–119
Februus	Macr. *Sat.* 1.13.3	Februa	Lyd. *mens.* 4.25 Mart. Cap. 2.149	Cognomen to Iuno in Mart. Cap.; Februus cthonic in Lydus	Radke 122–123 Vaan 208
Flusos (Florus)	Vetter 1.183	Flora			Latte 59
Fontanus	CIL 2.150	1) Fontana 2) Fonta ad aquas	1) CIL 2.150 2) CIL 11.6481; cf. 6494	*Fontano/ et Fontanae/ pro salut. Al/bi Fausti Albia/ Pacina v. s. a. l.*	Latte 60 Radke 131
Genius		Iuno		See discussion in chapter 4	
Honos	CIL 6.2044.5 (AD 66; Arval); dedication of cow (?)	Virtus		Axtell ("two cults . . . virtually one")	Pease 694–695 Axtell 21–22

APPENDIX TO CHAPTER 4 (*continued*)

Male Name	Ancient Source	Female Name	Ancient Source	Notes	Select Bibliography
?Hymenaeus	Catull. 61.9–10 Ov. *Her.* 21.157–168			Catullus depicts in dress of bride, Ovid of *matrona*. Mistaken for girl as youth (Serv. Auct. *Aen.* 4.99, Lact. Plac. 3.283, et al.)	Hersch 242–259 (258: "represents both sexes simultaneously")
Ianus		Iana	Tert. *nat.* 2.15 (lana *codd.*) Varro *rust.* 1.37.3 Macr. *Sat.* 1.9.8 (Nigidius)	Nigidius: Iana=Diana; Varro: Iana=*luna*; compare female form of Etruscan Culsans (de Grummond 2006: 147)	Roscher in Roscher 2.1:14 (doubts existence of Iana) Holland 224–226 (more optimistic)
Iugatinus	Aug. *civ.* 4.11	1) Iuga 2) Iugalis	1) Paul. Fest. p. 104 2) Serv. *Aen.* 4.16	Gods of marriage, but Aug. *civ.* 4.8 has Iugatinus in charge of *iuga montium*	Perfigli 159
?Iuppiter	CIL 11.3245; 9.5574	Iuventas [Iuventus]			Radke 162–163
?Iuppiter		Regen[ai] peai cerie iovia	Vetter no. 218	Cf. Lucanian inscr. διωϝιας διομανα[ς] ~ Iovia domina	Campanile 280–281, 284–285
Iuppiter Liber	Plin. *nat.* 36.43	Iuno Libera		See discussion in chapter 4	Kenner 157–158 Holland 217–221
Limentinus	Tert. *cor.* 13, *idol.* 15, *nat.* 2.15; Aug. *civ.* 4.8, 6.7; Osbern L xli 2=l 237	Lima	Arnob. 4.9	Gods of threshold	Radke 185
Lupercus		Luperca	Arnob. 4.3 (Varro)	Husband and wife	Radke 190–191 Cardauns 224–225

Male Name	Ancient Source	Female Name	Ancient Source	Notes	Select Bibliography
Maius	Macr. *Sat.* 1.12.17	Maia		Macrobius cites from *Fasti Tusculani*; gods of growth (cf. month of May)	Radke 192–194; cf. Bayet 1957: 112
Mamertus (Mars)	Lycophron 938, 1410	Mamersa	Lycophron 1417 (cf. 356, 985)		Radke 194–195 Wissowa 148 n. 7
Manes		Manes	E.g., Fest. p. 129, CIL 5.6710	ThLL vol. VIII 294.13–15, 295.57–58 (F. Bömer) lists over ten examples of feminine	Radke 195–196 Marbach 1060
Matutinus	Hor. *serm.* 2.6.20	Matutina			Radke 209
Mavors (Mars)		1) Maurta 2) Maurtia	1) CIL I² 49 2) Vetter no. 364b		Radke 209–210
Messor	Serv. Auct. *georg.* 1.21 (Fabius Pictor)	Messia	Tert. *spect.* 8.3	Neither Radke nor Wissowa link the two; clearly connected with "mowing" (*meto*) at harvest	Peter 204 Radke 216–217
Numisius	Several inscriptions	1) Numeries 2) Numeria	1) Non. p. 352 (Varro) 2) Aug. *civ.* 4.11; Osbern n 75	Radke: >**nome-*; gods of fate; in ancient references, feminine is goddess of quick birth or of numbers	Radke 233–235
Pales		Pales		See discussion in chapter 4	Radke 242–243
Pavor	Liv. 1.27.7 (Numa); Aug. *civ.* 6.10 (Seneca)	1) Paventia 2) Paventina	1) Aug. *civ.* 4.11 2) Tert. *nat.* 2.11	Female version governs children, male seemingly adult males	Radke 247 Wissowa 1916–1924c: 1341–1343
Pistor	Ov. *fast.* 6.349–394 Lact. *inst.* 1.20.33	Piistia	Vetter 1.147	Radke connects both to "pounding"	Radke 256–257

Male Name	Ancient Source	Female Name	Ancient Source	Notes	Select Bibliography
1) Pomo 2) Pomonus 3) Puemunus	1) CIL 10.531 (gender unclear) 2) Gloss. 5.93.25 3) Iguvine Tables	Pomona		Radke posits Illyrian origin	1) Radke 257, Wissowa 198–199 3) Radke 267–268
Praestes	CIL 14.3555 (Iuppiter) Ov. fast. 5.129–136 (Lares) ThLL X, 2 903. 53–904.6 (M. Pade)	1) Praestana 2) Praestita 3) Praestitia [4) Praestata/ Praestota]	1) Arnob. 4.3 2) CIL 9.4322 3) Tert. nat. 2.11 [4) Iguvine Tables]		Radke 261–262
Priapus		Pertunda	Aug. civ. 6.9		Radke 262 (cf. 295 s.v. Subigus)
Promitor	Aug. civ. 6.9 Serv. Auct. georg. 1.21	Prema	Aug. civ. 6.9 Tert. nat. 2.11	Ancient sources identify Promitor as agrarian, Prema as god of wedding night. Radke thinks both agrarian.	
Pudor	Hor. carm. saec. 57	Pudicitia		See discussion in chapter 4	
Robigus	Varro rust. 1.1.6 Fast. Praen. (CIL I² p. 236. 316–317); passim	Robigo	Ov. fast. 4.907; passim	Paul. Fest. p. 267 distinguishes Robigus = god from robigo = disease (cf. Ov. fast. 4.920: diva timenda)	Radke 273 (no mention of sex) Wissowa 196 Frazer 3: 406–407
Ruminus	Aug. civ. 7.11	Rumina	Aug. civ. 4.11 Sen. apud civ. 6.10	Seneca describes Rumina as a widow	Radke 274–275

Male Name	Ancient Source	Female Name	Ancient Source	Notes	Select Bibliography
Rusor	Aug. civ. 7.23 (Varro)	Rusina	Aug. civ. 4.8 (rura)	Rusor >ru- ("Nourisher") or rus; no modern source accepts Varro's etymology; Radke: Rusor/Rusina >*rudere ("Clod-Breaker")	Peter 220–221 Radke 276
Saturnus		Lua	Varro ling. 8.36 Gell. 13.23.2	Sources cite Lua as Lua Saturni	Radke 185–186
Semo (Sancus)		Salus (Semonia)	Macr. Sat. 1.16.8 CIL 6.30975 Fest. p. 309	Axtell discusses later identification with Hygieia and as Asclepius's consort	Wissowa 131–132 Axtell 13–15 Radke 286
Sentinus	Aug. civ. 7.2 Tert. nat. 2.11	Sentia	Aug. civ. 4.11	Sentia gives children sententia/sensus	Radke 287
Silvanus		Silvanae	Numerous inscriptions	Two-thirds of evidence from Pannonia; uncertain whether of local or Italian origin	Dorcey 42–48
1) Statilinus 2) Statanus	1&2) Non. p. 532.17–21 (Varro) 1) Aug. civ. 4.21	Statina	1) Tert. an. 39.2 2) Tert. nat. 2.11	Deity of first standing of child	Peter 143–144, 147, 224 Radke 292
Subruncinator	Serv. Auct. georg. 1.21 (Fabius Pictor)	Runcina	Aug. civ. 4.8 [Tert. nat. 2.11 seems to refer to different god]		Radke 275

APPENDIX TO CHAPTER 4 (*continued*)

Male Name	Ancient Source	Female Name	Ancient Source	Notes	Select Bibliography
1) Tellumo [2) Tellurus]	1) Aug. *civ.* 7.23 (Varro) [2) Mart. Cap. 1.49]	Tellus		Weinstock: both primitive Italic gods, later understood as "mother Earth" due to Greek influence (contra Usener 35)	Weinstock Radke 298 (doubts existence of Tellurus)
Venulus	Serv. *Aen.* 8.9	Venilia	Several references	Ancient sources give many etymologies for Venilia	Radke 16, 310–311 Peter 228–230 (Venilia consort of Neptunus) Courtney 1993: 139–140
Venus	Serv. *Aen.* 2.632 Macr. *Sat.* 3.8.1-3 (Laev. *poet.* 26, et alii)	Venus			
(Iuppiter) Victor		Victoria	CIL 6.2086.27 (Arval prayer)	Paired as *Iovi Victori . . . et Victoriae*	Wissowa 139–140 Axtell 15-17
Volumnus	Aug. *civ.* 4.21 Min. Fel. 25.8 Tert. *nat.* 2.11	1) Volumna 2) Voleta	1) Aug. *civ.* 4.21 2) Tert. *nat.* 2.11	God of children's will/desire (*voluntas*)	Radke 347, 348–349 (>*valetudo*?)
OTHER *Di consentes*	Enn. *ann.* 240-241			All twelve are in male/female pairs *except* Minerva/Venus	
?agricolarum duces	Varro *rust.* 1.1.4				

On consorts among *indigetes*, see Peter 185.58–186.45.
All references to "Radke" are to Radke 1979, where he includes full primary sources (and secondary through 1979); unless otherwise indicated, references to Wissowa are to Wissowa 1912.
Citations of primary sources are full for the rarer divinities, but more often selective, with emphasis on passages that provide evidence for androgyny.
"Select Bibliography" column cites only sources relevant to the issue of male/female pairs; fuller details for each deity may be found in standard works such as Peter 1890–1894, Radke 1979, and relevant entries in Roscher and RE.

Chapter 5

The Prodigious Hermaphrodite

INTRODUCTION

I begin with a joke that exploits the relationship that has been driving the preceding argument of this book: the consistent play in Latin between human sexuality and the grammatical rules that describe the gender of nouns. As discussed in chapter 1, in the second century AD a discourse on Latin grammar by a visibly addled scholar could command attention from members of the Roman elite awaiting an audience with the emperor (Gell. 4.1). Throughout the subsequent centuries, public demonstrations on grammar by a professional teacher continue to be of interest—and even in demand—on what may strike us as unexpected occasions.[1] The following epigram provides one instance. Composed by Ausonius in the fourth century AD, the poem describes a wedding benediction that has been solicited from a teacher of grammar:

> *Rufus vocatus rhetor olim ad nuptias,*
> *celebri ut fit in convivio,*
> *grammaticae ut artis se peritum ostenderet,*
> *haec vota dixit nuptiis:*
> *"et masculini et feminini gignite*
> *generisque neutri filios."* (Auson. 13.50 [Green])

> Rufus, a teacher of rhetoric, was once invited to a marriage, as often happens on a festive occasion. As a way of demonstrating his grammatical expertise he made the following toast at the wedding: "May you produce many children—both male and female . . . and neuter."[2]

This anecdote depicts a certain Rufus, the parodic stand-in for the pedantic scholar, attempting to display his grammatical erudition wittily in a public setting.[3] As often with Roman humor, more lies behind Rufus's blessing than would first appear. The surface absurdity of a neuter child is mitigated by the

---

[1] For weddings in particular see Russell 1979.

[2] Kay 2001: 174–175 discusses the epigram's unclear relationship with a contemporary poem of Palladas (*AP* 9.489: γραμματικοῦ θυγάτηρ ἔτεκεν φιλότητι μιγεῖσα / παιδίον ἀρσενικόν, θηλυκόν, οὐδέτερον). Mart. 11.19 also conflates sex with grammatical gender (Nobili 2002).

[3] Kay 2001: 168, 177 makes a good case for considering Rufus a fictional character.

fact that such an impossibility in fact represents the broadening of a rule that would have been known to much of Rufus's audience, namely that of "common gender." Grammatical treatises consider the morphologically masculine noun that Rufus uses here—*filius* (literally, "son")—to be equally applicable to a female "daughter" (normally denoted by the exclusively feminine designation *filia*)—and this rule is here extended, with inconceivable physiology but acceptable philology, to cover the theoretical possibility of "neuter" children.[1] The rhetor's juxtaposition *gignite/generis* in the final couplet also likely serves as a learned allusion to the ancient derivation of the noun *genus* ("grammatical gender") from verb forms such as *genero/gigno* ("to procreate"). In the context of our discussion of this etymology in chapter 1, another schoolteacher, Pompeius, forestalled objections from his students concerning the counterintuitiveness of applying this rule universally—what role, after all, can inanimate nouns have in sexual procreation? In Ausonius's epigram the grammarian Rufus responds to this concern by leaving open the possibility of a living and breathing neuter child.

Another poem from Late Antiquity seems self-consciously to carry still further the notion informing Rufus's joke by showing that a neuter human being is in fact *not* an impossibility. In the *Latin Anthology*, an anonymous epigrammatist wonders about the sexual status of a man who, castrated as a youth, comes to display feminine characteristics later in life.

> incertum ex certo sexum fert pube recisa,
>> quem tenerum secuit mercis avara manus.
> namque ita femineo eunuchus clune movetur,
>> ut dubites quid sit, vir [magis] an mulier.
> omnem grammaticam castrator sustulit artem,
>> qui docuit neutri esse hominem generis. (Anth. 109 = 98 SB)

> After having the genitals removed, his sex goes from certain to uncertain for the young man cut by a hand that is greedy for profit. For the eunuch walks with such an effeminate sway that you're not sure whether it's a man or a woman. The castrator has done away with the art of grammar, since he has shown that the word *homo* ("human being") has a neuter gender.

The castrator, the poet decides, had discovered a hitherto unknown grammatical rule by teaching that *homo*, the noun describing a human being, can in fact occur in the neuter gender. Once again the humor relies upon a single noun that commonly describes both females and males, in this case *homo*, being extended to cover the third, neuter, gender.[2]

It is not surprising, it is perhaps even inevitable, that the precious and learned realm of the epigram should concern itself with the sorts of language

---

[1] On *filius*, see NW 896.

[2] For parallels, see Kay 2001: 176; for *homo* applied to both men and women, see NW 897–898.

games that arise from ambiguous grammatical gender. And yet behind these instances of grammatical wit—indeed, centuries behind—lie complications when one turns to consider their wordplay from a literal standpoint. The issue of a child who is *neuter* in a strictly etymological sense—that is, one who can confidently be classified as "neither" male nor female—had already for centuries engendered heated debate outside the realm of the grammarians. Roman law, for example, treats this question, and it was a question that had to be taken seriously. Many fundamental principles of the legal system depended upon strict binary division of the sexes into male and female, including the institution of heirs (restricted to men). It is therefore unsurprising that the ambiguously sexed hermaphrodite presented a problem that threatened to undermine basic legal principles. Unlike in medicine, where the possibility of a third sex had theoretical justification, in law the existence of solely male and female actors, with no third option, was viewed as "not a natural fact but an obligatory norm."[3]

By examining the figure of the hermaphrodite, this chapter brings the phenomenon of fluid genders out of the hands of ancient scholars, pedants, and poets and into the world of the political elite. The notion of a third sex occupied members of Roman society in areas more critical to the Roman state's wellbeing than even its law codes. Like the androgynous nouns encountered in Latin poetry and the multi-sexed gods thought to populate the Roman pantheon, a human being of uncertain gender could have unimagined repercussions in the real world. Accordingly, my concluding chapter considers the change in attitudes toward the human hermaphrodite that our extant texts depict as occurring in the transition between the periods of the late Republic and early Empire.

DUAL SEXUALITY IN THE GREEK EAST

For centuries, scholars ancient and modern have enjoyed speculating about the potential ramifications of androgyny as it appears at both the divine and human levels. Before turning in detail to the culture-specific ways in which the Romans grappled with ambiguous sex in their own world, it will provide a helpful contrast to look at Greek approaches to the significance of androgyny. In the previous chapter, I touched briefly upon how the idea of androgynous gods developed in the Mediterranean world outside the specific Roman context. The survey in this section will treat a different selection of material, with the goal of better contextualizing a use of dual sexuality in the political life of the Roman Republic that is in many ways unique. The survey will consider in particular how a kind of symbolic androgyny manifests itself in human cult practice.[4]

---

[3] Thomas 1992: 85. The legal status of a castrated man was more complicated; see overview in Muth 2004: 307–308. I shall return to these legal issues in my conclusion.

[4] This section on the non-Roman evidence derives largely from Baumann 1955, Delcourt 1961

146 · Chapter 5

Various collections of Greek writings allegedly authored by the legendary singer Orpheus preserve a complex and multi-generational story of creation that differs in significant ways from the better-known theogony canonized by authors such as Hesiod. These Orphic texts, dating back as early as the fifth century BC and remaining popular throughout Late Antiquity, recount a tale in which divine androgyny appears at two distinct stages.[5] In an early phase of the Orphic cosmogony appears a primordial egg that is, according to the chief extant accounts, shaped by Chronos ("Time") out of his child, Chaos. From this egg emerges a single, androgynous being that bears many epithets, including *Protogonos* ("firstborn") and *Phanes* ("the one who makes manifest").[6] These two names indicate clearly the dual function of this creature both as the representative of a new stage of creation and as initiating, of its own accord, the subsequent stage. As a single being able to breed a new generation, Protogonos/ Phanes necessarily contains elements of both sexes.

The second stage of androgyny in the Orphic texts appears after Zeus begins to stabilize earlier divine conflicts over his succession by defeating the generation of gods prior to his own, that of the Titans. Experience has taught Zeus that superiority in physical strength provides insufficient assurance of a stable reign. He therefore decides to acquire powers from the past generations to supplement those of his own. In the more standard mythological accounts, Zeus swallows the pregnant goddess Metis so as literally to embody the "cunning" signaled by her name; as a result of this act, the goddess Athena is "born" from Zeus's head. In a similar fashion, the Zeus of the Orphic texts proceeds to swallow Protogonos/Phanes. In this way, Zeus embodies the androgynous procreative source that initiated the previous generation of gods and, as a result, he takes on both the active and passive capacities that were thought to typify the two sexes.[7] We can recognize driving this narrative a theme from the previous chapter, by which the possession of androgyny is envisaged as endowing a god with a fully realized perfection. In fact, by the early first century BC this feature of the reigning god has entered the poetry of the Roman Republic. In a poetic fragment that seems to derive from a hymn to Jupiter, Valerius Soranus includes among the characteristics of Jupiter's omnipotence his status as both male and female parent. Soranus conveys this omnipotence by simultaneously using a masculine and a feminine noun to describe the god ("All-powerful Jupiter, . . . / father and mother"; *Iuppiter omnipotens, . . . / progenitor genetrixque*).[8]

[1958], West 1983, and Brisson 2002 [1997]. Kenner 1970 offers the most detailed and balanced analysis of the cultic evidence.

[5] The most reliable account of these texts is West 1983; for speculation on possible pre-Greek origins of these episodes of androgyny, see Baumann 1955: 175–187.

[6] West 1983: 70–71, 202–207 provides a critical look at the various traditions; a more general treatment is in Delcourt 1961 [1958]: 67–70, Brisson 2002 [1997]: 85–96.

[7] West 1983: 89–90, 218–220; Brisson 2002 [1997]: 96–100.

[8] Valerius Soranus frg. 2 Blänsdorf, for which see Courtney 1993: 66–68.

Before turning to how this divine androgyny manifests itself in human cult practice, it is worth spending a few moments on a well-known passage of Plato that bears resemblance to Orphic doctrine and is commonly construed as referring to an analogous type of primordial androgyny.[9] In the *Symposium* (189c2–193d6) the character Aristophanes gives a speech that imagines the original state of human beings as comprising three different sets of joined pairs, in part female to female, in part male to female, and in part male to male.[10] Zeus comes to split these pairs as punishment for the arrogance displayed by human beings in believing themselves equal to the gods. The separation of the sexes and creation of the human physique in its current form result directly from this splitting. In addition to accounting for human physiology, the story provides an etiology for human desire and sexual attraction. What human beings call "love," Aristophanes concludes, is the emotional striving of these once united halves to relocate their original partner and become whole once again. Although this account does bear some resemblance to the Orphic tale—in particular Aristophanes's description of the original human life forms inhabiting a rounded body resembling an egg—androgyny in these Orphic texts is in fact securely attested only in the creation of divine, and not human, entities. No extant Orphic text preserves a belief in the earliest human beings possessing bodies of dual sex.[11] Furthermore, the original human beings in Plato's version are only one-third androgynous, with an equal number being unisex—male/male and female/female. In the Platonic context, in other words, primal androgyny constitutes only one feature of an ad hoc fable whose aim differs from that of the Orphic material: namely, to explain the origins of sexual attraction and, in particular, the inability of humans to recover for themselves that original state (Pl. *Symp.* 192c–e). The story offers no obvious guidance for understanding attitudes toward human androgyny in the ancient Mediterranean.

Elsewhere, however, Greek antiquity does provide accounts of practices that may aid in assessing the significance of hermaphroditic human beings at Rome. These practices occur among those elements of religious ritual that aim to contravene the accepted boundaries of sex and gender. Particularly illuminating are the instances of ritual cross-dressing that are reported to occur on diverse occasions. Scholars interested in biological androgyny have collected a wide array of evidence for private and public ritual in which both male and female participants adopt a form of transvestism. Although most of these practices are attested by authors writing later than the period they discuss, there seems no reason to doubt that the temporary ritual adoption of external characteristics of the opposite sex was prevalent in Greece throughout the archaic and classical

[9] See, for example, Baumann 1955: 175–180, Delcourt 1961 [1958]: 73–75, Brisson 2002 [1997]: 73–85.

[10] For the speech's relevance to Greek homosexuality, which is not my focus here, see discussion and bibliography in Skinner 2005: 129–131.

[11] West 1983: 164–166 summarizes the Orphic version of human origins.

periods. Examples include such anomalous injunctions as that the men of Lycia should wear women's clothing when in mourning, or that in Argos brides were expected to don a false beard when going to bed with their husbands.[12] These rituals are conventionally explained as apotropaic acts designed to ward off malevolent spirits during periods of transition—in the two examples cited, the transitions marked by death and marriage. Plutarch and Valerius Maximus, for instance, share the assumption that Lycian men mourn in women's clothing since excessive grief is unmanly and even emasculating; the unusual dress serves furthermore to remind the men to control their passions. In contrast with this explicit ancient testimony, Delcourt prefers to see the various instances of sexual elasticity such as these not as a protection against evil but as a celebration of longevity and fertility at periods of ritual initiation. This fecundity originates, she claims, in human mimicry of "symbolic androgyny," through which one sex appropriates the power of the other by adopting the dress or other traits expected of that sex.[13] Symbolic androgyny, in other words, evokes the sexual duality that the primal gods possessed at the fecund moments of primal creation.

Delcourt's argument for a single explanation arises from her belief that the same compulsions driving the paradigm of an aboriginal androgyny preserved in the Orphic texts also inform human behavior that transgresses sexual norms. By contrast Baumann, in his survey of the practice of ritual cross-dressing in cultures throughout the world, both contemporary and ancient, posits at least eight different explanatory models for the practice, and such multiple explanations provide a more balanced approach to the diverse Greek and Roman material.[14] Kenner, for example, has discussed thoroughly the two principal explanations for ritual transvestism given by ancient and modern scholars—namely, that such acts occur in imitation of the androgynous elements of divine figures such as Dionysos and Herakles (as Delcourt claims) or that they are meant to confuse demons (as in the claims that they are primarily apotropaic). Kenner not only deems both accounts relevant, but she also posits additional possibilities, such as that cross-dressing can enact sympathetic magic (e.g., a bride in male garb helps produce a male child).[15] It is impossible for us to decide among these explanations—and I suspect that it is likely that multiple explanations often converge to explain a single ritual act, depending upon date, context, and practitioner. What is common to all these cases of transvestism, however, is that transgressions of the boundary of sex and gender occur at moments of transi-

---

[12] Mourning: Val. Max. 2.6.13, Plut. *Mor.* 112f–113a; beard: Plut. *Mor.* 245f with Kenner 1970: 103–104.

[13] Delcourt 1961 [1958]: 16.

[14] Baumann 1955: 45–59.

[15] Kenner 1970: 111–148, who also discusses transvestism in the stories of Achilles and Theseus.

tion in the life of the individual and community. Kenner divides into two distinct types the occasions during which ritual transvestism regularly occurs.[16] The first centers on transitions in cultural or communal life, which would include ceremonies that mark occasions such as weddings and deaths. The second type occurs during transitions in the natural world; in fact, celebrations of the new year (whether calendrical or agricultural), clearly a time of potential uncertainty and anxiety among traditional societies, mark the time when ritual transvestism occurs most frequently in Greek and Roman antiquity.[17] And it is this second category, encompassing the relationship between androgyny and the cycles of the natural world, that will have most relevance for the Roman hermaphrodite.

Returning to those beings whose sexual duality subsists not in their costume but in the biology of their genitals, we find precious little indication of how these intersexed figures were perceived in regular ritual activity. If the recollection of an early phase of androgyny truly informs areas of cult activity, one would imagine that there would survive evidence that human androgynes received special treatment in the historical period. This, however, is not the case. According to Pliny, one Latin term describing such individuals, *hermaphroditus*, came to be the commonest word employed during the first century AD (Plin. *nat.* 7.34). This newly popular coinage, a loan word from Greek, derives from the name of the mythical creature Hermaphroditos. According to the most well-known version of the story, Hermaphroditos was a son of Hermes and Aphrodite whose youth and beauty attracted the nymph Salmacis.[18] After rejecting her advances, Hermaphroditos enters a spring to bathe, whereupon the hidden nymph leaps into the pool and attempts to rape the resisting young boy. Clinging to the struggling Hermaphroditos, Salmacis prays to the gods that they may never part. Her prayer granted, their male and female physiologies fuse into a single form.[19] At this point, however, the story takes an unusual turn. In contrast with the primordial examples of divine androgyny, which typically celebrate fecundity, the resulting androgynous creature Hermaphroditos became attached to a notion of sexual impotence. There is no mythical account of Hermaphroditos producing progeny; furthermore, the spring of Salmacis in which his transformation took place acquired the reputation of being able to make any male who drank from its waters somehow less of a man.[20] The consistent associations of this mythical prototype for the hermaph-

---

[16] Kenner 1970: esp. 102–112.

[17] Kenner 1970: 105–108.

[18] For the less well attested tradition that Hermaphroditos was born with two sets of genitals, see Diod. Sic. 4.6.5.

[19] Ov. *met.* 4.285–388 provides the most details; full references in Jessen 1912: 716–717.

[20] See esp. Fest. p. 329; for the nature of the spring, see Robinson 1999: 212–214; also Ov. *met.* 4.285–287. Vitr. 2.8.12 and Strabo 14.2.16 deny the possibility that the spring is enervating.

rodite, then, are those of an emasculated and infertile being, and in Rome the hermaphrodite may have also attracted the negative associations attaching to effeminate males who enjoy being sexually penetrated by other males.[21]

This tradition offers helpful perspective on the visual depictions of Hermaphroditos and hermaphrodites that survive from Greek and Roman antiquity. Terracotta votives of beings of dual sex datable to the third and second centuries BC have been found throughout Greece and Magna Graecia. Their precise function is unknown. One prominent authority hypothesizes that they were used to promote fertility. Such a hypothesis, however, would at first seem difficult to reconcile with the predominant associations between the hermaphrodite and sexual impotence and with description of the votives themselves as having "the unmuscled torso and small penis of a pre-pubescent boy."[22] The silent material evidence must remain open to interpretation. As we shall see, however, the human hermaphrodite at Rome possessed a range of features that also resist one simple functional explanation.

Modern anthropological studies supply sufficient reasons to be cautious about applying a single interpretation across cultures for attitudes toward intersexed individuals. The Navaho, for example, considered the birth of an androgynous child as a positive omen for the wealth and well-being of the child's family; among the Pokot of eastern Kenya, by contrast, those intersexuals not killed at birth live their lives outside the social life of the community as beings cursed by the gods.[23] The Sambia of New Guinea provide a definitively third option in their concept of the "third sex," comprising those adolescents identified as female at birth, but who acquire male sexual characteristics during puberty.[24] In an analogous fashion, one of the terms used to identify the neuter grammatical gender among the ancient Sanskrit grammarians is also normally employed to describe "sexless" creatures, such as eunuchs and hermaphrodites.[25] As Clifford Geertz remarks on this varying display of attitudes: "God may have made the intersexuals, but man has made the rest."[26] And yet as the studies of contemporary cultures also make clear, by paying special attention to context it is possible to determine what that human "making" consists of, and I cannot agree with Geertz's endorsement of the view that the Romans "regarded intersexed infants as supernaturally cursed." Accordingly, the polyvalence of modern attitudes to

[21] For the unlikely possibility that the fertility deity Mutunus Titunus was hermaphroditic see Wissowa 1912: 243 n. 7 (*unsicher*); Radke 1979: 225–226. On Hermaphroditos's effeminacy, see Robinson 1999: 214–217.

[22] Ajootian 1997: 227–229 (quotation from 228), who cites a Hellenistic inscription from Kos where the god is named alongside undisputed fertility deities such as Priapus and Pan.

[23] Edgerton 1964.

[24] Herdt 1994b: 419–445, who notes that, despite the presence of three sexes, the Sambia recognize only two genders.

[25] Wackernagel 1926–1928: 2.5.

[26] Geertz 1983: 84. His remarks on the Romans are on 81.

intersexed beings encourages me in the following sections to depart from these hypothetical reconstructions of the meaning of androgyny in Greek myth and ritual, concentrating instead on the function of the hermaphrodite in a context for which abundant evidence survives: the world of Roman Republican politics.

HERMAPHRODITES AS SIGNS IN REPUBLICAN ROME

During the Republic, every attested occurrence of an androgynous human being occurs in the context of the publicly investigated and sanctioned prodigy. The prodigy in Roman religion functioned as a particular kind of sign that, unlike oracles or similar omens, had a character that was essentially nonpredictive. In other words, although divinely ordained, it did not normally provide warnings about some specific future event.[27] Rather, the occurrence of a prodigy, and its acceptance by the state, signaled the recognition of an unspecific rupture of order in the natural world, an order marked in Latin by the term *pax deorum* (literally, "grace of the gods"). A second distinction between oracles and prodigies requires emphasis: whereas oracles most often predict a future event that cannot be avoided, the type of rupture indicated by a prodigy in the Roman world can indeed be countered if the Roman senate performs appropriate ritual activity in a timely fashion.[28]

This brief characterization reveals the importance of considering the Roman prodigy in its proper context. Luc Brisson, in a popular book on "sexual ambivalence" in ancient Greece and Rome, disregards the cultural specifics of human intersexuality across time and cultures when he asserts in his conclusion that, at least until the close of the Republic, the hermaphrodite constituted "a sign of divine anger that heralded the extinction of the human race, since it had become alien to itself and incapable of reproduction."[29] This conclusion rests in the Roman case on two insupportable premises. First, it ignores that in the Republic the androgyne prodigy belongs to a much larger class of "signs of divine anger," the majority of which it would be difficult to connect with issues of human reproduction. Talking cows and raining stones appear often, for example, and the commonest occurrence—lightning strikes—seems equally innocent of having an effect on the perpetuation of the human species.[30] It would seem instead that one possible trait uniting these apparently disparate prodigies is that they transgress normally stable boundaries—a talking animal borrows properties regularly identifiable as human, and stones are not normally

[27] North 1990: 60 considers instances where prophecy is an element of Roman divination more generally. Compare Cicero's discussion of the ancient etymology of *prodigium* from *praedico* (*nat.* 2.7, *div.* 1.93; see too *Phil.* 4.10).

[28] Bloch 1964 concisely outlines this and other unique features of Roman divination.

[29] Brisson 2002: 147.

[30] Wülker 1903: 6–26 offers a full list of prodigies attested by ancient sources.

associated with weather phenomena.[31] In the particular case of the hermaphrodite, the boundary violated stands between the normally distinct sexes of male and female. Such boundary crossing is what Livy implies in describing unusual births, including that of a hermaphrodite, as an instance of "nature wandering into procreative areas that belong to another."[32] Just as the breaking of the boundaries of grammatical gender increased the perceived power of Roman poets, and just as the adoption of dual sexual characteristics by a god marked an acme of authority, so too the breaking of boundaries in the case of the hermaphrodite can be interpreted as a mark of its sacred character rather than of its impiety. Second, Brisson's statement ignores the basic nature of the Roman prodigy. Far from representing the physical manifestation of a divine anger that will cause the "extinction of the human race," in this particular instance the crossing of sexual boundaries indicates to the Roman audience that something is not right with the world, but that that something can be remedied. Far from being destructive, the hermaphrodite provides a means by which divine anger can be appeased.

In his discussion of attitudes toward monstrous human births in Rome, Garland concludes that "no ancient author sheds any light on the crucial question as to whether in Roman society the deformed were perceived to be evil in and of themselves or whether the evil which they testified to and in some sense symbolised was external to their deformity."[33] While it is true that an explicit ancient discussion of this issue is lacking, consideration of how prodigies are presented nevertheless offers perspective on which alternative—as evil embodied or as evil portended—better reflects public practice in Rome. Garland's distinction can perhaps best be illustrated through an analysis of the ambivalent force of the adjective in an English phrase such as "disastrous portent." The most straightforward interpretation involves taking "disastrous" as an adjective describing an attribute that the portent possesses. For instance, the pestilence and famine of 165 BC constituted a disaster in and of itself and so was a "disastrous portent" in this first sense. Simultaneously, however, these events of 165 were also thought to portend further disasters, with the result that the Sibylline books ordered the people to make sacrifice in their local shrines (Obseq. 13). In this latter case, the portent was also "disastrous" in the sense that it is interpreted by religious authorities as portending disaster. Numerous examples of this kind of proleptic sense of a prodigy could be cited, where the prodigiousness of an event lies in its unexpected character rather than in any immediate promise of danger from the prodigy itself. Consider, for instance, unusual cloud formations or trees growing in uncustomary places. One would be hard put to imagine how phenomena such as these presented by themselves any seri-

---

[31] Rosenberger 1998: 107–126.
[32] Liv. 31.12.8: *errantis . . . in alienos fetus naturae.*
[33] Garland 1995: 72.

ous danger to the Roman state. Nevertheless, prodigies of this type were reviewed by the priestly colleges and by the senate in Rome.[34] Although one inevitably finds ancient texts (or modern authors such as Brisson) melding cause and effect by characterizing the signifying event as itself evil rather than as portending evil, it is its function as indicating possible future unrest that characterizes the typical Republican prodigy.

NAMING THE HERMAPHRODITE

The earliest attested appearance of a human androgyne in the Roman world dates to a time of extreme danger for the Roman state. Livy includes among the prodigies recorded for the year 209 BC bloodied water at the Alban Lake and a series of lightning strikes occurring throughout the Italian peninsula, while at Privernum a bull spoke and a vulture descended to enter a shop in the town's forum. At Sinuessa it rained milk, and a child was born with an elephant's head. Livy's prodigy lists normally offer no more information than the kind of bare description given here; among these entries, however, the birth of a human hermaphrodite at Sinuessa prompts a brief but significant digression:

> *natum ambiguo inter marem ac feminam sexu infantem, quos androgynos volgus, ut pleraque, faciliore ad duplicanda verba Graeco sermone appellat.* (Liv. 27.11.4–5)

> An infant was born possessing a sex somewhere between male and female. The common people refer to these [with the Greek term] *androgynus* since, as often occurs elsewhere (*ut pleraque*), the Greek language is more adept at making compound words.

Biological uncertainty engenders philological uncertainty. The appearance of the androgyne has created a linguistic problem: how does one name such a creature? Since Latin cannot produce a noun to describe accurately the intersexed child, recourse is had to Greek. It must be noted that this adoption of the loan word *androgynus* is not based on any overwhelming parallel between Greek and Roman treatments of the phenomenon being named. Livy makes clear that such cross-language borrowing occurs often (*ut pleraque*), and indeed it is well attested from the earliest stages of Latin, in particular in its lower registers.[35] Nevertheless, Livy's need to account for the form here must mean that the word, like the phenomenon, would have rung oddly in the average Roman ear.

The meaning of the noun *androgynus*—literally, "man-woman"—nicely mirrors the condition of the infant, as a compounded word standing in for a

---

[34] Wülker 1903: 11, 20–21.

[35] Clackson and Horrocks 2007: 197–198; for the abundant examples already in Plautus, see Palmer 1954: 81–84.

compounded body. The same holds true for the other Greek loanword that, as Pliny the Elder testifies, would come to replace it: *hermaphroditus*, apparently formed by compounding the proper name of the male god Hermes with that of the female Aphrodite.[36] Although the extant occurrences of each noun do not allow us to judge with confidence Pliny's claim about the displacement of the word *androgynus* by *hermaphroditus*, the change would most logically accord with the growing popularity of Hermaphroditus, the eponymous figure of myth, depictions of whom experienced an increase beginning in the second century BC.[37] There also occurs occasionally a native Latin alternative to these Greek borrowings, and it is not difficult to see why speakers may have found these alternatives unsatisfactory. The adjective *semimas*, literally "half-male," obfuscates the biology of these prodigies when compared with the Greek synonyms, as is shown by the simultaneous application of this same word, like that of *semivir*, to eunuchs and other men for whom masculinity is either deficient or derided as such.[38] In the twenty-first century, medical practice continues to underscore the importance of correct vocabulary, where the analogous designation in English has shifted over a short period of time from "hermaphrodite" to "intersexual" to "disorders of sex development" (DSD), the term now generally accepted, albeit tenuously.[39] While in ancient Rome the debate over terminology did not center on human rights as it does today, I would argue, here as elsewhere, that the Romans too saw the importance of accurate terminology. Although in Latin the signifier for the hermaphrodite is almost inexpressible, at Rome the signification remains clear.

THE OFFICIAL PRODIGY PROCESS OF THE LATE ROMAN REPUBLIC

"What should we say about the birth of an androgyne? Wasn't this a kind of fateful warning?"[40] So remarks the character of Quintus Cicero when listing the various ways in which human beings are able to perceive the divine indirectly communicating with themselves—through phenomena such as earthquakes, lightning bolts, sweating statues. Quintus's remarks about Roman signs follow a discussion of how all the best-regulated states in human history have relied upon some sort of divination in ordering their respective societies. In most cases, Quintus observes, the form of divination adopted reflects local consider-

---

[36] Plin. *nat.* 7.34, mentioned above and discussed in the concluding section below. For opposing explanations of the origin of the name *Hermaphroditos*, see Jessen 1912: 717–718, Herrmann 1916–1924, 1: 2314–2317.

[37] Ajootian 1990: 283, 285.

[38] Full list of the various Latin terms for hermaphrodite at Luterbacher 1904: 25 n. 39; Plin. *nat.* 11.263 explicitly distinguishes a *semivir* from hermaphrodites and eunuchs.

[39] Reis 2009: 153–160.

[40] Cic. *div.* 1.98: *quid? ortus androgyni nonne fatale quoddam monstrum fuit?*

ations—since the Egyptians and Babylonians live on open plains, they became particularly adept at astrology, whereas the density of the atmosphere in Etruria makes its inhabitants especially skilled at reading weather signs (*div.* 1.93). Romans, by contrast, most often heed those prodigies that continual practice and collected experience have allowed them to be the most competent in interpreting (*div.* 1.97; cf. 1.3–5). It is here, in his assertion of the validity of divination at Rome as an empirically tested procedure, that Quintus places his remark about hermarphrodites. Just as ritual cross-dressing occurred in Greek cult at key moments of transition for the individual and community, so too did the appearance of a human hermaphrodite at Rome attract particular attention at crucial periods when the Roman state was undergoing a crisis.[41] Yet this is where any close similarities between Greece and Rome end. As Quintus implies in his survey of the origins of different types of divination, the interpretation of a hermaphrodite's appearance during the Roman Republic stands in a historical and epistemological category that is entirely its own.

This difference in the treatment of hermaphrodites can be clearly illustrated from a story preserved in Phlegon of Tralles, who compiled a chronicle of marvels during the reign of the Roman emperor Hadrian in the second century AD. Some time in late fourth-century BC Greece, Phlegon recounts, an Aetolian magistrate named Polycritus died, leaving a newly married bride with child.[42] In due time the widow gave birth to an infant with a double set of genitals, male and female. The child was taken to the city center, where various types of seers deliberated about what the child's birth portended for the city and in what manner it should be treated. Burning the mother and child together at the state's borders is mentioned as a possibly suitable response. Before any decisive action could be taken, the ghost of Polycritus appeared at the assembly, devoured the infant save for its head, and returned to the underworld. The child's disembodied head thereupon renders a prophecy of destruction and devastation to the stunned onlookers.

Three points of this synopsis should be emphasized. First, the assembled Aetolians consider the child a matter of public importance but, as details in the narrative make clear, this importance stems not from androgyny per se but from the symbolism of the relationship between the parents, with the father having held a high political office and the mother being from Locria, a state allied with Aetolia during that period. Second, the Aetolians interpret the dual-sex body of the child as a symbol for some kind of division that the state will soon suffer; in other words, the androgyne metaphorically embodies a direct indication of some future event. Third, the proposal before the citizen assembly to kill the infant seems to be carrying the day, until averted by the apparition of

[41] Breglia Pulci Doria 1983: 77 ("gli anni in cui [l'androgino] appare, sono anni sempre legati ad eventi particolarmente gravi per lo stato").
[42] For details I rely on Hansen 1996: 85–101.

the child's dead father. The execution of the child, in other words, would likely have proceeded to completion if not for intervention of the supernatural. Similar procedures characterize the other known appearances of hermaphrodites in the Greek world: first, the affected community meets to determine how the sexual anomaly can help determine future events at a precise historical moment and, second, each prodigy receives a treatment particular to the circumstances. The Roman response to the hermaphrodite invokes none of these procedures.[43] Rather, in all extant Republican instances, the precise identity of the parents is irrelevant (indeed, names are never given in the sources), the appearance of the portent is not predictive of a specific future outcome, the Roman senate—not a popular assembly—renders the ultimate decision, and the androgyne seems never to have been directly put to death.

There existed for the androgyne prodigy in the Republican period a set process by which the hermaphrodite was reported, investigated, and treated.[44] The following description provides a synthesis of the formal steps taken in this assessment.[45] The process begins when a witness or witnesses report the existence of the hermaphrodite, in most cases soon after birth, to a magistrate who, in our extant sources, is normally a praetor or consul.[46] As in all cases of anomalous births, sources pass over in silence the identity of both the parents and of the informant (when it is not an elected official).[47] This anonymity would seem further to underscore that, unlike the Greek case narrated by Phlegon, the significance of the birth applies not to an individual or particular family, but to the community as a whole. The relevant magistrate then brings the case to the attention of the senate in Rome, which chooses either to consider it, or to reject it with no further action. If accepted for official consideration, the senate relays the information to a priestly body for examination. In the case of hermaphrodites, that body is either the haruspices or the *decemviri sacris faciundis* (later expanded to *quindecimviri*). It is even probable that in many if not all cases the dual-sexed body becomes the responsibility of these two groups combined. The hermaphrodite is the only prodigy that receives such privileged treatment.[48] In the concluding step of the prodigy process, it is always the senate that has the ultimate say in whether to accept the recommendations for expiation made by

---

[43] Breglia Pulci Doria 1983: 58–66, in particular her conclusion that "L'atteggiamento greco di fronte al prodigio in genere e la pratica nei confronti dell'androgino non permettono quindi di far risalire l'uso romano a quello greco" (66). Contrast Brisson 2002 [1997]: 14, who erroneously conflates Greek and Roman practice in treating this episode.

[44] Explicitly political motivations behind the treatment of prodigies have been the object of much speculation; see especially Günther 1964: 209–236, MacBain 1982 (127–135 on hermaphrodites), Breglia Pulci Doria 1983 (88–166 on hermaphrodites), Rasmussen 2003: 219–239.

[45] I follow principally Wissowa 1912: 391–394; for details, see Rosenberger 1998: 17–90.

[46] For the sixteen to eighteen hermaphrodite prodigies, four are explicitly attested as not newborns: Liv. 31.12.6 (age 16), 39.22.5 (age 12); Obseq. 34 (age 8), 36 (age 10).

[47] Allély 2003: 147–148; this does not apply to all prodigies.

[48] MacBain 1982: 127–135.

these officials or, as occurs in some cases, to reject their suggestions entirely. This final stage, marking the senators as ultimate arbiters, underscores yet again the unmistakable connection perceived by the Romans between the prodigy and matters of state.

The hermaphrodite also stands out from among other known prodigies by the fact that, for each separate appearance, the expiatory ritual recommended by the priests is normally, and perhaps always, identical. This is not the case for non-human hermaphrodites. For animals, the expiation ritual seems to differ from that carried out for human beings, and no specific provisions survive regarding the fate of the animals.[49] In the numerous other cases of unusual human birth as well, when details are given the expiation ritual differs from that used consistently for the androgyne.[50] The means of elimination of the non-androgyne also differs in the one case for which such detail is provided: in 136 BC male conjoined twins were cremated and their ashes sent out to sea (Obseq. 25).

In his account of 207 BC, Livy provides a clear outline of the special procedure reserved for androgyne prodigies. Following the successful expiation of an earlier series of portents, alarm is revived by a miraculous birth about fifty miles southeast of the capital:

nuntiatum Frusinone natum infantem esse quadrimo parem, nec magnitudine tam mirandum quam quod is quoque, ut Sinuessae biennio ante, incertus, mas an femina esset, natus erat. id vero haruspices ex Etruria acciti foedum ac turpe prodigium dicere: extorrem agro Romano, procul terrae contactu, alto mergendum. vivum in arcam condidere provectumque in mare proiecerunt. decrevere item pontifices, ut virgines ter novenae per urbem euntes carmen canerent. (Liv. 27.37.5–7)

It was reported [to the senate] that a child had been born at Frusino identical to a four-year old. But its size was not so marvelous as the fact that, as at Sinuessa two years earlier, it too had been born indistinguishable between male or female. The haruspices, summoned from Etruria, declared the child to be a dreadful and hideous prodigy. [They recommended] that it be cast from Roman territory, far from contact with the earth, and submerged in the sea. They deposited it alive in a chest, brought it to the sea, and cast it in. The pontifices, for their part, declared that three bands of nine girls each should process through the city singing a song.

The coordination of the various official bodies is to be noted: the senate understands the significance of this birth; the haruspices, summoned by the senate, recommend expiation; the pontifical college adds a procession to the ceremony; finally, we read later in the passage that the *decemviri* offered their expertise as well, in part by supervising a second procession that the pontifices had ordered

---

[49] Liv. 27.4.11, 15; 28.11.3, 5.
[50] Breglia Pulci Doria 1983: 78–80; Rosenberger 1998: 109–110.

(27.37.13). All priestly bodies that specialize in prodigies—both foreign and native—assist in the expiatory proceedings for the hermaphrodite.

The elaborate ritual proved successful, as Livy indicates explicitly with the opening words of the next chapter: "the gods were duly appeased" (27.38.1: *deis rite placatis*). The evident success on this occasion presumably helps explain why the procedure was to remain standard for subsequent appearances. For the remainder of the Republic, in all cases but one where the disposal of the hermaphrodite is detailed, it is put aboard a ship and cast out to sea.[51] Even in the one case where Livy seems to imply that the hermaphrodite was killed by direct human intervention, there is good reason to assume that the historian is in fact referring to the standard ritual of casting to sea, but is being imprecise.[52] From a modern perspective one assumes, of course, that any child cast out to sea alone, much less a newborn, would soon meet with death. But it is a mistake to project this attitude back onto the Romans who, according to Livy, made sure to ascertain that the child was alive at the time of its relegation (27.37.6: *vivum*). In addition to performing expiation while the child is living, the ritual contains a second essential element: transporting the intersexed being out to sea, where the purifying water prevented any future consequences from being visited upon the Romans.[53] Indeed, the importance placed upon both the watery element and the preservation of the androgyne's life receives support from the manner in which the haruspices treat a prodigy of 171 BC that also centers on the unexpected genital formation of a young human being. Pliny tells us that a girl who had changed into a boy was taken off to a deserted island (*nat.* 7.36). Presumably the slight change in the procedure of banishment is attributable to the fact that the child was of an age—perhaps at the onset of puberty—where he could have saved himself if simply left to his own resources on a boat.[54]

A possible explanation for the preservation of life, however temporary that preservation may have been, will be considered in the next section. I will close this introductory discussion of the hermaphrodite prodigy during the Republic by considering yet one final way in which it constitutes a unique sign. The Romans considered most instances of excessive or seemingly unnatural sexuality as a means by which an individual could receive protection from malevolent spirits. In the visual realm, images of figures such as Priapus sporting an erec-

[51] Brisson 2002: 26–27 provides a convenient table, Allély 2003: 151–153 a discussion.

[52] Liv. 39.22.5, describing the killing of a twelve-year old hermaphrodite in Umbria in 186 BC (*id prodigium abominantes arceri Romano agro necarique quam primum iusserunt*; Obseq. 3). There are also textual problems (Briscoe 2008: 296–297). For the assumption that the normal expiation occurred, see MacBain 1982: 128–129, Rosenberger 1998: 132 and n. 15.

[53] Purifying effect of water: Allély 2003: 152 ("l'eau ayant valeur cathartique, le spectre de l'enfant ne la traverserait pas, et en conséquence n'inquiéterait pas les vivants"); Smith 1913: 470–471 cites abundant parallels.

[54] For other instances of sex change receiving different expiation rites, see Liv. 24.10.10–13 (214 BC), Diod. Sic. 32.12.2 (c. 90 BC).

tion (or sometimes multiple erections), of stylized female genitalia, and of non-standard sexual activity (such as male pygmies publicly engaged in anal sex) served an apotropaic purpose, warding off the evil eye from individuals, domiciles, and public gathering places.[55] Sexual gestures, too, such as the phallic image of the erect middle finger or the "fig" gesture representing penile penetration, seem to have originated as an analogous form of protection, as did the common phallic amulet, or *fascinum*, worn around the neck.[56] In contrast, there is no convincing evidence that the Romans of the Republic attributed apotropaic properties to the hermaphrodite.[57] They appear throughout the historical record not as talismans for personal protection, but as signs proffered by the gods to the state that something is not right with the world.

THE CONCEPT OF *SACER* AND PUNISHING THE SACRED

The appearance of a human being displaying characteristics of both sexes presents a conundrum toward which societies throughout history have adopted various attitudes. Infanticide offers a particularly draconian approach; in recent years it has become increasingly clear that a second common alternative does not resolve the issue satisfactorily either, namely that of assigning to the newborn a fixed sex of either male or female, an assignment that can inflict significant psychological damage on the intersexed individual.[58] The Roman treatment considered in this chapter represents a third option—handing the hermaphrodite over to political and religious authorities. Although hardly a preferable one, this approach, like those of exposure and of fixed sexual assignment, stems from its own set of assumptions and beliefs.

As we have seen, the parents or other members of the community during the Roman Republic were compelled neither to kill directly nor to expose to the elements an infant of mixed sex immediately upon discovery. This restraint does not arise from simple compassion, however, nor does it represent a general Roman attitude toward unusual births. In fact, the rearing of such a child stands contrary to the known provisions of archaic law. Cicero tells us that the

---

[55] Clarke 1998: 130–136 with bibliography, Williams 1999: 92–93; for eroticized pygmies, see Clarke 2007: 74–81.

[56] Middle finger: Corbeill 2004: 5–6; "fig" gesture: Sittl 1890: 102–103, 123; *fascinum*: Adams 1982: 63–64 (cf. Clarke 2007: 69–73).

[57] See, e.g., Delcourt 1966: 39; Ajootian 1997: 230–231 provides good evidence for seeing such a function of the hermaphrodite in the *anasyromenos* pose found on adult figures from second-century BC Delos.

[58] For sex assignment of hermaphrodites (and other intersexed individuals) among a range of traditional and modern societies, see the survey in Baumann 1955: 14–44; from the voluminous bibliography on the topic in Western culture I have found particularly stimulating Barbin 1980, Herdt 1994a, Herdt 1994b, Dreger 1998.

Twelve Tables of the fifth century BC prescribed that any child marked by a deformity (*insignis ad deformitatem*) should be immediately dispatched.[59] Dionysius of Halicarnassus, writing a generation after Cicero, provides additional details for a similar law that he attributes to Rome's first king. To ensure that his new city's population would grow, Romulus forbade the infanticide of children below the age of three "unless the child was disfigured or a monster."[60] The parents could not, however, expose even such a disfigured or monstrous child unless it was shown to the five nearest neighbors, who had to offer consent. In the context of Romulus's desire to populate his new state, this final proviso seems intended primarily to prevent families from killing healthy children. At the same time, however, it would have provided an opportunity for communities to detect marvelous births, such as hermaphrodites, that could be brought to the attention of the government in Rome. Elected officials would then take charge of whether such a baby had relevance to issues currently confronting the state. An illuminating parallel for this type of ambivalent attitude toward the intersexed child—undesired, and yet charged with potential significance—can be found among the Pokot of eastern Africa, as observed by the anthropologist Robert Edgerton in the early 1960s. Although most intersexed Pokot children are exposed or smothered at birth, the decision to permit some to live is attributed to a divine impersonal force called *torurut*, which protects the child from harm.[61] As in Rome, such protection belongs only to the hermaphrodite, as all other unusual births—children born without limbs or eyes, or having other deficiencies—are disposed of without hesitation. "But who can know what torurut intended for intersexed infants?"[62] In the case of both the ancient Romans and the twentieth-century Pokot, the compulsion toward infanticide, toward eliminating a child with an insecure future, yields to recognizing the potential relevance that mixed sexual characteristics may have in determining the will of the divine toward the community.

This connection between divine will and dual sexuality in humans prompts a consideration of archaic Roman views of what constitutes the sacred. The hermaphrodite cannot normally reproduce sexually, nor is it likely to be married, two factors that would cause a Roman to consider such a creature as a potential outcast from human society. As a result, the special treatment accorded the child at birth requires explanation. Some parallels from Rome's historical period provide a perspective on this treatment. The liminal sexuality of the hermaphrodite may be compared with that of another anomalous group of

---

[59] Cic. *leg.* 3.19 = Lex XII Tab. 4.1 Crawford (in analogy with the elimination of the tribunate by the *decemviri* in 451: [the tribunate was] *cito necatus, tamquam ex XII Tabulis insignis ad deformitatem puer*; see too Sen. *dial.* 3.15.2); on the conjecture *necatus*, see Crawford 1996: 630, Dyck 2004: 495.

[60] Dion. Hal. 2.15.2: πλὴν εἴ τι γένοιτο παιδίον ἀνάπηρον ἢ τέρας; Allély 2003: 129–130.

[61] Edgerton 1964: 1295–1297.

[62] Edgerton 1964: 1296.

the Republican era, the priests that served the Magna Mater. Imported to Rome during the Second Punic War following consultation of both the Sibylline books and the Delphic oracle—once again, at a time of communal crisis—this cult had many features that the Romans deemed exotic: the goddess was represented by an aniconic rock; although a foreign import, Magna Mater received a temple within Rome's sacred boundaries (*pomerium*); and, in a move that the Romans found particularly outrageous, the priests of the Magna Mater, or Galli, consisted of men who had undergone a ritual of voluntary self-castration.[63] These "illegitimate women" and "half-men," dancing through Rome to the percussion of exotic instruments, allegedly engaging in assorted forms of deviant sexual activity, received attention in Roman literature across a wide variety of genres.[64] Roman texts show perplexity with, and even repulsion at, the self-inflicted sexuality of the Galli, to such an extent that legislation barred native-born Romans from serving as priests.[65] Nevertheless, these religious figures were tolerated as something inconstruable and, therefore, as members of the realm of the sacred.

In a similar fashion, Delcourt has noted that the sacredness of androgyny in antiquity resides in its embodying the polar opposites of being both a biological monstrosity and an awe-inspiring mystery of nature.[66] Such a conception recalls ancient and modern discussions of the Latin term *sacer*, a word that ultimately survives in the English "sacred," but with original connotations that are foreign to current English usage.[67] The earliest explicit testimony of the realm of the *sacer*, dating probably to the Late Republic, makes clear that an object is *sacer* if it has been given over to the gods in accordance with conventional state practice; private offerings, in contrast, cannot belong to the category of the *sacer*.[68] Several passages in Livy indicate that, from the first years of the Republic, the adjective could apply to persons as well.[69] The Twelve Tables also preserve this notion; in what seems at first an oxymoron, in being "dedicated to the gods," the *sacer homo* can be killed with impunity.[70] A passage from the late-antique author Macrobius provides a final link between the Roman sacred and

[63] Full citations at Sanders 1972: 999–1008.

[64] E.g., Catull. 63.27 (*notha mulier*); Iuv. 6.513 (*semiviri*); Williams 1999: 128 ("Perhaps the ultimate scare-figure of Roman masculinity was the *gallus* or castrated priest of Cybele"; further 176–177).

[65] Dion. Hal. 2.19.5.

[66] Delcourt 1966: 11 ("l'androgyne occupe donc les deux pôles du sacré"); 1961: 43–45. For the notion of the sacred as both maleficent and beneficent, see the famous account of Girard 1977.

[67] For a critical review of modern scholarship see Jacob 2006: 523–534.

[68] Fest. p. 321: *Gallus Aelius ait sacrum esse, quocumque modo atque instituto civitatis consecratum sit, sive aedis, sive ara, sive signum, sive locus, sive pecunia, sive quid aliud quod dis dedicatum atque consecratum sit: quod autem privati[s] suae religionis causa aliquid earum rerum deo dedicent, id pontifices Romanos non existimare sacrum.*

[69] Ogilvie 1970: 500–501.

[70] Lex XII Tab. 8.10 Crawford, with Crawford 1996: 690. This use was already unusual in Mac-

androgyne prodigies. In attempting to explain the semantic development of *sacer* as applied to human beings, Macrobius reasons that, just as the ancients did not wish for a sacred animal to be outside the precinct of the gods, so too were sacred humans "returned" to gods via their death.[71] Although modern scholars tend to ignore Macrobius's rationalization that the soul of the consecrated man is somehow "owed" to the gods, his basic reasoning corresponds well with modern investigations into the concept. Benveniste has identified the Roman *sacer* as a concept unique among other early Indo-European cultures, and concludes that the creation of the *sacer* involves transferring an object or person from the human domain to the divine.[72]

The parallels between the concept of *sacer* and the hermaphrodite prodigy are not precise, however. Significantly, the hermaphrodite, once identified as a prodigy, cannot be put to death with impunity, but is reserved for the exclusive judgment of the gods; furthermore, I know of no instance in which the adjective *sacer* is applied to the androgyne prodigy. Nevertheless, the distinction between belonging exclusively to either divine or human realms, a distinction upon which the Roman concept of the sacred depends, matches well the special space occupied by the hermaphrodite. Although a monster, it may not be killed upon birth as the law ordains for other unusual children. Rather, a decision of the state allows it to be given over to the gods for judgment.

A parallel that has been frequently cited for the disposal of the hermaphrodite is the punishment for the act of *parricidium* (murder of a close relative or associate). In this instance, the resemblance includes not only structural parallels but a shared vocabulary for the process of removing the condemned—be it an infant or an adult murderer—from human society.[73] The bizarre form of punishment for the *parricida* has received much scholarly attention, but for our purposes it is the similarities rather than the differences between these two proceedings that are of interest: the basic form involves sewing the perpetrator into a sack (sometimes with a dog, rooster, snake, and ape) and throwing the sack into a river while the parricide is still alive. As with the hermaphrodite, the condemned is not literally killed but immersed in water for extinction at the hands of natural elements. Again, in both cases the possibility for survival, however unlikely, is not ruled out. An early imperial declamation, in fact, makes explicit that the death of the *parricida* is contingent upon guilt; the gods will somehow miraculously preserve the life of one wrongfully accused (Sen.

---

robius's day (*Sat.* 3.1.5: *non ignoro quibusdam mirum videri quod, cum cetera sacra violari nefas sit, hominem sacrum ius fuerit occidi*).

[71] Macr. *Sat.*3.7.7: *quem ad modum igitur, quod sacrum ad deos ipsos mitti non poterat, a se tamen dimittere non dubitabant, sic animas, quas sacras in caelum mitti posse arbitrati sunt, viduatas corpore quam primum illo ire voluerunt.*

[72] Benveniste 1969: 2.179–207; Girard 1977: 262–265 maintains against Benveniste that the same claim applies to early Greek concepts of the sacred.

[73] Cloud 1971: 35–36 offers the best discussion; see too, e.g., Breglia Pulci Doria 1983: 52–57.

contr. 7.1.5–10). It has been proposed that the unusual punishment of the parricide originates in the notion that the perpetrator is a *homo sacer*: as he is dedicated to the gods, it is with the divine element that the ultimate judgment lies.[74] If so, this provides another reason to characterize the androgyne prodigy as, at the very least, analogous with the *sacer*.

A final parallel for the expiation of the hermaphrodite lies in a third class of portentous human being: the unchaste Vestal Virgin. Ancient sources record two to four occasions during which the violation of a Vestal's virginity represented a prodigy that signaled a rupture in the *pax deorum*.[75] Plutarch provides a clear account of the measures taken by the Roman state to expiate this physical violation. As with the hermaphrodite, the priests do not harm the condemned Vestal directly, but bury her alive near one of the city gates in a burial chamber that comes equipped with means of sustenance: "In it are placed a couch laid out with coverlets and a burning lamp, along with small portions of the essentials for staying alive such as bread, water in a jug, milk, and olive oil, as if they are making expiation for the starvation of a body that had been devoted to the greatest sacred rites."[76] The penalty is designed in such a way that responsibility for the death of a sacred being does not fall on the community, and Plutarch notes in another context that priests regularly honor with rites and offerings the place that an unchaste Vestal has been buried.[77] Just as the hermaphrodite represents a violation of the natural order whose ultimate fate the Romans choose to dedicate to the gods, so too is retribution for an alleged violation of the Vestal placed outside the realm of human responsibility.[78] There is also a possibility that the original punishment for the unchaste Vestal involved not burial, but casting her into a body of flowing water, as was done with the hermaphrodite and the parricide. According to Ennius's *Annales,* Ilia, the mother of Romulus and Remus, was a Vestal Virgin whose intercourse with the god Mars caused her to be thrown into the Tiber along with her children.[79] Another resemblance between the two punishments is worth mentioning: the verb *neco* is commonly used in the killing of these prodigies. In this case the verb denotes a death that is achieved bloodlessly through the deprivation of the means for survival—air, food, water—for both the buried Vestal and the cast-

---

[74] Fowler 1911: 59; for an assessment of these arguments see Cloud 1971: 26–36.

[75] Liv. 22.57.2–6 (216 BC); Obseq. 37 (114 BC). Wülker 1903: 22 also includes Val. Max. 8.15.12, Plin. *nat.* 7.120 (292 and 219 BC).

[76] Plut. *Numa* 10.5: κεῖται δὲ ἐν αὐτῷ κλίνη τε ὑπεστρωμένη καὶ λύχνος καιόμενος, ἀπαρχαί τε τῶν πρὸς τὸ ζῆν ἀναγκαίων βραχεῖαί τινες, οἷον ἄρτος, ὕδωρ ἐν ἀγγείῳ, γάλα, ἔλαιον, ὥσπερ ἀφοσιουμένων τὸ μὴ λιμῷ διαφθείρειν σῶμα ταῖς μεγίσταις καθιερωμένον ἁγιστείαις.

[77] Plut. *mor.* 287A; cf. Parker 2004: 586, with parallel expiations and further bibliography.

[78] The alleged uncertain gender of the Vestals provides another similarity with the hermaphrodite; see Beard 1980 and 1995.

[79] Porph. Hor. *carm.* 1.2.17–18: *Ilia auctore Ennio in amnem Tiberim iussu Amu[l]ii regis Albanorum praecipitata*; similar testimony at Serv. *Aen.* 1.273, Mythogr. 1.30.

off hermaphrodite.[80] Yet again the human hermaphrodite stands apart from other prodigies as it aligns with the Vestal, whose violation offers one of the greatest threats to Rome's own sense of vulnerability.[81]

THE END OF THE PRODIGY PROCESS

René Girard's famous characterization of the sacrificial victim as a liminal figure that "should belong both to the inside and the outside of the community" applies well to the androgyne prodigy in Rome.[82] Originating within human society, the hermaphrodite leaves that community when the senatorial process entrusts the prodigy to the gods. A clear ancillary proof that the hermaphrodite inhabited such a conceptual framework of simultaneous exclusion and consecration is offered by the ways in which our texts describe the breakdown of the prodigy process as concurrent with the breakdown of the republican form of government. The rise of a powerful individual, such as the Roman emperor, rests unquietly with any implications external to that individual that the gods perceive problems with the state of affairs at Rome. As a result, with the rise of Octavian's autocracy, each prodigy had to be incorporated into a new logic regarding the relationship between human politics and the more-than-human world. As we shall see, in the presence of a single ruler, signs from the gods encourage the Romans to look on the bright side of life.

A fading of the mystique attending human androgyny can be detected in various areas of Roman society—in religious ritual and law, for example—beginning with the Augustan age. It is at this same point, and not coincidentally I will suggest, that the state-sanctioned prodigy process falls into abeyance. Livy makes the change explicit in his account of the year 169 BC, immediately before providing, as he often does, the annual list of prodigies:

> non sum nescius ab eadem neglegentia qua nihil deos portendere vulgo nunc credant, neque nuntiari admodum ulla prodigia in publicum neque in annales referri. ceterum et mihi vetustas res scribenti nescio quo pacto antiquus fit animus, et quaedam religio tenet, quae illi prudentissimi viri publice suscipienda censuerint, ea pro indignis habere, quae in meos annales referam. (Liv. 43.13.1–2)

> I am not ignorant that prodigies are no longer publicly announced or recorded in the official annals. From the same neglect arises the common belief that the gods do not provide warnings [to human beings]. But as I write about events of old, I acquire as it were an ancient frame of mind, and a certain religious awe prevents me from considering unworthy of recording in my history the kinds of things that the wisest men of those days thought should be taken up for the public good.

[80] Adams 1990: 235–238 (unwanted infants), 243 (Vestals), 249; Adams 1991: 105–106.
[81] Parker 2004.
[82] Girard 1977: 272.

Writing probably some time in the second decade BC, Livy provides contemporary testimony not only for the abeyance of the prodigy process during the Augustan age but, of equal importance, for how this abeyance reflects a broader change of attitude toward the divine. The loss of the prodigy process stems "from the same neglect" (*ab eadem neglegentia*) that refuses to recognize any relationship between odd occurrences in nature and the will of the gods.[83] Livy's lament about the waning belief in prodigies as divine signs receives firm support from other extant texts, which record for the seventy-eight years between 36 BC and AD 42 only one example of the official state expiation of a prodigy. The trend continues beyond this period as well, with few official prodigies recorded for the remainder of the first century and scarcely any for the second.[84]

Although Livy maintains a discreet silence over possible causes, independent evidence makes clear one source of this neglect. Under the autocratic rule initiated by Augustus, as prodigies of relevance to the state receive decreased attention, there appears in their place an increased focus on the private omen. Our sources characterize these omens as having bearing not on Rome as a whole but on the family and close associates of the *princeps*.[85] As a further irony, those types of unnatural phenomena that have now been classified as private omens often resemble the state prodigies investigated and expiated during the Republican period. What does change, however, and significantly, is their interpretation; signs that once signaled disruption can now bring hope.[86] Such a convenient approach to the divine had already been discernible as early as the first century BC, when individuals who had attained unusual prominence in the Republic came to recognize that the normal prodigy process could relay messages potentially damaging to their reputations as competent leaders. When Sulla and Julius Caesar were dictators, for example, they circumvented the senate-based procedures by consulting private diviners. The omens detected by these hired seers, while resembling prodigies, were construed no longer as disrupting the *pax deorum* but as indicating positive approval of each dictator's reign.[87]

With the dawning of the Augustan age this autocratic approach emerges once again. A single example will illustrate clearly how the new political organization ushered in a new perception of the natural world.[88] For the year 193 BC Livy records among a series of inauspicious prodigies a flood of the Tiber that caused a number of buildings near the Capitoline hill to collapse.[89] The

[83] For a defense of the MS. reading *qua* see W-M *ad loc.*, Davies 2004: 47 n. 64.

[84] Wülker 1903: 71 (Dio 54.19.7 records the sole Augustan example; cf. Obseq. 71).

[85] Günther 1964: 275–285; Rosenberger 1998: 210–240 offers a thorough discussion.

[86] In addition to the examples given by Günther and Rosenberger (in note above and text below), see Février 2003: 50–57 on animal signs.

[87] Günther 1964: 227, 232–233; North 1990: 69–71.

[88] I owe this example to Linderski 1993: 63–64; see further Davies 2004: 46–51, and Feeney 2007: 140–142 on portents in Tacitus.

[89] Liv. 35.9.2–5; see too Dio 39.61 (54 BC).

priestly college of the *decemviri* recommended from the Sibylline books a series of elaborate expiatory rites, including a nine-day festival (*novemdiale*), a ceremony of supplication at the temples of all the gods (*supplicatio*), and a purification of the entire city (*lustratio*). The symbolism of the inundation is clear: the particular areas affected by the Tiber waters indicate that the gods forecast a threat to the very heart of Rome's political and mercantile center. In 27 BC an overflow of the Tiber occurred of equally impressive proportions, covering all the low-lying areas of the city. This nighttime event, however, had followed closely upon a particularly auspicious moment earlier that day: the senate voting to bestow upon Octavian the honorific title "Augustus." Dio tells us that the haruspices, one of the main bodies consulted in the Republican prodigy process also, prophesied from this flood "that [Augustus] would grow greatly and would hold the entire city under his command."[90] Not only is a natural disaster construed as a positive sign for Rome but the very prophecy of the haruspices figures "Augustus" as the flood itself, since Dio's verb αὐξήσοι, translated here as "grow," provides a clear allusion to Octavian's newly acquired title. Nature no longer needs to be reckoned with when the ruler himself becomes perceived as nature's embodiment.

THE IMPERIAL FUTURE OF THE ROMAN HERMAPHRODITE

As floods and other oddities of nature come to be construed as occurring in accordance with imperial objectives, the hermaphrodite too changes roles during the post-Republican period. One area in which such change occurs is in the kinds of ruminations of the jurists with which this chapter opened. In the context of law, the hermaphrodite is first mentioned by the jurist Ulpian in the early third century AD.[91] Considering that, according to our sources, androgynous human beings during the Republic rarely matured beyond puberty, and that those adult specimens who were discovered were promptly removed from society, it comes as a surprise to see hermaphrodites translated from an area of divine concern to one of human legislation. The jurists too, it turns out, see the need to eliminate the hermaphrodite. And yet this intersexual being now represents not a rupture in the order of the gods but a legal conundrum. Since hermaphrodites can be considered in a sense both male and female, how is one to settle, for instance, matters of inheritance, where men and women have distinct rights? The legal solution is to rule that, for the purposes of Roman law, a third sex is impossible. Consequently, the sexual organs predominating in any

---

[90] Dio 53.20.1: ἀπ᾿ αὐτοῦ οἱ μάντεις ὅτι τε ἐπὶ μέγα αὐξήσοι καὶ ὅτι πᾶσαν τὴν πόλιν ὑποχειρίαν ἕξοι προέγνωσαν.

[91] Thomas 1992: 84–85.

given hermaphrodite came to define unambiguously that person's legal sexual category. If male genitals predominate, the hermaphrodite may establish an heir; if female genitals, then the hermaphrodite becomes indisputably female in the eyes of the law.[92] In legal contexts, the androgyne now presents not a mystery to ponder, but a biological puzzle that is able to offer one, and only one, correct solution.

Extant artistic representations of the hermaphrodite also offer evidence for changed perceptions. As always, however, this silent material can offer only hints. In her survey of extant representations of the mythical Hermaphroditos (and of human hermaphrodites) from the Greek and Roman worlds, Ajootian notes that it is difficult to reconstruct a consistent attitude toward the subject. During the last three centuries before the Common Era, when expiation of androgynes is best attested, numerous images of androgynous human figures were produced. This includes one common type that humorously depicts an "amorous wrestling match" between a satyr and hermaphrodite, a subject that Ajootian judges to be incongruous with a period of hermaphroditic prodigies.[93] It is worth noting, however, that these scenes represent figures in a clearly mythical context and that they develop from Greek prototypes that may date back as early as the fifth century BC.[94] By contrast, the famous type of the hermaphrodite resting alone, prone on a couch, seems to gain in effect by placing it in a context outside the mythical. It is accordingly intriguing that all extant versions of this category of sculpture date from the first and second centuries AD, suggesting "some specific impulse for the generation of the type primarily for a Roman clientele."[95] These sculptures in the round, inviting the viewer to admire the beauty of an apparently female form before being surprised by the unexpected male genitalia, prompt a response far removed from the response of the Roman senate only a few centuries earlier. Material representations too suggest changed perceptions between Republic and Empire.

Among textual material, Pliny the Elder provides the most explicit reference to the hermaphrodite's fate. After listing various forms of multiple births, concluding with a set of septuplets born to a woman in Egypt, Pliny devotes one sentence to an additional category:

> *gignuntur et utriusque sexus quos hermaphroditos vocamus, olim androgynos vocatos et in prodigiis habitos, nunc vero in deliciis.* (Plin. *nat.* 7.34)

---

[92] Ulp. *dig.* 1.5.10: *quaeritur: hermaphroditum cui comparamus? et magis puto eius sexus aestimandum, qui in eo praevalet*; cf. 28.2.6.2. The distinction matches the way in which moderns distinguish sex in contemporary situations (Kessler and McKenna 2006).

[93] Ajootian 1990: 284, referring to an Italian relief vase from the Hellenistic period (catalogue number 64a–b).

[94] Ajootian 1990: 278–279.

[95] Ajootian 1990: 276, who also argues for the viewing experience that I describe in the next sentence.

> There are also those that we call "hermaphrodites," produced with the characteristics of each sex. They were once called "androgynes" and classed among the prodigies, but now they are considered playthings (*in deliciis*).[96]

Pliny notes a similar phenomenon later in his encyclopedia when he mentions Nero as the first person to display hermaphroditic quadrupeds; to see the emperor riding on such marvels (*ostentis*) was deemed a sight not to be missed (11.262). The progression in attitudes that Pliny describes in these passages, from awe of the sacred to curiosity for nature's oddities, recalls Delcourt's formulation concerning developing attitudes toward cross-dressing in the Greek and Roman worlds. Originally involving the separation of individual from group for some now-lost ritual significance—fertility, perhaps, or the averting of evil—"once the meaning was forgotten, the attribute misinterpreted, transvestism necessarily degenerated into buffoonery and license. That is, indeed, the fate of everything that touches on the sexual life." As with the hermaphrodite, attitudes evolve from reverence and fear into open derision, "leaving no place for any intermediate feeling."[97]

Pliny's remark reveals a new phase in how androgynous human beings were perceived, and in so doing it marks the terminal end of a familiar progression. The hermaphrodite has followed a path parallel with its linguistic and divine analogues, from acceptance of sexual multiplicity to a need to situate sex and gender in explicit categories. Being neither male nor female, the hermaphrodite no longer belongs to the divine, and among humans it does not fit a heterosexual paradigm. A similar arc from inclusivity to the creation of discrete categories has also been noted for the development of human sexual behavior between the Republic and early Empire. In contrast with the earlier period, where the erotic impulse of poets such as Catullus depicts a man's choice of sexual object as dependent not on biological sex, but on "issues of status and property," by the time of the Augustan poet Ovid one finds an "exclusive interest in the possibilities of coupling between males and females."[98] In modern terms, the period witnesses the birth of heterosexuality as a normative concept. The development parallels the fate of nouns of fluid gender and of gods of androgynous power, which derived their significance from origins in an obscure time of mixed sex and gender. Another phenomenon can now join this group. After the end of the Republic, the dual sexuality of the hermaphrodite loses all ties to divine mystery.

---

[96] For the range of meanings of *deliciae*, from object of diversion to source of sexual pleasure, see Adams 1982: 171, 196–197, 220.

[97] Delcourt 1961: 14; see too Février 2003: 59–61 (on animal prodigies). Contrast Brisson 2002: 2, who characterizes the transition from a Republican time of "cruel religious superstition" to the Empire, where hermaphrodites have become "an agreeable fluke of nature and were put on show as freaks"; Garland 1995: 70–72.

[98] Habinek 1997: 31.

CONCLUSION

Saint Augustine's discussion of the hermaphrodite offers a convenient conclusion, uniting as it does this book's themes of grammar, divine power, human bodies with dual sexuality, and the origins of human culture. As with the Roman senate of the Republican era, the mere existence of the hermaphrodite puzzles Augustine, and forces him to ponder why his God would intentionally produce such a creature. He does not doubt that the hermaphrodite represents a true phenomenon since, although appearances are rare, they nevertheless occur at regular intervals.[99] He is confused, however, by terminology, just as the earlier Romans described by Livy were at a loss when first devising a name to describe an androgyne child. Augustine's hesitation, however, is of a different sort. He expresses uncertainty over which grammatical gender he should use to describe such a creature: "both sexes are present, with the result that it is unclear from which of these sexes they should receive their designation. Everyday usage has prevailed that they should be named in the preferred gender, the masculine."[100] Once again the Latin speaker desires grammatical gender to derive from biological sex and, in a confused instance such as this, Augustine must rely on the practice of past speakers, just as Latin's earliest speakers decided that a tree (*arbor*) is feminine, despite all contradictory morphological evidence.

Augustine also resembles the Roman grammarians in his explanation for the early history of the hermaphrodite. Like these scholars, who must create a narrative explanation for the origins of fluid gender since they are continually confronted with the phenomenon in poetic texts, Augustine posits an origin that goes back to the beginning of time. Regardless of their appearance, he says, hermaphrodites too must be descendants of Adam.[101] The narrative is familiar: scholarship seeks an explanation for an unusual phenomenon, one distinguished by an uncharacteristically dual sexuality, and finds it at the origin of culture, where, scholars are confident, it fits in with an early worldview. While it is impossible to account for all aspects of the phenomenon, confidence remains that the explanation offers a key to understanding external nature. Sex (and grammatical gender, of course) is everything.

[99] Aug. *civ.* 16.8: *androgyni . . . quamvis admodum rari sint, difficile est tamen ut temporibus desint; gen. ad litt.* 3.22.34. Cf. Lucr. 5.837–839.

[100] Aug. *civ.* 16.8: *sic uterque sexus apparet ut ex quo potius debeant accipere nomen incertum sit; a meliore tamen, hoc est a masculino, ut appellarentur loquendi consuetudo praevaluit.* For the notion of the masculine as the "default" gender, see Vaahtera 2008: 257–261.

[101] Aug. *civ.* 16.8 (on the entire variety of human beings that differ in some way): *verum quisquis uspiam nascitur homo, id est animal rationale mortale, . . . ex illo uno protoplasto originem ducere nullus fidelium dubitaverit.*

Abbreviations

B = C. Barwick. 1964. *Flavii Sosipatri Charisii artis grammaticae libri V.* 2nd ed. Leipzig: B. G. Teubner.

CIL = 1862–. *Corpus Inscriptionum Latinarum.* Berlin: De Gruyter et al.

CLE = F. Buecheler. 1895, 1897. *Anthologia Latina. Pars posterior: Carmina Latina Epigraphica.* Leipzig: B. G. Teubner.

DK = H. Diels and W. Kranz. 1951–1952. *Die Fragmente der Vorsokratiker.* 6th ed. Berlin: Weidmann.

GG = *Grammatici Graeci.* 1867–1910. 3 vols. Leipzig: B. G. Teubner.

ILS = H. Dessau. 1892–1916. *Inscriptiones latinae selectae.* 5 vols. Berlin: Weidmann.

Keil = H. Keil ed. 1857–1880. *Grammatici Latini.* 7 vols. Leipzig: B. G. Teubner.

LHS = M. Leumann, J. B. Hofmann, and A. Szantyr. 1972–1979. *Lateinische Grammatik.* Handbuch der Altertumswissenschaft 2: 2. Revised edition. Munich: Beck.

LIMC = H. C. Ackerman and J.-R. Gisler ed. 1981–2009. *Lexicon Iconographicum Mythologiae Classicae.* 8 vols. Zurich and Munich: Artemis Verlag.

LSJ = H. G. Liddell and R. Scott. 1968. *A Greek–English Lexicon.* 9th ed. Rev. by H. S. Jones and R. McKenzie, with supplement. Oxford: Oxford University Press.

Mazzarino = A. Mazzarino. 1955. *Grammaticae romanae fragmenta aetatis Caesareae.* Turin: Loescher.

NW = F. Neue. 1902. *Formenlehre der lateinischen Sprache. Erster Band: Das Substantivum.* 3rd ed. Rev. by C. Wagener. Leipzig: O. R. Reisland.

ORF = H. Malcovati. 1953. *Oratorum Romanorum fragmenta liberae rei publicae.* 3rd ed. Turin: Paravia.

Osbern = P. Busdraghi et al., eds. 1996. *Osberno: Derivazioni.* 2 vols. Spoleto: Centro Italiano di Studi sull' Alto Medioevo.

RE = A. Pauly and G. Wissowa ed. 1894–1963. *Real-encyclopädie der classischen Altertumswissenschaft.* 24 vols. Stuttgart: J. B. Metzler.

Roscher = W. H. Roscher ed. 1916–1924. *Ausführliches Lexikon der griechischen und römischen Mythologie.* 6 vols. Leipzig: B. G. Teubner.

SNG France = *Sylloge Nummorum Graecorum, Cabinet des Médailles, Bibliothéque Nationale.* Paris: Bibliothéque Nationale 1983–.

ThLL = *Thesaurus linguae Latinae.* 1900–. Leipzig: B. G. Teubner.

W-M = W. Weissenborn and H. J. Müller ed. 1880–1911. *Titi Livi ab urbe condita libri.* 6 vols. 2nd ed. Berlin: Weidmann.

Works Cited

Adams, J. N. 1982. *The Latin Sexual Vocabulary*. Baltimore: Johns Hopkins University Press.

———. 1983. "Words for 'Prostitute' in Latin." *Rheinisches Museum* 126: 321–358.

———. 1990. "The Uses of *neco* I." *Glotta* 68: 230–255.

———. 1991. "The Uses of *neco* II." *Glotta* 69: 94–123.

———. 2003. *Bilingualism and the Latin Language*. Cambridge: Cambridge University Press.

———. 2007. *The Regional Diversification of Latin, 200 BC–AD 600*. Cambridge: Cambridge University Press.

———. 2013. *Social Variation and the Latin Language*. Cambridge: Cambridge University Press.

Ahl, F. 1985. *Metaformations. Soundplay and Wordplay in Ovid and Other Classical Poets*. Ithaca, NY: Cornell University Press.

Ahlquist, A. 1996. " 'Gender' in Early Grammar," in V. Law and W. Hüllen, eds. *Linguists and their Diversions: A Festschrift for R. H. Robins on His 75th Birthday*. Münster: Nodus Publikationen. 43–52.

Ajootian, A. 1990. "Hermaphroditos." LIMC 5.1: 268–285; 5.2: 190–198.

———. 1997. "The Only Happy Couple: Hermaphrodites and Gender." In A. Koloski-Ostrow and C. Lyons, eds. *Naked Truths: Women, Sexuality, and Gender in Classical Art and Archaeology*, 220–242. London: Routledge.

Albrecht, K. 1895 and 1896. "Das Geschlecht der hebräischen Hauptwörter." *Zeitschrift für die alttestamentliche Wissenschaft* 15: 313–325; 16: 41–121.

Allardice, J. 1929. *The Syntax of Terence*. Oxford: Oxford University Press.

Allély, A. 2003. "Les enfants malformés et considérés comme *prodigia* à Rome et in Italie sous la République." *Revue des études anciennes* 105: 127–156.

Allen, J. 2005. "The Stoics on the Origin of Language and the Foundations of Etymology." In D. Frede and B. Inwood, eds. *Language and Learning*, 14–35. Cambridge: Cambridge University Press.

Ammassari, A. 1987. *Il Salterio latino di Pietro*. Rome: Città Nuova. 3 vols.

Arnott, W. G. 1959. "The Author of the Greek Original of the *Poenulus*." *Rheinisches Museum* 102: 252–262.

Axelson, B. 1945. *Unpoetische Wörter: Ein Beitrag zur Kenntnis der lateinischen Dichtersprache*. Lund: H. Ohlssons Boktryckeri.

Axtell, H. 1907. *The Deification of Abstract Ideas in Roman Literature and Inscriptions*. Chicago: University of Chicago Press.

Bailey, C. 1947. *Titi Lucreti Cari De rerum natura libri sex*. 3 vols. Oxford: Oxford University Press.

Balty, J. 1990. "Ingenium." LIMC 5.1: 657, 5.2: 440.

Barbin, H. 1980. *Herculine Barbin: Being the Recently Discovered Memoirs of a Nineteenth-Century French Hermaphrodite*. Trans. R. McDougall, introduction M. Foucault. New York: Pantheon Books.

Bardon, H. 1973. *Catulli Veronensis carmina.* 2nd ed. Leipzig: B. G. Teubner.

Bartelink, G. 1980. *Liber de optimo genere interpretandi (Epistula 57): Hieronymus, ein Kommentar.* Leiden: E. J. Brill.

Barwick, K. 1922. *Remmius Palaemon und die römische "Ars grammatica."* Leipzig: B. G. Teubner.

Bastien, P. 1992. *Le buste monétaire des empereurs romains.* 3 vols. Wetteren: Éditions numismatiques romaines.

Bauer, H. 1920. "Das Geschlecht von *finis.*" *Glotta* 10: 122–127.

Baumann, H. 1955. *Das doppelte Geschlecht: ethnologische Studien zur Bisexualität in Ritus und Mythos.* Berlin: D. Reimer.

Bayet, J. 1957. *Histoire politique et psychologique de la religion romaine.* Paris: Payot.

Baynes, L. 2002. "Philo, Personification, and the Transformation of Grammatical Gender." *Studia Philonica* 14: 31–47.

Beall, S. 2001. "*Homo fandi dulcissimus*: The Role of Favorinus in the *Attic Nights* of Aulus Gellius." *American Journal of Philology* 122: 87–106.

Beard, M. 1980. "The Sexual Status of Vestal Virgins." *Journal of Roman Studies* 70: 12–27.

———. 1987. "A Complex of Times: No More Sheep on Romulus' Birthday." *Proceedings of the Cambridge Philological Society* 33: 1–15.

———. 1995. "Re-reading (Vestal) Virginity." In R. Hawley and B. Levick, eds. *Women in Antiquity: New Assessments,* 166–177. London: Routledge.

Beard, M., J. North, and S. Price. 1998. *Religions of Rome.* 2 vols. Cambridge: Cambridge University Press.

Benveniste, É. 1969. *Le vocabulaire des institutions indo-européennes.* 2 vols. Paris: Éditions de Minuit.

Bergk, T. 1870. *Auslautendes D im alten Latein: ein Beitrag zur lateinischen Grammatik.* Halle: Mühlmann.

Bertholet, A. 1934. *Das Geschlecht der Gottheit.* Tübingen: Mohr.

Bieber, M. 1945. "*Honos* and *Virtus.*" *American Journal of Archaeology* 49: 25–34.

Blanco-Freijeiro, A. 1971. "El mosaico de Mérida con la alegoria del Saeculum Aureum." In J. Alsina, ed. *Estudios sobre el mundo helenístico,* 153–178. Seville: Publicaciones de la Universidad.

Blank, D. 1998. *Sextus Empiricus: Against the Grammarians.* Oxford: Oxford University Press.

Blänsdorf, J., W. Morel, and C. Büchner ed. 1995. *Fragmenta Poetarum Latinorum Epicorum et Lyricorum praeter Ennium et Lucilium.* 3rd ed. Stuttgart and Leipzig: B. G. Teubner.

Bloch, R. 1964. "Liberté et déterminisme dans la divination romaine." In M. Renard and R. Schilling, eds. *Hommages á Jean Bayet,* 89–100. Brussels: Latomus.

Bögel, T. 1966. "Lateinisch *arbor* in der Entwicklung zum Maskulinum und Personennamen um Ausonius." *Helikon: Rivista di tradizione e cultura classica* 6: 37–50.

Boll, F., and W. Gundel. 1916–1924. "Sternbilder, Sternglaube und Sternsymbolik bei Griechen und Römern." In Roscher 6: 867–1071.

Bonfante, L. 1981. "Etruscan Couples and Their Aristocratic Society." In H. Foley, ed. *Reflections of Women in Antiquity,* 323–343. New York: Gordon and Breach.

———. 1997. *Corpus Speculorum Etruscorum. U.S.A. 3: New York, The Metropolitan Museum of Art.* Rome: "L'Erma" di Bretschneider.

Bordenache Battaglia, G., and A. Emiliozzi. 1979. *Le ciste prenestine*. Vol. 1. Rome: Consiglio Nazionale delle Ricerche.

Boroditsky, L., L. Schmidt, and W. Phillips. 2003. "Sex, Syntax, and Semantics." In Gentner and Goldin-Meadow, eds., 61–80.

Bouché-Leclerq, A. 1871. *Les pontifes de l'ancienne Rome*. Paris: A. Franck.

Bourdieu, P. 1990. *The Logic of Practice*. Trans. R. Nice. Stanford: Stanford University Press.

Boussaada Ahlem, J. 1992. "Le culte de *Liber Pater* en Afrique à la lumière de l'épigraphie." *Africa Romana* 9: 1049–1065.

Boyce, G. 1942. "Significance of the Serpents on Pompeian House Shrines." *American Journal of Archaeology* 46: 13–22.

Bozzi, M., and A. Grilli. 1995. *Regola del Maestro*. 2 vols. Brescia: Paedeia.

Breglia Pulci Doria, L. 1983. *Oracoli sibillini tra rituali e propaganda (Studi su Flegonte di Tralles)*. Naples: Liguori.

Brelich, A. 1949. *Die geheime Schutzgottheit von Rom*. Zurich: Rhein-Verlag. Albae Vigiliae 6.

Briscoe, J. 2008. *A Commentary on Livy, Books 38–40*. Oxford: Oxford University Press.

Brisson, L. 2002 [1997]. *Sexual Ambivalence: Androgyny and Hermaphroditism in Graeco-Roman Antiquity*. Trans. J. Lloyd. Berkeley: University of California Press.

Brock, S. 1979. "Aspects of Translation Technique in Antiquity." *Greek, Roman, and Byzantine Studies* 20: 69–87.

Brown, R. D. 1987. *Lucretius on Love and Sex*. Leiden: E. J. Brill. Columbia Studies in the Classical Tradition 15.

Brugmann, K. 1889. "Das Nominalgeschlecht in den indogermanischen Sprachen." *Internationale Zeitschrift für allgemeine Sprachwissenschaft* 4: 100–109.

———. 1897. *The Nature and Origin of the Noun Genders in the Indo-European Languages*. Trans. E. Robbins. New York: C. Scribner's Sons.

Bruhl, A. 1953. *Liber Pater: Origine et expansion du culte dionysiaque à Rome et dans le monde romain*. Paris: E. de Boccard.

Burton, D. 2005. "The Gender of Death." In E. Stafford and J. Herrin, eds. *Personification in the Greek World: from Antiquity to Byzantium*, 45–68. Aldershot, England: Ashgate. Publications of the Centre for Hellenic Studies (King's College, London) 7.

Buslepp, C. 1916–1924. "Teiresias." In Roscher 5: 178–207.

Bussmann, H. 1995. "*Das* Genus, *die* Grammatik und—*der* Mensch: Geschlechterdifferenz in der Sprachwissenschaft." In H. Bussmann and R. Hof, eds. *Genus: Zur Geschlechterdifferenz in den Kulturwissenschaften*, 114–160. Stuttgart: Alfred Kröner.

Butler, J. 1990. *Gender Trouble: Feminism and the Subversion of Identity*. New York: Routledge.

Campanile, E. 1991. "Note sulle divinità degli italici meridionali e centrali." *Studi classici e orientali* 41: 279–297.

Camps, W. A. 1965. *Propertius: Elegies, Book IV*. Cambridge: Cambridge University Press.

Canciani, F. 1994. "Senatus." LIMC 7.1: 727–730; 7.2: 535–538.

Capdeville, G. 1971. "Substitution de victimes dans les sacrifices d'animaux à Rome." *Mélanges de l'École Française de Rome. Antiquité* 83: 283–323.

Cardauns, B. 1976. *M. Terentius Varro: Antiquitates Rerum Divinarum*. Wiesbaden: Franz Steiner.

Cartault, A. 1898. *La flexion dans Lucrèce*. Paris: Ancienne Librairie Germer Baillière et Compagnie. Bibliothèque de la Faculté des Lettres de l'Université de Paris 5.

Catone, N. 1964. *Grammatica enniana*. Florence: Vallechi.

Cavazza, F. 1981. *Studio su Varrone etimologo e grammatico*. Florence: La nuova Italia.

Cèbe, J.-P. 1987. *Varron, Satires Ménippées. 8: Marcopolis-Mysteria*. Rome: École Française de Rome.

Champeaux, J. 1982. *Fortuna. Recherches sur le culte de la Fortune à Rome et dans le monde romain des origines à la mort de César*. 2 vols. Rome: École Française de Rome. Collection de l'École Française de Rome 64.

Chin, C. 2008. *Grammar and Christianity in the Late Roman World*. Philadelphia: University of Pennsylvania Press.

Clackson, J., and G. Horrocks. 2007. *The Blackwell History of the Latin Language*. Oxford: Blackwell.

Clark, A. 2007. *Divine Qualities: Cult and Community in Republican Rome*. Oxford: Oxford University Press.

Clarke, J. R. 1998. *Looking at Lovemaking: Constructions of Sexuality in Roman Art, 100 B.C.–A.D. 250*. Berkeley and Los Angeles: University of California Press.

———. 2007. *Looking at Laughter: Humor, Power, and Transgression in Roman Visual Culture, 100 B.C.–A.D 250*. Berkeley and Los Angeles: University of California Press.

Cloud, J. D. 1971. "*Parricidium*: From the *lex Numae* to the *lex Pompeia de parricidiis*." *Zeitschrift der Savigny-Stiftung für Rechtsgeschichte* 88: 1–66.

Coker, A. 2010. "Aspects of Grammatical Gender in Ancient Greek." Diss. University of Manchester.

Corbeill, A. 1996. *Controlling Laughter: Political Humor in the Late Roman Republic*. Princeton: Princeton University Press.

———. 2008. "*Genus quid est?* Roman Scholars on Grammatical Gender and Biological Sex." *Transactions of the American Philological Association* 138: 75–105.

Corbett, G. 1991. *Gender*. Cambridge: Cambridge University Press.

Courtney, E. 1980. *A Commentary on the* Satires *of Juvenal*. London: The Athlone Press.

———. 1985. "Three Poems of Catullus." *Bulletin of the Institute of Classical Studies* 32: 85–100.

———. 1993. *The Fragmentary Latin Poets*. Oxford: Oxford University Press.

Crawford, M. 1974. *Roman Republican Coinage*. 2 vols. Cambridge: Cambridge University Press.

Crawford, M., ed. 1996. *Roman Statutes*. 2 vols. London: Institute of Classical Studies. Bulletin of the Institute of Classical Studies, Suppl. 64.

Cristofani, M. 1993. "Sul processo di antropomorfizzazione nel pantheon etrusco." *Miscellanea etrusco-italica, 9–21*. Rome: Consiglio nazionale delle ricerche. Quaderni di archeologia etrusco-italica 22.

———. 1997. "Masculin/féminin dans le théonymie étrusque." In F. Gaultier and D. Briquel, eds. *Les Etrusques, les plus religieux des hommes*, 209–219. Paris: Documentation Française.

Davies, J. P. 2004. *Rome's Religious History: Livy, Tacitus and Ammianus on Their Gods*. Cambridge: Cambridge University Press.

de Grummond, N. 1991. "Etruscan Twins and Mirror Images: The Dioskouroi at the Door." *Yale University Art Bulletin* 11–31.

————. 2006. *Etruscan Myth, Sacred History, and Legend.* Philadelphia: University of Pennsylvania Museum of Archaeology and Anthropology.

de Grummond, N., and E. Simon ed. 2006. *The Religion of the Etruscans.* Austin: University of Texas Press.

Delcourt, M. 1961 [1958]. *Hermaphrodite. Myths and Rites of the Bisexual Figure in Classical Antiquity.* Trans. J. Nicholson. London: Studio Books.

————. 1966. *Hermaphroditea. Recherches sur l'être double promoteur de la fertilité dans le monde classique.* Brussels: Latomus. Collection Latomus 86.

Della Corte, F. 1976. "Catullo, la vite e l'olmo." *Maia* 28: 75–81.

Deutscher, G. 2010. *Through the Language Glass: Why the World Looks Different in Other Languages.* New York: Metropolitan Books.

Dever, W. G. 2005. *Did God Have a Wife? Archaeology and Folk Religion in Ancient Israel.* Grand Rapids: William B. Eerdmans.

Devoto, G. 1932. "Nomi di divinità etrusche: I. Fufluns." *Studi Etruschi* 6: 243–260.

Dickey, E. 2007. *Ancient Greek Scholarship.* Oxford: Oxford University Press.

Dionisotti, A. C. 1984. "Latin Grammar for Greeks and Goths." *Journal of Roman Studies* 74: 202–208.

Dixon, R. M. W. 1982. *Where Have All the Adjectives Gone? And Other Essays in Semantics and Syntax.* Berlin: Mouton. Janua linguarum 107.

Dorcey, P. 1992. *The Cult of Silvanus: A Study in Roman Folk Religion.* Leiden: E. J. Brill. Columbia Studies in the Classical Tradition 20.

Dreger, A. 1998. *Hermaphrodites and the Medical Invention of Sex.* Cambridge, MA: Harvard University Press.

Dubuisson, M. 1984. "Le latin est-il une langue barbare?" *Ktema* 9: 55–68.

Dumézil, G. 1956a. "Le *curtus equos* de la fête de Pales et la mutilation de la jument Víspalā." *Eranos* 54: 232–245.

————. 1956b. *Déesses latines et mythes védiques.* Brussels: Latomus. Collection Latomus 25.

————. 1962. "Les deux Palès." *Revue des études latines* 40: 109–117.

————. 1970. *Archaic Roman Religion.* 2 vols. Trans. P. Krapp. Chicago: University of Chicago Press.

Dunbabin, K. 1999. *Mosaics of the Greek and Roman World.* Cambridge: Cambridge University Press.

Dyck, A. 1996. *A Commentary on Cicero, "De Officiis."* Ann Arbor: University of Michigan Press.

————. 2004. *A Commentary on Cicero, "De Legibus."* Ann Arbor: University of Michigan Press.

Edgerton, R. 1964. "Pokot Intersexuality: An East African Example of the Resolution of Sexual Incongruity." *American Anthropologist* 66: 1288–1299.

Erbse, H. 1969–1988. *Scholia graeca in Homeri* Iliadem *(scholia vetera).* 7 vols. Berlin: Walter de Gruyter.

Ernout, A. 1956. "Coniectanea." *Studi italiani di filologia classica* 27–28: 119–122.

Fantham, E. 2009. *Latin Poets and Italian Gods.* Toronto: University of Toronto Press.

Farrell, J. 2001 *Latin Language and Latin Culture: From Ancient to Modern Times.* Cambridge: Cambridge University Press.

Fedeli, P. 1980. *Sesto Properzio: il primo libro delle Elegie.* Florence: L. S. Olschki. Studi, Accademia toscana di scienze e lettere La Colombaria 53.

Feeney, D. 1991. *The Gods in Epic: Poets and Critics of the Classical Tradition*. Oxford: Oxford University Press.

———. 1998. *Literature and Religion at Rome*. Cambridge: Cambridge University Press.

———. 2007. "The History of Roman Religion in Roman Historiography and Epic." In J. Rüpke, ed. *A Companion to Roman Religion*, 129–142. Malden, MA, and London: Blackwell.

Fehling, D. 1956. "Varro und die grammatische Lehre von der Analogie und der Flexion." *Glotta* 35: 214–270.

———. 1965. "Zwei Untersuchungen zur griechischen Sprachphilosophie." *Rheinisches Museum* 108: 212–229.

Fernández Castro, M. 1986. "Chaos." LIMC 3.1: 188–189.

Février, C. 2003. "Le bestiaire prodigieux. Merveilles animales dans les littératures historique et scientifique à Rome." *Revue des études latines* 81: 43–64.

Fischer-Hansen, T. 2009. "Artemis in Sicily and South Italy: A Picture of Diversity." In T. Fischer-Hansen and B. Poulsen, eds. *From Artemis to Diana: The Goddess of Man and Beast*, 207–260. Copenhagen: Museum Tusculanum Press. Acta Hyperborea 12.

Flemming, R. 2000. *Medicine and the Making of Roman Women*. Oxford: Oxford University Press.

Fodor, I. 1959. "The Origin of Grammatical Gender." *Lingua* 8: 1–41, 186–214.

Fögen, T. 2000. *"Patrii sermonis egestas." Einstellungen lateinischer Autoren zu ihrer Muttersprache*. Munich and Leipzig: Saur.

Fontenrose, J. 1959. *Python: A Study of Delphic Myth and Its Origin*. Berkeley: University of California Press.

Fordyce, C. 1961. *Catullus*. Oxford: Oxford University Press.

———. 1977. *P. Vergili Maronis Aeneidos libri VII–VIII*. Oxford: Oxford University Press.

Forni, G. 1953. "ΙΕΡΑ ε ΘΕΟC CΥΝΚΛΗΤΟC. Un capitolo dimenticato nella storia del Senato Romano." *Atti della Accademia nazionale dei Lincei, Classe di Scienze morali, storiche e filologiche, Memorie*. Ser. 8.5: 49–168.

Fowler, W. W. 1911. "The Original Meaning of the Word *Sacer*." *Journal of Roman Studies* 1: 57–63.

Foxhall, L. 1998. "Natural Sex: The Attribution of Sex and Gender to Plants in Ancient Greece." In L. Foxhall and J. Salmon, eds. *Thinking Men: Masculinity and Its Self-representation in the Classical Tradition*, 57–70. London and New York: Routledge.

Fraenkel, E. 1917. "Das Geschlecht von *dies*." *Glotta* 18: 24–68.

———. 1955. "*Vesper adest* (Catullus LXII)." *Journal of Roman Studies* 45: 1–20.

Frazer, J. G. 1929. *Publii Ovidii Nasonis Fastorum libri sex*. 5 vols. London: Macmillan.

Fröhlich, T. 1991. *Lararien- und Fassadenbilder in den Vesuvstädten*. Mainz: von Zabern.

Funaioli, H. 1907. *Grammaticae romanae fragmenta*. Leipzig: B. G. Teubner.

Gabba, E. 1963. "Il latino come dialetto greco." In *Miscellanea di studi alessandrini in memoria di Augusto Rostagni*, 188–194. Turin: Bottega d'Erasmo.

Garcia de Diego López, V. 1945, 1946a, and 1946b. "Orientaciones sobre el género en latín." *Anales de la Universidad Hispalense* 8.3: 115–146; 9.1: 129–175; 9.2: 155–176.

Garland, R. 1995. *The Eye of the Beholder: Deformity and Disability in the Graeco-Roman World*. Ithaca, NY: Cornell University Press.

Geer, R. 2011. *"Invitus, regina"*: *Aeneas Cast as the Unwilling and Unfit Hero*. M.A. thesis, University of Kansas.

Geertz, C. 1983. "Common Sense as a Cultural System." In *Local Knowledge: Further Essays in Interpretive Anthropology*, 73–93. New York: Basic Books.

Gentner, D., and S. Goldin-Meadow, eds. 2003. *Language in Mind: Advances in the Study of Language and Thought*. Cambridge, MA: MIT Press.

Getty, R. J. 1933, "*Insomnia* in the Lexica." *American Journal of Philology* 54: 1–28.

Girard, R. 1977. *Violence and the Sacred*. Trans. P. Gregory. Baltimore: Johns Hopkins University Press.

Gomperz, T. 1901–1912. *Greek Thinkers: A History of Ancient Philosophy*. Trans. L. Magnus and G. Berry. 4 vols. London: John Murray.

Goold, G. P. 1981. "Two Notes on Catullus 1." *Liverpool Classical Monthly* 6.9: 233–238.

Goud, T. 1995. "Who Speaks the Final Lines? Catullus 62: Structure and Ritual." *Phoenix* 49: 23–32.

Gratwick, A. 1982. "Drama." In E. J. Kenney and W. Clausen, eds. *The Cambridge History of Classical Literature II: Latin Literature*, 77–137. Cambridge: Cambridge University Press.

Green, P. 1979. "Strepsiades, Socrates, and the Abuses of Intellectualism." *Greek, Roman, and Byzantine Studies* 20: 15–25.

Grevisse, M. 1969. *Le bon usage: grammaire française*. 9th ed. Gembloux, Belgium: Duculot.

Grimm, J. 1890. *Deutsche Grammatik*. Vol. 3, 2nd ed. G. Roethe and E. Schröder. Gütersloh: C. Bertelsmann.

Guittard, C. 2002. "*Sive deus sive dea*: les Romains pouvaient-ils ignorer la nature de leurs divinités?" *Revue des études latines* 80: 25–54.

Günther, R. 1964. "Der politisch-ideologische Kampf in der römischen Religion in den letzten zwei Jahrhunderten v. u. Z." *Klio* 42: 209–297.

Gutzwiller, K. 1992. "Callimachus' *Lock of Berenice*: Fantasy, Romance, and Propaganda." *American Journal of Philology* 113: 359–385.

Habinek, T. 1997. "The Invention of Sexuality in the World-City of Rome." In T. Habinek and A. Schiesaro, eds. *The Roman Cultural Revolution*, 23–43. Cambridge: Cambridge University Press.

Haffter, H. 1934. *Untersuchungen zur altlateinischen Dichtersprache*. Berlin: Weidmann. Problemata: Forschungen zur klassischen Philologie 10.

Hanfmann, G. 1951. *The Season Sarcophagus in Dumbarton Oaks*. 2 vols. Cambridge, MA: Harvard University Press.

Hansen, W. 1996. *Phlegon of Tralles' Book of Marvels*. Exeter: University of Exeter Press.

Hanssen, J. 1942. "Remarks on Euphony—Cacophony and the Language of Virgil." *Symbolae Osloenses* 22: 80–106.

Hardie, P. 1994. *Virgil, Aeneid Book IX*. Cambridge: Cambridge University Press.

Harless, G. 1816. *M. Tullii Ciceronis ad Quintum Fratrem Dialogi Tres De Oratore*. Leipzig: Weidmann.

Harrison, S. 2005. "Altering Attis: Ethnicity, Gender and Genre in Catullus 63." In Nauta and Herder, eds., 11–24.

Harrison, S., J. Hilton, and V. Hunink. 2001. *Apuleius: Rhetorical Works*. Oxford: Oxford University Press.

Harrod, S. 1909. *Latin Terms of Endearment and of Family Relationship: A Lexicographical Study Based on Volume VI of the* Corpus Inscriptionum Latinarum. Diss., Princeton University.

Heraeus, W. 1937. "Die Sprache des Petronius und die Glossen." In J. B. Hofmann, ed. *Kleine Schriften,* 52–150. Heidelberg: Carl Winter.

Herdt, G. 1994a. "Introduction." In G. Herdt, ed. *Third Sex, Third Gender: Beyond Sexual Dimorphism in Culture and History,* 21–81. New York: Zone Books.

———. 1994b. "Mistaken Sex: Culture, Biology and the Third Sex in New Guinea." In G. Herdt, ed., 419–445. New York: Zone Books.

Herescu, N. 1960. *La Poésie latine: étude des structures phoniques.* Paris: Les Belles Lettres.

Herrmann, P. 1916–1924. "Hermaphroditos." In Roscher 1: 2314–2342.

Hersch, K. 2010. *The Roman Wedding: Ritual and Meaning in Antiquity.* Cambridge: Cambridge University Press.

Hockett, C. F. 1958. *A Course in Modern Linguistics.* New York: Macmillan.

Hodgman, A. 1902. "Noun Declension in Plautus." *Classical Review* 16: 294–305.

Holford-Strevens, L. 2003. *Aulus Gellius: An Antonine Scholar and his Achievement.* Rev. ed. Oxford: Oxford University Press.

Holland, L. 2011. "Family Nomenclature and Same-Name Divinities in Roman Religion and Mythology." *Classical World* 104: 211–226.

Hollis, A. S. 2007. *Fragments of Roman Poetry, c. 60 BC–AD 20.* Oxford: Oxford University Press.

Hölscher, T. 1986. "Clementia." LIMC 3.1.295–299, 3.2.230.

Horsfall, N. 1981. "Aspects of Virgilian Influence in Roman Life." *Atti del convegno mondiale scientifico di studi su Virgilio* 2: 47–63. Rome.

———. 1991. *Virgilio: l'epopea in alambicco.* Naples: Liguori. Forme, materiali e ideologie del mondo antico 31.

———. 2008. *Virgil,* Aeneid *2: A Commentary.* Leiden: E. J. Brill. Mnemosyne suppl. 299.

Houghton, L. 2009. "Sexual Puns in Ovid's *Ars* and *Remedia.*" *Classical Quarterly* 59: 280–285.

Hutchinson, G. 2006. *Propertius: Elegies, Book IV.* Cambridge: Cambridge University Press.

Innes, D. 1988. "Cicero on Tropes." *Rhetorica* 6: 307–325.

Jacob, R. 2006. "La question romaine du *sacer.* Ambivalence du sacré ou construction symbolique de la sortie du droit." *Revue historique* 308: 523–588.

Jakobson, R. 1959. "On Linguistic Aspects of Translation." In R. Brower, ed. *On Translation,* 232–239. New York: Oxford University Press.

Janan, M. 2001. *The Politics of Desire: Propertius IV.* Berkeley: University of California Press.

Janko, R. 1992. *The Iliad: A Commentary. Volume IV: books 13–16.* Cambridge: Cambridge University Press.

Jeanneret, M. 1917. "La langue des tablettes d'exécration latines. Première partie." *Revue de philologie* 41: 5–153.

Jespersen, O. 1967. *Growth and Structure of the English Language.* 9th ed. Oxford: Blackwell.

Jessen, O. 1912. "Hermaphroditos." RE 8: 714–721.

Jocelyn, H. D. 1964. "Ancient Scholarship and Virgil's Use of Republican Latin Poetry I." *Classical Quarterly* 14: 280–295.

———. 1967. *The Tragedies of Ennius: The Fragments*. Cambridge: Cambridge University Press.

———. 1984 and 1985. "The Annotations of M. Valerius Probus." *Classical Quarterly* 34: 464–472; 35: 149–161, 466–474.

Jonge, C. de. 2008. *Between Grammar and Rhetoric: Dionysius of Halicarnassus on Language, Linguistics, and Literature*. Leiden: E.J. Brill.

Josephson, Å. 1950. "*Casae litterarum.*" *Studien zum Corpus Agrimensorum Romanorum*. Uppsala: Almqvist & Wiksells.

Kaster, R. 1978. "Servius and *Idonei Auctores.*" *American Journal of Philology* 99: 181–209.

———. 1988. *Guardians of Language: The Grammarian and Society in Late Antiquity*. Berkeley: University of California Press.

———. 1995. *C. Suetonius Tranquillus: "De Grammaticis et Rhetoribus.*" Oxford: Oxford University Press.

Katz, J. 2007. *The Invention of Heterosexuality*. Chicago: University of Chicago Press.

Kay, N. M. 2001. *Ausonius: Epigrams*. London: Duckworth.

Kendon, A. 1991. "Some Considerations for a Theory of Language Origins." *Man* n.s. 26: 199–221.

Kenner, H. 1970. *Das Phänomen der verkehrten Welt in der griechisch-römischen Antike*. Klagenfurt: Geschichtsverein für Kärnten.

Kessler, S. J., and W. McKenna. 2006. "Toward a Theory of Gender." In S. Stryker and S. Whittle, eds. *The Transgender Studies Reader*, 165–182. New York: Routledge. Orig. publ. in S. J. Kessler and W. McKenna, *Gender: An Ethnomethodological Approach*, 142–169. Chicago: University of Chicago Press 1985.

Keulen, W. 2009. *Gellius the Satirist: Roman Cultural Authority in Attic Nights*. Leiden: E. J. Brill. Mnemosyne suppl. 297.

Kiss, D. Forthcoming. "Catullo 1.2, Servio e Guglielmo da Pastrengo." *Quaderni Urbinati di Cultura Classica*.

Klotz, A. 1931. "Zu Catull." *Rheinisches Museum* 80: 342–356.

Knauer, G. 1964. *Die Aeneis und Homer. Studien zur poetischen Technik Vergils mit Listen der Homerzitate in der Aeneis*. Göttingen: Vandenhoeck & Ruprecht. Hypomnemata 7.

Koenen, L. 1993. "The Ptolemaic King as a Religious Figure." In A. Bulloch et al., eds. *Images and Ideologies: Self-Definition in the Hellenistic World*, 25–115. Berkeley: University of California Press.

Koterba, L. 1905. *De sermone Pacuviano et Acciano*. Vienna: F. Deuticke. Dissertationes Philologae Vindobonenses 8: 3.

Krenkel, W. 2002. *Marcus Terentius Varro, Saturae Menippeae*. St. Katharinen: Scripta Mercaturae. Subsidia Classica 6.

Kretschmer, P. 1924. "Dyaus, Ζεύς, Diespiter und die Abstrakta im Indogermanischen." *Gnomon* 13: 101–114.

Kroll, W. 1959. *C. Valerius Catullus*. 3rd ed. Stuttgart: B. G. Teubner.

Krostenko, B. 2001. *Cicero, Catullus, and the Language of Social Performance*. Chicago: University of Chicago Press.

Lakoff, G. 1986. "Classifiers as a Reflection of Mind." In C. Craig, ed. *Noun Classes and Categorization*, 13–52. Philadelphia: John Benjamins.

Lakoff, G. 1987. *Women, Fire, and Dangerous Things: What Categories Reveal about the Mind.* Chicago: University of Chicago Press.

Latte, K. 1960. *Römische Religionsgeschichte.* Munich: C. H. Beck. Handbuch der Altertumswissenschaft 5: 4.

Lehmann, W. 1989. "Problems in Proto-Indo-European Grammar: Residues from Pre-Indo-European Active Structure." *General Linguistics* 29: 228–246.

Linderski, J. 1993. "Roman Religion in Livy." In W. Schuller, ed. *Livius. Aspekte seines Werkes,* 53–70. Konstanz: Universitätsverlag Konstanz.

———. 1995. *Roman Questions: Selected Papers.* Stuttgart: F. Steiner.

Lindsay, W. 1903. *Nonii Marcelli De conpendiosa doctrina libri XX.* 3 vols. Leipzig: B. G. Teubner.

Ling, R. 1983. "The Seasons in Romano-British Mosaic Pavements." *Britannia* 14: 13–22.

Löfstedt, B. 1961. *Studien über die Sprache der langobardischen Gesetze. Beiträge zur frühmittelalterlichen Latinität.* Stockholm: Almqvist & Wiksell. Studia Latina Upsaliensia 1.

Lomanto, V. 1998. "Varrone e la dottrina del genere." In U. Rapallo and G. Garbugino, eds. *Grammatica e lessico delle lingue "morte,"* 89–105. Allesandria: Edizioni dell' Orso.

López Monteagudo, G. 1997. "Saeculum." LIMC 8.1: 1071–1073, 8.2: 724.

Loraux, N. 1992. "What Is a Goddess?" In Schmitt Pantel, ed., 11–44, 481–489.

Lunelli, A. 1969. *Aerius: Storia di una parola poetica (varia neoterica).* Rome: Edizioni dell' Ateneo.

Luterbacher, F. 1904. *Der Prodigienglaube und Prodigienstil der Römer.* Repr. 1967, Darmstadt: Wissenschaftliche Buchgesellschaft.

MacBain, B. 1982. *Prodigy and Expiation: A Study in Religion and Politics in Republican Rome.* Wetteren: Imprimerie Universa. Collection Latomus 177.

Malcovati, H. 1953. *Oratorum Romanorum fragmenta liberae rei publicae.* 3rd ed. Turin: Paravia.

Maiden, M. 2013. "Morphological Persistence." In M. Maiden et al., eds. *The Cambridge History of the Romance Languages,* 155–214. Cambridge: Cambridge University Press.

Maltby, R. 1991. *A Lexicon of Ancient Latin Etymologies.* Leeds: Cairns.

Mankin, D. 2011. *Cicero, "De Oratore" Book III.* Cambridge: Cambridge University Press.

Marache, R. 1952. *La critique littéraire de langue latine et le développement du goût archaïsant au IIe siècle de notre ère.* Rennes: Plihon.

Marbach, E. 1894–1963. "Manes." RE 14.1: 1050–1060.

Massaro, M. 1998. "Gli epigrammi per L. Maecius Pilotimus e A. Granius Stabilio (*CIL,* I², 1209 e 1210)." *Epigraphica* 60: 183–206.

Matasović, R. 2004. *Gender in Indo-European.* Heidelberg: Universitätsverlag Winter.

McCracken, G. 1947. "*Arnobius Adversus Genera*—Arnobius on the Genders." *Classical Journal* 42: 474–476.

———. 1949. *Arnobius of Sicca: The Case against the Pagans.* 2 vols. Westminster, MD: Newman Press.

McNeill, R. 2010. "*Cum tacent, clamant*: The Pragmatics of Silence in Catullus." *Classical Philology* 105: 69–82.

Meershoek, G. Q. A. 1966. *Le latin biblique d'après Saint Jérôme; Aspects linguistiques de la rencontre entre la Bible et le monde classique*. Nijmegen-Utrecht: Dekker and Van de Vegt.

Meillet, A. 1920. "Les noms du 'feu' et de l''eau' et la question du genre." *Mémoires de la Société linguistique de Paris* 21: 249–256.

Ménage, G. 1715. *Menagiana*. 3rd ed. Paris: Chez Florentin Delaulne.

Mohrmann, C. 1965 (1949). "Les origines de la latinité chrétienne à Rome," *Études sur le latin des chrétiens*. Rome: Edizioni di storia e letteratura. 3: 67–126. 3 vols. Orig. publ. in *Vigiliae Christianae* 3: 67–106, 163–183.

Morena, P. 1990. "Kairos." LIMC 5.1: 921–926, 5.2: 597–598.

Mühmelt, M. 1965. *Griechische Grammatik in der Vergilerklärung*. Munich: C. H. Beck. Zetemata 37.

Müller, L. 1894. *De re metrica poetarum latinorum praeter Plautum et Terentium libri septem*. 2nd ed. Leipzig: Ricker.

Muth, R. 2004. "Kastration." *Reallexikon für Antike und Christentum* 20: 285–342.

Nauta, R. 2005. "Catullus 63 in a Roman Context." In Nauta and Harder, eds., 87–119.

Nauta, R., and A. Harder, eds. 2005. *Catullus' Poem on Attis: Text and Contexts*. Leiden: E. J. Brill.

Nettleship, H. 1886. "The Study of Latin Grammar among the Romans in the First Century A.D." *Journal of Philology* 15: 189–214.

Niedermann, M. 1937. *Consentii Ars de barbarismis et metaplasmis; Victorini fragmentum De soloecismo et barbarismo*. Neuchâtel: Neocomi Helvetiorum.

Nisbet, R., and M. Hubbard. 1970. *A Commentary on Horace: Odes Book I*. Oxford: Oxford University Press.

———. 1978. *A Commentary on Horace: Odes Book II*. Oxford: Oxford University Press.

Nobili, M. 2002. "'Solecismi' di Marziale: *Epigr.* 11, 19 e 5, 38." In *"Arma virumque . . ."*: *studi di poesia e storiografia in onore di Luca Canali*, 121–136. Pisa: Istituti Editoriali e Poligrafici Internazionali.

Norden, E. 1913. *Agnostos Theos. Untersuchungen zur Formengeschichte religiöser Rede*. Leipzig: B. G. Teubner.

North, J. A. 2007. 1990. "Diviners and Divination at Rome." In M. Beard and J. A. North, eds. *Pagan Priests*, 49–71. Ithaca, NY: Cornell University Press.

———. 2007. "Why Does Festus Quote What He Quotes?" In F. Glinister and C. Woods, eds. *Verrius, Festus, and Paul: Lexicography, Scholarship, and Society*, 49–68. London. Bulletin of the Institute of Classical Studies 93.

Ogilvie, R. M. 1970. *A Commentary on Livy, Books 1–5*. Oxford: Oxford University Press.

O'Hara, J. J. 1996. *True Names: Vergil and the Alexandrian Tradition of Etymological Wordplay*. Ann Arbor: University of Michigan Press.

Orr, D. 1978. "Roman Domestic Religion: The Evidence of the Household Shrines." *Aufstieg und Niedergang der römischen Welt* II 16.2: 1557–1591.

Ortner, S. 1974. "Is Female to Male as Nature Is to Culture?" In M. Z. Rosaldo and L. Lamphere, eds. *Woman, Culture, and Society*, 67–87. Palo Alto, CA: Stanford University Press.

Pagels, E. 1978. "The Gnostic Vision." *Parabola* 3.4: 6–9.

———. 1979. *The Gnostic Gospels*. New York: Vintage Books.

Pallottino, M. 1955. *The Etruscans*. Trans. J. Cremona. Harmondsworth, UK: Penguin.

Palmer, L. R. 1954. *The Latin Language*. London: Faber and Faber.

Panayotakis, C. 2010. *Decimus Laberius: The Fragments*. Cambridge: Cambridge University Press.

Panofsky, E. 1939. *Studies in Iconology: Humanistic Themes in the Art of the Renaissance*. Oxford: Oxford University Press.

Parker, H. 2004. "Why Were the Vestals Virgins? Or the Chastity of Women and the Safety of the Roman State." *American Journal of Philology* 125: 563–601.

Paxson, J. 1998. "Personification's Gender." *Rhetorica* 16: 149–179.

Pease, A. 1955. *M. Tulli Ciceronis De Natura Deorum*. 2 vols. Cambridge, MA: Harvard University Press.

Pellizzari, A. 2003. *Servio: storia, cultura e istituzioni nell' opera di un grammatico tardoantico*. Florence: L. S. Olschki.

Perfigli, M. 2004. *"Indigitamenta": Divinità funzionali e funzionalità divina nella religione romana*. Pisa: Edizioni ETS.

Peter, R. 1890–1894. *"Indigitamenta* und *Indigetes."* In Roscher 2: 1, 129–233.

Pfiffig, A. 1975. *Religio etrusca*. Graz: Akademische Druck- und Verlagsanstalt.

Pighi, G. 1954. "I nomi delle divinità iguvine." *Rivista di filologia e di istruzione classica* 32: 225–261.

Prescendi, F. 2002–2010. "Pales." In H. Cancik and H. Schneider, eds. *Brill's New Pauly: Encyclopedia of the Ancient World: Antiquity*, 10: 385.

Quinn, K. 1973. *Catullus: The Poems*. 2nd ed. London: Macmillan.

Radke, G. 1956. "*Aurea funis.*" *Gymnasium* 63: 82–86.

———. 1979. *Die Götter Altitaliens*. Münster: Aschendorff. 2nd ed. Fontes et commentationes 3.

Rasmussen, S. 2003. *Public Portents in Republican Rome*. Rome: "L'Erma" di Bretschneider. Analecta Romana Instituti Danici 304.

Rawson, E. 1985. *Intellectual Life in the Late Roman Republic*. Baltimore: Johns Hopkins University Press.

Reis, E. 2009. *Bodies in Doubt: An American History of Intersex*. Baltimore: Johns Hopkins University Press.

Reitzenstein, R. 1893. *Epigramm und Skolion: Ein Beitrag zur Geschichte der alexandrinischen Dichtung*. Giessen: J. Ricker.

Renehan, R. 1998. "On Gender Switching as a Literary Device in Latin Poetry." In P. Knox and C. Foss, eds. *Style and Tradition: Studies in Honor of Wendell Clausen*, 212–229. Stuttgart and Leipzig: B. G. Teubner.

Rilke, R. M. 1977. *Briefe an Nanny Wunderly-Volkart*. Frankfurt am Main: Insel. 2 vols.

Rives, J. 1992. "The *Iuno Feminae* in Roman Society." *Echos du Monde Classique* 36: 33–49.

Rix, H. 1998. "Teonimi etruschi e teonimi italici." *Annali della Fondazione per il Museo Claudio Faina* 5: 207–229.

Roberts, W. Rhys. 1901. *Dionysius of Halicarnassus: The Three Literary Letters*. Cambridge: Cambridge University Press.

———. 1910. *Dionysius of Halicarnassus: On Literary Composition*. London: Macmillan and Company.

Robinson, M. 1999. "Salmacis and Hermaphroditus: When Two Become One (Ovid, *Met.* 4.285–388)." *Classical Quarterly* 49: 212–223.

Romeo, I. 1997. "Genius." LIMC 8.1.599–607, 8.2.372–377.

Rosén, H. 1999. *"Latine loqui": Trends and Directions in the Crystallization of Classical Latin.* Munich: Wilhelm Fink Verlag.

Rosenberger, V. 1998. *Gezähmte Götter. Das Prodigienwesen der römischen Republik.* Stuttgart: Franz Steiner Verlag. Heidelberger Althistorische Beiträge und Epigraphische Studien 27.

Rothstein, M. 1898. *Die Elegien des Sextus Propertius.* 2 vols. Berlin: Weidmann.

Rousselle, R. 1987. "Liber-Dionysus in Early Roman Drama." *Classical Journal* 82: 193–198.

Rubin, G. 1975. "The Traffic in Women: Notes on the 'Political Economy' of Sex." In R. Reiter, ed. *Toward an Anthropology of Women,* 157–210. New York: Monthly Review Press.

Rüpke, J. 2007. *Religion of the Romans.* Trans. R. Gordon. Malden, MA: Polity Press.

Russell, D. A. 1979. "Rhetors at the Wedding." *Proceedings of the Cambridge Philological Society* 205: 104–117.

Sanders, G. M. 1972. "Gallos." *Reallexikon für Antike und Christentum* 8: 984–1034.

Scheid, J. 2003 [1999]. "Hierarchy and Structure in Polytheism: Roman Methods of Conceiving Action." In C. Ando, ed. *Roman Religion,* 164–189. Trans. P. Purchase. Edinburgh: Edinburgh University Press. Orig. publ. as "Hiérarchie et structure dans le polythéisme romain: Façons romaines de penser l'action." *Archiv für Religionsgeschichte* 1 (1999) 184–203.

Schenkeveld, D. 1996. "Charisius, *Ars grammatica* I.15: The Introduction." In P. Swiggers and A. Wouters, eds. *Ancient Grammar: Content and Context,* 17–35. Leuven and Paris: Peeters.

———. 1998. "The Idea of Progress and the Art of Grammar: Charisius *Ars grammatica* 1.15." *American Journal of Philology* 119: 443–459.

———. 2004. *A Rhetorical Grammar: C. Iulius Romanus, Introduction to the* Liber de adverbio. Leiden: E. J. Brill.

Schilling, R. 1979. "Genius et ange." In *Rites, cultes, dieux de Rome.* Paris: Klincksieck. 415–443. German version at *Reallexikon für Antike und Christentum* 10 (1976) 52–83.

Schmitt Pantel, P., ed. 1992. *A History of Women in the West. I. From Ancient Goddesses to Christian Saints.* Trans. A. Goldhammer. Cambridge, MA: Harvard University Press.

Schultz, C. 2006. *Women's Religious Activity in the Roman Republic.* Chapel Hill: University of North Carolina Press.

Schulze, W. 1934. "Beiträge zur Wort- und Sittengeschichte," *Kleine Schriften,* 189–210. Göttingen: Vandenhoeck & Ruprecht. Orig. publ. in *Sitzungsberichte der Preußischen Akademie der Wissenschaften* 1918: 769–791.

Schwyzer, E. 1966. *Griechische Grammatik,* vol. 2 *Syntax und syntaktische Stilistik.* 3rd ed. rev. Ä. Debrunner. Munich: C. H. Beck. Handbuch der Altertumswissenschaft 2: 1.

Scullard, H. H. 1981. *Festivals and Ceremonies of the Roman Republic.* Ithaca, NY: Cornell University Press.

Setaioli, A. 2004. "Interpretazioni stoiche ed epicuree in Servio e la tradizione dell'esegesi filosofica del mito e dei poeti a Roma (Cornuto, Seneca, Filodemo)." *International Journal of the Classical Tradition* 10: 335–376; 11: 3–46.

Setaioli, A. 2008. "Stoic and Epicurean Interpretations in Servius's Commentary on Vergil." In S. Casali and F. Stok, eds. *Servio: stratificazioni esegetiche e modelli culturali / Servius: Exegetical Stratifications and Cultural Models*, 159–178. Brussels: Latomus. Collection Latomus 317.

Shapiro, H. A. 1993. *Personifications in Greek Art: The Representation of Abstract Concepts, 600–400 BC*. Zurich: Akanthus.

Sharrock, A. 2008. "*Aemulatio*: The Critic as Intertext." In S. Casali and F. Stok, eds. *Servio: stratificazioni esegetiche e modelli culturali / Servius: Exegetical Stratifications and Cultural Models*, 8–23. Brussels: Latomus. Collection Latomus 317.

Siebenborn, E. 1976. *Die Lehre von der Sprachrichtigkeit und ihren Kriterien. Studien zur antiken normativen Grammatik*. Amsterdam: B. R. Grüner.

Sihler, A. 1995. *New Comparative Grammar of Greek and Latin*. Oxford: Oxford University Press.

Simon, E. 1984. "Laran." LIMC 2.1: 498–505, 2.2: 374–378.

———. 2006. "Gods in Harmony: The Etruscan Pantheon." In N. de Grummond and E. Simon, eds., 45–65.

Sittl, C. 1890. *Die Gebärden der Griechen und Römer*. Leipzig: B. G. Teubner.

Skinner, M. 1997. "*Ego mulier*: The Construction of Male Sexuality in Catullus." In J. Hallett and M. Skinner, eds. *Roman Sexualities*, 129–150. Princeton: Princeton University Press.

———. 2005. *Sexuality in Greek and Roman Culture*. Malden, MA, and Oxford: Blackwell.

Skutsch, O. 1985. *Annals of Q. Ennius*. Oxford: Oxford University Press.

Sluiter, I. 1990. *Ancient Grammar in Context: Contributions to the Study of Ancient Linguistic Thought*. Amsterdam: VU University Press.

Smith, K. F. 1913. *The Elegies of Albius Tibullus*. New York: The American Book Company.

Smith, R. R. R. 2013. *The Marble Reliefs from the Julio-Claudian Sebasteion*. Darmstadt and Mainz: Philipp von Zabern. Aphrodisias VI.

Stafford, E. 1998. "Masculine Values, Feminine Forms: On the Gender of Personified Abstractions." In L. Foxhall and J. Salmon, eds. *Thinking Men: Masculinity and Its Self-representation in the Classical Tradition*, 43–56. London and New York: Routledge.

Sterne, L. 1956. *The Life and Opinions of Tristram Shandy, Gentleman*. Boston: Houghton Mifflin.

Stotz, P. 1998. *Handbuch zur lateinischen Sprache des Mittelalters; vol. 4, Formenlehre, Syntax und Stilistik*. Munich: C. H. Beck.

Swain, S. 2004. "Bilingualism and Biculturalism in Antonine Rome: Apuleius, Fronto, and Gellius." In L. Holford-Strevens and A. Vardi, eds. *The Worlds of Aulus Gellius*, 3–40. Oxford: Oxford University Press.

Syndikus, H. P. 1984. *Catull: Eine Interpretation*. 3 vols. Darmstadt: Wissenschaftliche Buchgesellschaft. Wege der Forschung 46.

Szemerényi, O. 1969. "Etyma Latina II (7–18)." In *Studi linguistici in onore di Vittore Pisani*, 963–994. Brescia: Paideia.

Talbert, R. 1984. *The Senate of Imperial Rome*. Princeton: Princeton University Press.

Taylor, L. R. 1967. "Aniconic Worship among the Early Romans." In G. Hadzsits, ed. *Classical Studies in Honor of John C. Rolfe*, 305–314. Philadelphia: University of Pennsylvania Press.

Thomas, R. 1988. *Virgil: "Georgics."* 2 vols. Cambridge: Cambridge University Press.

Thomas, Y. 1992. "The Division of the Sexes in Roman Law." In Schmitt Pantel, ed., 83–137, 492–503.

Thomson, D. F. S. 1998. *Catullus, Edited with a Textual and Interpretative Commentary.* Phoenix Suppl. 34. Toronto: University of Toronto Press.

Tolkiehn, J. 1901. "Die inschriftliche Poesie der Römer." *Neue Jahrbücher für das klassische Altertum* 7: 161–184.

Tommasi Moreschini, C. 1998. "L'androginia divina e i suoi presupposti filosofici: il mediatore celeste." *Studi classici e orientali* 46: 973–998.

———. 2001. "*Deus utraque sexus fecunditate plenissimus:* divinità androgine nel mondo classico e cristiano." *Atti e Memorie dell'Accademia Toscana di scienze e lettere* 66: 11–25.

Torelli, M. 1986. "La religione." In M. Pallottino et al., eds. *Rasenna: storia e civiltà degli Etruschi*, 159–237. Milan: Libri Scheiwiller.

Tran, V. 1994. "Ouranos." LIMC 7.1: 132–136.

Tränkle, H. 1960. *Die Sprachkunst des Properz und die Tradition der lateinischen Dichtersprache.* Wiesbaden: F. Steiner. Hermes Einzelschriften 15.

Trappes-Lomax, J. 2007. *Catullus: A Textual Reappraisal.* Swansea: The Classical Press of Wales.

Treggiari, S. 1994. "Putting the Bride to Bed." *Echos du monde classique* 13: 311–331.

Truffaut, F. 1968. *Jules and Jim.* Trans. N. Fry. New York: Simon and Schuster.

Usener, H. 1896. *Götternamen: Versuch einer Lehre von der religiösen Begriffsbildung.* Bonn: F. Cohen.

Vaahtera, J. 2008. "On Grammatical Gender in Ancient Linguistics—The Order of Genders." *Arctos* 42: 247–266.

Vaan, M. de. 2008. *Etymological Dictionary of Latin and the Other Italic Languages.* Leiden: E. J. Brill.

Väänänen, V. 1982. *Introduzione al latino volgare.* Trans. A. Silvestri. 3rd ed. Bologna: Pàtron.

Vainio, R. 1999. *Latinitas and Barbarisms according to the Roman Grammarians.* Turku: Painosalama Oy.

Van Sickle, J. 1968. "About Form and Feeling in Catullus 65." *Transactions of the American Philological Association* 99: 487–508.

Vardi, A. 2001. "Gellius against the Professors." *Zeitschrift für Papyrologie und Epigraphik* 137: 41–54.

Varner, E. 2008. "Transcending Gender: Assimilation, Identity, and Roman Imperial Portraits." In S. Bell and I. Hansen, eds. *Role Models in the Roman World: Identity and Assimilation*, 185–205. Ann Arbor: University of Michigan Press.

Vetter, E. 1953. *Handbuch der italischen Dialekte. I. Band: Texte mit Erklärung, Glossen, Wörterverzeichnis.* Heidelberg: Carl Winter.

Wackernagel, J. 1926–1928. *Vorlesungen über Syntax.* 2 vols. 2nd ed. Basel: Birkhäuser.

Wagenvoort, H. 1947. *Roman Dynamism: Studies in Ancient Roman Thought, Language, and Custom.* Oxford: Blackwell.

Walters, B. 2011. "Metaphor, Violence, and the Death of the Roman Republic." Diss. University of California, Los Angeles.

Weinstock. S. 1934. "Terra Mater und Tellus." RE 5A: 1.791–806.

Welch, T. S. 2005. *The Elegiac Cityscape: Propertius and the Meaning of Roman Monuments*. Columbus: The Ohio State University Press.

West, M. L. 1978. *Hesiod: Works and Days*. Oxford: Oxford University Press.

———. 1983. *The Orphic Poems*. Oxford: Oxford University Press.

———. 2007. *Indo-European Poetry and Myth*. Oxford: Oxford University Press.

White, D. 1980. "The Method of Composition and Sources of Nonius Marcellus." *Studi Noniani* 8: 111–211.

Wilkinson, L. P. 1963. *Golden Latin Artistry*. Cambridge: Cambridge University Press.

Williams, C. A. 1999. *Roman Homosexuality: Ideologies of Masculinity in Classical Antiquity*. Oxford: Oxford University Press.

Winterbottom, M. 1994. *De officiis M. Tulli Ciceronis*. Oxford: Oxford University Press.

Wiseman, T. P. 1979. *Clio's Cosmetics: Three Studies in Greco-Roman Literature*. Leicester: Leicester University Press.

———. 2000. "Liber: Myth, Drama and Ideology in Republican Rome." In C. Bruun, ed. *The Roman Middle Republic: Politics, Religion, and Historiography, c. 400–133 B.C.*, 265–299. Rome: Institutum Romanum Finlandiae. Acta Instituti Romani Finlandiae 23.

Wissowa, G. 1904. "De feriis anni Romanorum vetustissimi observationes selectae." In *Gesammelte Abhandlungen zur römischen Religions- und Stadtgeschichte*, 154–174. Munich: C. H. Beck.

———. 1912. *Religion und Kultus der Römer*. Munich: C. H. Beck. 2d ed. Handbuch der klassischen Altertumswissenschaft 5: 4.

———. 1916–1924a. "Liber," "Libera." In Roscher 2.2: 2021–2030.

———. 1916–1924b. "Pales." In Roscher 3.1: 1276–1280.

———. 1916–1924c. "Pallor und Pavor." In Roscher 3.1: 1341–1343.

———. 1916–1924d. "Tellus." In Roscher 5: 331–345.

———. 1916–1924e. "Tutela." In Roscher 5: 1304–1307.

Wittig, M. 1985. "The Mark of Gender." *Feminist Issues* 5.2: 3–12.

Woodcock, E. C. 1959. *A New Latin Syntax*. Cambridge, MA: Harvard University Press.

Woytek, E. 1970. *Sprachliche Studien zur Satura Menippea Varros*. Vienna: Böhlau. Wiener Studien Beiheft 2.

Wright, H. W. 1917. "The *Sacra Idulia* of Ovid's *Fasti*: A Study of Ovid's Credibility in Regard to the Place and the Victim of This Sacrifice." Diss. University of Pennsylvania.

Wülker, L. 1903. *Die geschichtliche Entwicklung des Prodigienwesens bei den Römern*. Leipzig: Emil Glausch.

Yaguello, M. 1978. *Les mots et les femmes: essai d'approche socio-linguistique de la condition féminine*. Paris: Payot.

Zetzel, J. 1981. *Latin Textual Criticism in Antiquity*. Salem N. H.: Ayer.

Zubin, D. A., and K.-M. Köpcke. 1984. "Affect Classification in the German Gender System." *Lingua* 63: 41–96.

This index includes all passages from Greek and Roman works that are cited in the text or notes (*excluding* those in the appendix to chapter 4). Latin authors and works are cited according to the *Index* of the *Thesaurus linguae Latinae* (Leipzig: B. G. Teubner, 1990), Greek according to the *Oxford Classical Dictionary* (Oxford: Oxford University Press, 2003) 3rd ed., rev.

General Index

Roman names are listed according to the form commonly used in English. For a listing of Greek and Latin passages cited in text and notes, see *Index locorum*. The appendix to chapter 4 has not been considered for this index.